excellence in Freight Transport

How to better manage domestic and international logistics transport

excellence in
Freight Transport

How to better manage domestic and international logistics transport

Stuart Emmett

Contents

About this book

In writing this book, I have endeavoured not to include anything that, if used, would be injurious or cause financial loss to the user. The user is strongly recommended, before applying or using any of the contents, to check and verify their own company policy/ requirements. No liability will be accepted by the author or publisher for the use of any of the contents.

It can also happen, in a lifetime of learning and meeting people, that the original source of an idea or information has been forgotten. If I have actually omitted, in this book, to give anyone credit they are due, I apologise and hope they will make contact so that I can correct the omission in future editions.

In the book, besides the usual text, I have also included many Case Studies, Action Times, and Exercises. These are to encourage reader interaction with the text, and above all to stimulate "reflection", an often omitted part of personal learning and development.

Additionally, included are Training Topics, as it can be useful to ensure that all people involved in companies have a common understanding of what is involved. The Training Topics therefore give examples of training contents to facilitate a common understanding.

About the author

My interest in transport goes back to childhood and was fostered and matured during employment. Starting out in shipping and forwarding in the days of conventional cargo shipping in the early 1960s, an early responsibility of mine was arranging transport to the docks. We were quickly forced to change to Roll On Roll Off and Lift On Lift Off methods, as containers and trailer methods of transport largely took over and also moved activities inland. Looking after containers for a service to Norway was an early main responsibility at what seems now, a tender age. Containers to Canada and a CP Ships agency were also involved.

With the UK making the decision to join to the EU in 1972, this changed my work and I moved into consultancy, giving transport advice to those people who, previously, had only traded in the UK, and now had the view that the whole continent was soon to become a domestic market. This consultancy work was also widened out to include worldwide export/ import movements.

After completing studies with the Open University in 1978, we moved out to Nigeria where I was employed by the largest Forwarding/Ships Agency Company there, with over 1000 staff in Lagos alone. I was involved in import clearing, containers de-consolidation/ warehousing, and lighterage and road transport of strategic imports. Not a dull place to work, and fascinating also to be able to work where skills in Forwarding and Transport were highly appreciated and well rewarded.

My time there ran its course, and upon return to the UK, I took one year out to complete an MSc in Transport studies at Cranfield, before joining a third party company in a Commercial Development role, dealing with companies like Heinz, Pedigree Petfood, Boots the Chemist etc. on UK Transport/Warehousing works, as well as running vehicles into Europe for freight forwarders.

This role continued until 1990 when I moved into Training, with work associated largely with the then Institute of Logistics and Distribution Management (now the Chartered Institute of Logistics and Transport).

After being a Director of Training for nine years, I then chose to become a freelance independent mentor/coach, trainer and consultant. Trading under the name of Learn and Change Limited, I now enjoy working on six continents, principally in Africa and the Middle East, but also in the Far East, Europe and North and South America.

Additional to undertaking training, I also am involved with one-to-one coaching/mentoring, consulting, writing, assessing and examining for professional institutes' qualifications. This has included being Chief Examiner on the Graduate Diploma of the Chartered Institute of Purchasing and Supply, and as an external university examiner for an MSc in Purchasing and Logistics.

My own journey to today, whilst an individual one does not happen, thankfully, without other peoples' involvement. I smile when I remember so many helpful people. So to anyone who has ever had contact with me, please be assured you will have contributed to my own learning, growing and developing.

Finally I remain grateful to Barry Crocker, MSc Programme Leader, Purchasing and Logistics, of Salford University, for his support and expert editorial eye in this book, and who, at all times, has a most valuable contribution to make, not the least of which is friendship and humour.

I am married to the lovely Christine, with two cute adult children, Jill and James; James is married to Mairead, who is also cute. We are, additionally, the proud grandparents of three girls (the totally gorgeous twins Megan and Molly, and their younger sister, Niamh).

I can be contacted at stuart@learnandchange.com or by visiting www.learnandchange.com.

I do welcome any comments.

Stuart Emmett

1: Importance of Freight Transport

Introduction

Transport is the method by which goods (or people) move from one location to another and it is an essential function in product supply chains as it provides the physical movement between the suppliers and customers. This movement can be for raw materials, sub-assemblies/work in progress, or for the finished goods; it can take place over shorter distances on a national basis, or the movement can be over longer distances and on a global basis.

Transport costs may represent a substantial part of the price of goods. When, however, a holistic view of supply chain management is taken, it will be necessary to consider the total costs/service levels involved, also including the activities of buying, making and the selling of products. Transport costs, when examined holistically, may therefore not be the main cost.

Transport is often a barometer of an economy; accordingly, any changes in industrial structures and any changes in the consumer tastes and demand, will all affect transport operations. Additionally, changes within supply chain management techniques, such as Just In Time (JIT), will also mean changes have to be made in transport operations and strategy. A number of reasons can contribute to the growth in freight transport:

- General economic growth
- Specialisation and more outsourcing between separated parties
- Differentiation in product ranges giving more variety of products
- Centralised stock holding meaning greater transport distances are involved
- Increased use of "make to order" and "just in time" methods of production meaning more frequent deliveries of smaller lots that "delivered as required"
- Move from a single UK country scope to European and global perspectives, involving sales to different and more dispersed markets; and, additionally, involving sourcing from optimal places, irrespective of geographical locations

The environmental impact of transport receives attention by legislators. This can involve increased restrictions to operating methods as well as in technical aspects of vehicle design. Transport is subject to political influences and resources and is involved in the lobbying for these scarce financial resources. The technology involved with transport in the future would seem to be one that pursues closer monitoring of vehicle performance either in terms of satellite location technology or in the technical aspects of the vehicle design. All such technology currently exists, if not universally used. Tagging and identifying of individual goods/ packages is technically available, and if the time sensitive/reliability requirements of supply chain management continue, then increased usage of such technology may occur.

Transport is a service and therefore an enabler or a means to an end. To ensure the end is going to be found, the following are examples of what can be continually needed from the enabling supply side of the transport service. Many of these go beyond the provision of just a transport service, and emphasise the connectivities involved and the need for these to be recognised by alert 21st century transport companies.

Customer Service aspects
- Improvements in on-time delivery to the customer's customer
- Reduction in product life cycle
- Reduction in stock-outs

Management aspects
- Reduction in overhead costs
- Increased productivity levels
- Increased flexibility

Cost Reduction aspects
- Reduction in overall freight costs
- Reduction in landed costs and total product costs
- Reduction in lead times

Production aspects
- Reduction in raw material costs
- Increased use of capacity and flexibility
- Reduction in inventory levels

Information aspects
- Increased visibility and access to information
- Improved customer service levels to their customer
- Improved ability to respond to customer demand

As mentioned, many of these go beyond the pure provision of a transport service and emphasise the links of transport to the holistic business aspects of the supply chain.

Supply Chain Management

The term Supply Chain is the process which integrates, coordinates and controls the movement of goods and materials from a supplier to a customer and to the final consumer. The essential point with a supply chain is that it links all the activities between suppliers and customers to the consumer in a timely manner. Supply chains, therefore, involve the activities of buying/sourcing, making, moving, and selling. The supply chain "takes care of business" following from the initial customer/consumer demand. Nothing happens with supply until there is an order; it is the order that drives the whole process. Indeed some people logically argue that the term supply chain could be called the demand chain. Additionally, as supply chain management is all about the flow of goods and information, then perhaps a better analogy than chain is a pipeline, as this better emphasises flow.

It is also important to realise that each company has not one supply chain, but many, as it deals with different suppliers and has different customers. For each finished product, whilst some of the buying, making, moving and selling processes will be identical or very similar, the total supply chain for each product will be different. Multiple supply chain management is therefore a better description - but it is a cumbersome one. In supply chain management, therefore, there are many different supply chains to manage. This can mean using many different methods of arranging transport.

The Supply Chain or the Demand Pipeline

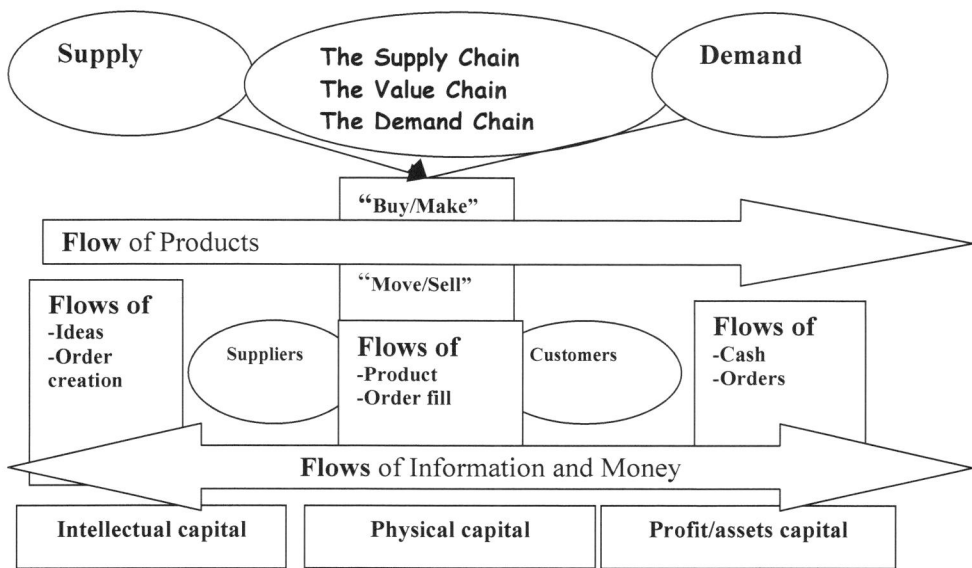

Definitions

Definitions can be important to clarify thought, and especially so when one person understands a term to mean one thing, but another person understands the same term differently. This has been happening for example, in the UK from the early 2000s with the word Logistics. This term, which originally encompassed the whole supply chain, as shown in the previous definition of the supply chain, is now being referred to by many companies as a new name for transport, or for warehousing/stores or for distribution. Third party transport companies are also beginning to call themselves supply chain management companies. Confusing, isn't it?

In the UK, one can observe the new name on a freight transport vehicle that before was called "Fred Smith Transport," is now called "Fred Smith Logistics". Logistics can therefore be a confusing word - additionally, some people use the term logistics to describe their own internal company process, and use the supply chain term when they are dealing with external suppliers/ customers. At the risk of further confusion, others also call their internal logistics processes their internal supply chain!

Distribution is meant to be about delivering the right goods to the right place at the right time and at the right cost. This definition is the "rights of distribution" and represents in a simple way, the objectives for distribution. Distribution therefore involves the combining of transport with warehousing, and is a term that is often applied to mainly finished goods. However, it may also by used by suppliers who are delivering product to their customer, perhaps of raw materials and semi-finished work-in-progress goods. Suppliers are also concerned with getting the "rights" correct, and as far as that supplier is concerned, the raw materials can be, for them, the finished goods.

Meanwhile, when readers hear the three terms of logistics, supply chain and distribution, they are strongly recommended to ensure they have the full understanding of what the originator means when they are using the word. This can be very important and prevent confusions; for example, "Fred Smith Logistics" is unlikely to have a clue about whether to outsource the manufacture of sub-assemblies, or whether these be manufactured internally. This would often be strategic supply chain decision (but then again, some would say it is strategic logistics decision).

Strategic aspects of Transport

Transport management is often thought of as being just an operational day-to-day job. However, it should also be involved in the longer strategic aspects of a business. Transport has a critical part to play in supply chain management, and it can only play this part if it is involved in the strategic aspects of the business. This will involve being aware of the expected development of the business in terms of the future:
*   production
*   product
*   suppliers
*   customers
*   and all the associated product volumes and through puts

Then, transport management is able to more fully assess situations and make important contributions to the decision making process. The following illustrates the recent evolutions in freight transport:

Pre-1980	1980-2000	Post 2000
Physical Transportation	**Evolution of Logistics**	**Supply Chain Management**
Regulated market	Deregulated market	Global market
Cost-based pricing	Price-based costing	Financial reengineering
Low cost of capital	Awareness of high inventory cost	Total cost of sales
Inventory carried	Lower stocks / make to order production	Total inventory reduced

Inflation and Deregulation → Globalisation and Reengineering →

Customers

I mentioned, earlier, the importance of the customer order, as it is only the order from the customer that triggers all the activity in the supply chain, logistics, stores, or distribution processes. Without a customer order, none of these process or activities is required. The customer is also interested not in buying products, but in buying *delivered* products.

It should be appreciated that customer service levels are a variable and each customer service variable has a cost associated with it. The relationship between cost and service is rarely a linear straight line, but more of an exponential curve. So, a ten per cent increase in service may mean a cost increase of 15 or over 50 per cent. For example, in transport we pay more for first class mail than for second class mail, and we pay more for a service offering an overnight parcel delivery than for a three day or a deferred delivery.

Customer Value

Customers will place a value of many aspects of the total service offering with transport being involved in the physical delivery. Value is also placed by customers against quality, the cycle lead-time and the cost and the service levels. Perception is reality: customers can see these as being inter-related, or may view them independently. It is, therefore, important for a business to understand the specific reality as seen by the customer.

The following are the aspects of the four customer value criteria:

Quality is "performing right first time every time" and involves:
*   Meeting requirements
*   Fitness for purpose
*   Minimum variance
*   Elimination of waste
*   Continuous improvement culture

Service, is about "continually meeting customer needs as the market changes", and involves:
*   Support available
*   Product availability
*   Flexibility
*   Reliability
*   Consistency

Cost, is about knowing what the costs really are and then looking at how to reduce them. This involves the:
*   Design of product
*   Manufacturing process
*   Distribution process
*   Administration process
*   Stock levels

5

Cycle lead-time is about knowing what the lead times really are and then looking for ways to reduce them. This involves considering:

- Time to market
- Time from order placement to time available
- Response to market forces
- Days of Stock cover

A business therefore, ideally will try to improve the quality and the service, whilst, reducing the cost and lead times. All of the aspects are inter-related and connected and for example, it matters not to the majority of customers whether the goods are transported by road, rail, sea, air or multimodal or intermodal modes. The above factors are what they really value. The transport mode used is a means to these ends and outcomes.

The Value Chain

Michael Porter, of Harvard Business School, in his book **Gaining Competitive Advantage (1998: Free Press)** introduced this concept in 1985. From the diagram below, you will see this has large implications for logistics/ supply chain/ distribution and transport.

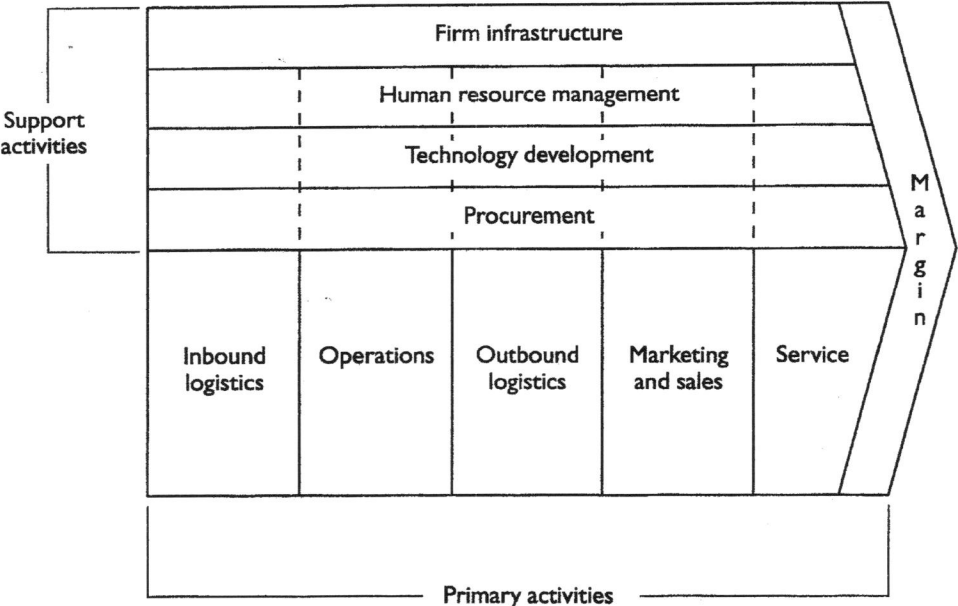

The Value Chain
(Reproduced with permission Cheltenham Tutorial College)

This divides into primary and support activities as follows:

Primary Activities
- Inbound logistics covering stores, warehousing, handling and stock control
- Operations covering production and packing and all activities that transfer inputs into outputs
- Outbound logistics include transport and warehouse networks to get products to customers
- Marketing and sales cover the methods by which customers know about and purchase products
- Service includes the support for all activities such as installation, returns.

Support Activities
- Procurement includes the buying and purchasing of products as well as all other resources
- Technology covers things information and communications technology (ICT) and research and development (R&D)
- Human Resource management covers all aspects concerned with personnel
- Infrastructure covers finance, legal and other general management activities

Porter then expanded this concept of a Value Chain into a Value System. This consists of a series of linked value chains. By this joining together of value chains into a value system, in effect we create a supply chain. Where the value actually is, according to Porter, is dependant on the way that a customer uses the product and not just totally on the costs incurred into buying, making and moving it. These costs including all the raw materials and activities that create the product, which then that represent its value. But after this, it is only when the product is purchased that the value can be measured; and finally, it is not until the product is at the final customer/consumer that the real value is to be found.

Part of the difficulty here is that each individual organisation in the supply chain will attempt to define value themselves by looking at its own profitability. Each company will, in turn, carry on this definition to their suppliers and as the value definition moves back up the chain it will become distorted. Indeed, one of the reasons for companies to try to work together more closely with suppliers and customers, is to have a constant view of value throughout the supply/value chain.

Therefore, we have seen that costs are added during the buying, making and the moving activities, and that ultimate/real value is only found when the product is with the customer. Meanwhile, value has been added by improving the product, by changing its form, moving it to a different place, and all this has occurred over time. Therefore, we can see that value is added by:

- Making it faster by changing the form
- Moving it faster to the place required
- Doing it faster by time changes
- Ultimate value comes after the movement to the customer

The following diagram shows how cost and value are added in the supply chain process.

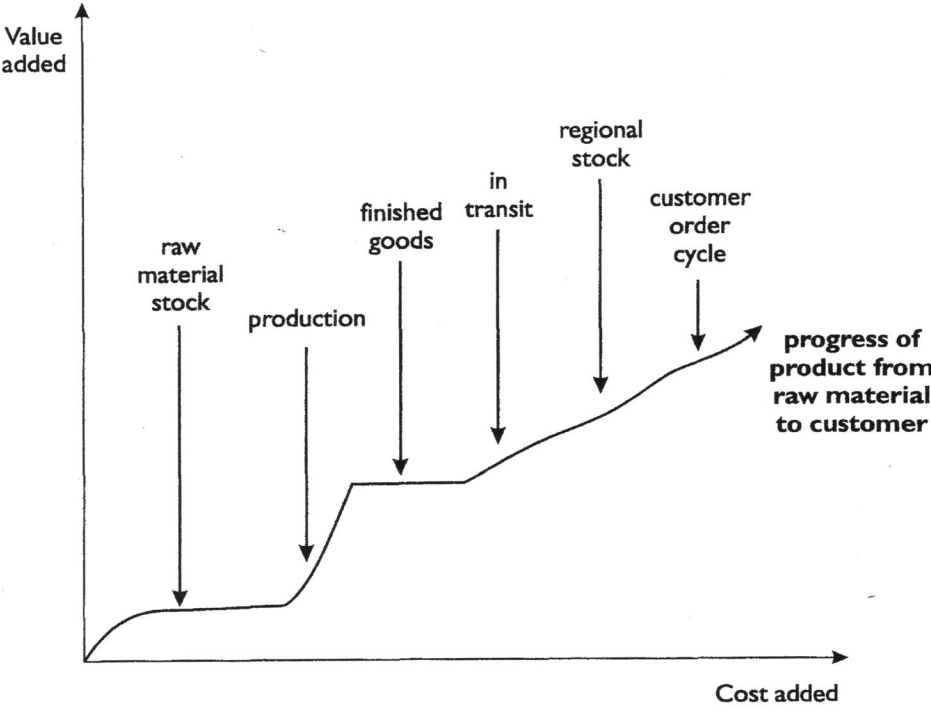

Cost and Value adders in the Supply Chain
(Reproduced with permission Cheltenham Tutorial College)

Clearly, this diagram shows that goods being stored are incurring cost and are not adding value. Whilst this will generally be the case, if those goods being stored were appreciating in value, then this would not apply. This would however, only apply for a very limited range of products, such as with bullion in non-inflation times, and with works of art. The diagram emphasises that movement to the customer as quickly as possible whilst accounting for associated cost levels, is what really counts in adding value.

Transport Statistics

Government publishes, each year, a series of statistics on vehicle numbers, and movements of freight by mode. One of the main measures used for freight movements is how much freight is moved and over what distance. This is done by recording the Tonnes lifted and the Tonnes moved by tonne/kilometres (which is simply a measure of how many tonnes are moved by how many kilometres.) So for example 100 tonne kilometres could be, 100 tonnes moving one kilometre, 1 tonne moving 100 kilometres, 20 tonnes moving 5 kilometres, etc).

As these statistics are reported each year, of course yearly variations are found, but the general trends stay very similar, and the following statistics are a composite representation of recent figures to give indications. Full details can be found be accessing www.dft.gov.uk.

UK Freight by mode by Tonnes Moved and Tonnes Lifted (in Tonne KM)

Mode	Tonnes Lifted	Tonnes Moved
Road	82%	59%
Rail	5%	8%
Pipeline	7%	4%
Water inland and coastal	6%	29%

The situation is very similar with the EU:

UK/EU Freight by Mode by Tonnes Lifted

Mode	UK	EU
Road	82%	80%
Rail	5%	5%
Pipeline	7%	5%
Water-inland/coastal	6%	
Water-inland		3%
Intra EU		7%

The dominance of road transport can be seen in the above tables, and we shall be examining this further in the next chapter on transport modes. Meanwhile, the interaction of freight transport vehicles on the roads with other road users is interesting:

UK Vehicle Population

Vehicle	Million
Cars	26.50
Vans under 3.5 tonne GVW	3.10
Trucks over 3.5 tonne GVW	0.45

On total vehicles registered (this also includes motorbikes and crown/exempt vehicles), cars represent some 79% of vehicles registered, vans 9.4% and trucks 1.3%.

Road freight can be undertaken by operators moving their own goods with their own vehicles (known as private or own account operators); or by using third party companies (these are variously known as public hauliers, or as some prefer to be called, LSPs - logistics service providers or 3PL - third party logistics). The division between these private/public operators is as follows:

UK Own Account/Third Party Split

	By tonnes moved	By vehicle ownership
Own Account/Private	38%	65%
Third Party/Public	62%	35%

It can be seen here that the third party companies move more goods with fewer vehicles, indicating they have more satisfactory productivity levels.

Case Study: The UK road haulage freight industry

The road transport mode is the dominant method of transport within the UK. From the varied statistics available it is possible to build up a picture of a typical road transport/ haulage company; such analysis begs the question: is it an "industry apart" instead of it being a "cottage industry"? Please note rounded off figures are given in this analysis, and whilst year-by-year individual and precise figure are available, the aim here is too show the trends and give a general picture. As such therefore it is not representative on any specific year but of trends over recent years.

General
- Road accounts for over 80% of all the tonnes lifted
- Operates around 450 000 vehicles over 3.50 tonne GVW
- Comprises around 96 000 individual companies
- About 80% of companies operate under 10 vehicles
- Less than 100 companies operate more than 500 vehicles
- Users spend around £45 billion per annum on road freight

Public/Private operators
- Publics hauliers move 72% of tonne kilometres and 62% of tonnes lifted and own 35% of the vehicles registered
- Private operators move 28% of tonne kilometres, 38% of tonnes lifted and own 65% of the vehicles registered

Public hauliers therefore move more freight, further with fewer vehicles than private operators.

Freight Services/Commodities moved
- A wide range of services are offered from 1 kilo parcels to 1000 tonne plus abnormal loads
- Three commodity groups account for over 50% of the tonnes lifted (crude minerals, food-drink-tobacco and building materials)

Vehicle Journeys and Productivity
- The average vehicle journey is 54 miles
- The average vehicle travels 25 000 miles per annum
- 75% of journeys are loaded
- The average payload per trip is 9.1 tonnes
- The average vehicle moving time per working day is 3.47 hours.
- Conversely, the average vehicle non moving time per working day is 4.73 hours
- Rigid vehicles average 9.4 mpg with articulated vehicles averaging 8.0 mpg

Vehicle Types
- Rigid vehicles account for 73% of the vehicles licensed but move only 27% of tonne kilometres

- Articulated vehicles move 72% of tonne kilometres with only 28% of the vehicles licensed

Financial/General measures
- Public hauliers return 14.9% ROCE and 4.6% margin.
- Those public hauliers of over £10 million turnover, return up to a 4 times better ROCE and a 3 time better margin, than those public hauliers having a turnover of under £3 million.
- 10 public hauliers account for around 10% of total user spending on road freight
- Almost 96000 other companies (public and private) account for the balance 90% of user spending

Transport and the Economy

In the UK and Europe, there is a close relationship between freight movement and economic growth measured by gross domestic product (GDP). Road haulage as the dominant mode has important and wide-ranging effects on supply chain management simply because of the fact that other modes, and particularly rail transport, are currently such an imperfect substitute. In particular:
- Rail transportation and inland waterway transportation are not generally able to offer the same quality (in terms of speed, flexibility, availability and reliability) as road transportation.
- The capacity of rail transportation is not sufficient to guarantee a smooth transportation of those goods, which are currently transported by road.

The nature of the transport service demanded will depend to some extent on the nature of the materials transported. The important elements here are as follows:
- nature of product
- value density
- perishable nature (physically and economically)
- hazardousness physical characteristics (size, liquid, gas)

The structural characteristics of the supply chain systems, which are of most significance in determining the sensitivity of the transport system, are:
- number and location of facilities, including production plants, warehouses and transfer facilities
- the transportation modes currently used
- number and location of the suppliers
- size and location of inventories
- size and location of the customers information systems employed

Road freight transport has an integral and dominant part in the economy and therefore any changes made which affect this dominance will have knock-on impacts to the whole economy.

Meanwhile the link of transport into a supply chain can be seen further in the following case study:

Case Study: Post-Kogeko NL: Fresh beginnings

Dutch logistics company Post-Kogeko has carved itself a niche market in transporting fruit and vegetables across Europe.

"We should be the DHL of fruit and vegetables, not on a worldwide scale but in Europe," Erik Janse, commercial director of Maasdijk based temperature-controlled logistics company Post-Kogeko, explains. "We must build up a structure so we can conquer Western Europe." Janse is referring to DailyFresh Logistics, a joint venture the company runs alongside fellow transport firms Visbeen and Norfolkline.

DailyFresh Logistics was set up in 1998 with the aim of bringing together the three main companies delivering temperature-controlled food from Holland to the UK and Ireland. "Our drivers were on the same ferries as theirs and they regularly spoke," explains Janse. "After they got off the ferries, they drove to the same markets and retailers in London, Bristol and Manchester. Our owners got together and debated why they were competing against each other." The solution for Post-Kogeko, which had survived independently since being formed by Dirk Post in 1979, was to join forces with its one-time rivals. "Instead of sending three trucks to the UK, we decided to send just one. Every partner agreed this was the best way to optimise the logistics flow."

Ten years on and with an annual turnover of €80m and major UK customers such as Tesco, Morrison's and Sainsbury's, Janse hails DailyFresh as "one of the great joint-venture successes in logistics".

Main markets

DailyFresh has two main logistics centres: Dunkirk, France, and Poeldijkin the Netherlands. It distributes throughout Eastern and Southern Europe, but its main markets are Benelux, northern France and the UK. "In some joint-ventures there is some freedom in what you put into the network and what you keep for yourself. That is not want we wanted. Either you do everything with DailyFresh or you do nothing and that has been the main contributor to our success. We have all lost a bit of our old identity but we have a new one in DailyFresh," Janse says.

DailyFresh sends between 100 and 150 trailers a day to the UK and it aims to increase this by 10% every year. But the past 12 months have been challenging. "The pound is very expensive and that has affected fruit and vegetable exports," Janse remarks. Customers are demanding that food is transported quicker and with more emphasis on quality. "There are tighter timeframes in which we have to work and we have to cope with increased concerns about early and late deliveries in urban areas," he explains. However, the main challenge is the seasonality of the work. "The high season is between April and September. During that time we double our transport volume and it's a tough job."

More than wheels

Post-Kogeko has a fleet of 400 trucks and 500 trailers. It buys 40 extra trucks for the start of the high season and then sells the same number of old vehicles in September. The fleet is primarily Scania. "It makes quality trucks. The standard of construction is the best," Janse declares.

The company's motto is 'More Than Wheels' and joint-ventures have been the lifeblood of its development.

Coolboxx, another JV, was launched in 2004 on a similar basis to DailyFresh with partners Visbeen and Geest North Sea Line.
"We saw that short-sea container operators such as Geest were bringing alternatives to trailers on the market, such as the 45ft high cube reefer container. We thought we could wait and suffer from this or ask Geest if we could put something together," explains Janse. "It has the knowledge of intermodal and Visbeen and we have the knowledge of fridge transport. It is a profitable venture and we now have 350 containers running." Janse has clear thoughts about the value of joint ventures. "Every company has its own benefits. If you compete on the little things that you do differently then the only thing you achieve is worse rates. But if you join forces you give the customer a good logistics option. You can keep rates at a normal level and earn some money. "Fear in the transport business has always been bigger than the willingness to help each other. If you can do it a better way, then why don't we all do it together?"

Post-Kogeko doesn't just exist with joint ventures; it distributes chilled and frozen products throughout Benelux and offers truck-washing facilities to third parties. Given the company's reliance on the UK, it may surprise some that it doesn't have a depot here, Janse says it had an office in Felixstowe but it was closed in 2002 and operations returned to the Netherlands. "It was too expensive. You need an office manager and planners and the benefits were low. We can follow our drivers when they are in the UK from in the Netherlands using track and trace. If 90% of the time you don't see your drivers then why have an office?" he states.

Of the company's 550 drivers, 60 are from the UK "The wages here are not that different from the UK," Janse says. "We pay them the same as our Dutch drivers. UK drivers say they work for us because they like the way we treat them. We give our drivers the best equipment and communications in their cab because we need them to do the work. We respect them."

Business costs

Respect or no respect, drivers' wages are usually the biggest cost to any business and Post-Kogeko is no different "Fuel is also getting very expensive, that and wages are 80% of our costs," remarks Janse. "Our customers are willing to pay a fuel surcharge at the moment, but it is changing. If they don't earn enough, it will be difficult to get more from them; the arguments are starting." Unsurprisingly he sympathises with the fuel prices raced by UK hauliers, "The idea of different fuel prices throughout Europe is not good. It is ridiculous that you pay more in the UK than we do in the Netherlands. But the answer is not a UK vignette; you have to organise these things through Brussels. The EU must neutralise the differences between fuel prices in our countries," he says. "The high prices affect us when we refuel in the UK."

Another UK problem also experienced in the Netherlands is driver shortage; there is a shortage of approximately 5,000 drivers' there. "It causes us difficulties," says Janse. "Our part of the Netherlands is a busy area and everyone is looking for staff."

Post-Kogeko's solution is to train warehouse or office staff as truck drivers. "Once a week we teach them how to drive a truck and get a licence. Then when they are ready and are familiar with the company they can drive our trucks," he explains.

Using Eastern European drivers to plug the gap is not an option. "We have had some requests and we tried two Polish drivers. But you have to understand the language and things such as street signs and employing these drivers did not work for us," he says. However, Eastern European operators are proving harder to ignore. "It is difficult to compete with them on long-distance traffic; it is more profitable for companies to use them. But that is partly why we started Coolboxx. In five years' times these long routes will be taken over by rail and sea operators," Janse predicts.

Port congestion
Easing the problems of port congestion will help in this aim. "The Port of Rotterdam now has floating docks that have containers on them that are shipped to Germany for onward truck use. In this way you avoid trucks going through Holland and Belgium. This is all avoidable trucking capacity and with wages and fuel rates rising the less we drive the better."

This is where the talk of the future begins. The expectation is to increase Post-Kogeko's turnover, minus the joint ventures, from €60m (£47m) to S90m (£71m) with new contracts. The company is also looking for other joint ventures but it is dedicated to expanding the reach of DailyFresh.

Janse says: "The UK gets food imports from all over the Continent: our Dunkirk warehouse must be the axle for these imports from Spain, Germany and Italy. We want to be the supply chain coordinator for Western Europe."

Source: Motor Transport 27 March 2008

Government Policy

Freight movement is inevitably caught up with access to infrastructure, for example, road developments. Effective access for people and for goods is essential to maintain high standards of living, including giving choice. However Government strategy has continually faltered in recent years and a formal strategic transport framework is non-existent as legislation is delayed and funding remains constrained. Growing affluence and ever-increasing demands for higher standards of living leads to an increase in car ownership, increasing pressure on a strained road system, and to the need for a widening range of goods to be available at reasonable prices.

There are conflicts here as, and contrary to majority public opinion, the road congestion and the slowing of traffic on overcrowded roads is more because of increased public car travel, and not due to increase in road freight vehicle movements; even at an admitted simplistic level, 26 million cars vie with around 400 000 freight vehicles, a ratio of about 60 to one.

Availability of goods in the UK is largely met by road freight, and disruption to such services soon causes effects: witness for example the fuel strikes in 2000, when in a matter of days, supermarkets ran out of goods. Such is the important role of road freight transport in the UK. Whilst we have the ability to move large quantities of data at the speed of light electronically virtually any where in the world, until we have figured out a way to do this for raw materials, sub assemblies/work in progress, or for the finished goods, then road freight transport will remain a most vital and critical part of the UK economy. The following two case studies illustrate this important aspect

Case Study: Transport links all company activities

The Company manufactures beds in the north of England. These are sold by major and multiple retails stores and DIY sheds; but are delivered direct to homes in all national locations upon receipt of orders direct from the stores. Typically 60% of volume is delivered from the north to the south east of England.

The order pattern process is:
- Order received from retailer
- Delivery day is confirmed, usually in 8 days time
- Countdown planning happens from this delivery date:
  - Day 1: order received
  - Day 2: production planning completed
  - Day 3/4: make to order production is undertaken
  - Day5: vehicle is loaded
  - Day 6-8: delivery is undertaken

It will be seen here that the customer order literally triggers the whole process, with production planning working back from the customer delivery date. It is virtually the case, that the transport routing and scheduling programming determines the production planning.

The vehicles used are demountable drawbars with a ratio of 4 bodies to one vehicle unit/ trailer. These are double manned and each vehicle completes 90/100 deliveries per week. They have a high utilisation as the following crewing shift patterns are worked:
- 3 weeks on and one week off.

- Week 1: Sunday to Friday
- Week 2: Sunday to Friday
- Week 3: Monday to Saturday
- Week 4: off

This gives a wide range of delivery date options.

Case Study: Importance of specialised transport - temperature controlled distribution

The aim of temperature-controlled distribution may be described as to create a micro controlled climate within the total distribution chain. The object of this controlled climate being to prevent the commodities being handled suffering from deterioration.

Commodities deteriorate more quickly in hotter and humid climates. Consequently the total design of the temperature controlled distribution system needs to be undertaken carefully, and then run and controlled strictly.

System Design

Important factors to consider in the design and operation of a temperature controlled distribution system for food commodities are summarised below:

- Climatic hazards
  - Humidity
  - Temperature
  - Rain
  - Light (UV)
- Biological hazards
  - Insects/Mites/Rodents/Birds
  - Moulds
  - Bacteria
- Product Composition
- Mechanical hazards
  - Handling Process
  - Transport Process
  - Sampling Process
- Other hazards
  - Design of Vehicles/Warehouses
  - Pilferage
  - Working Practices

Reliability of operations (on mechanical and other hazards) and the reliability of control over climatic and biological hazards are of paramount importance, if the system is to maintain product hygiene durability.

Types of Temperature Control

Various types of temperature control are needed and these may be summarised as below:

Type	Temperature	Product examples
Frozen	-30° to -10°C	Meat, fish
Chilled	-5° to 0°C	Fresh Meat, fish, poultry
Cool	-1° to 5°C	Dairy Produce
Cold	5° to +15°C Below Ambient	Citrus Produce

A temperature controlled distribution system therefore operates in a wide range of controlled conditions. The technical hardware equipment and the management "software" needed to maintain such "internal" conditions within a varying range of "external" ambient temperatures will be explored further.

Cool/Cold Storage (-1 to +15 C)

This temperature band prevents the rapid spoilage which is found when products are handled under ambient temperature conditions. Whilst microbiological spoilage is not completely prevented, the respiration rates in fresh fruit and vegetables are considerably reduced. Biochemical changes are therefore slowed down and the storage life is increased. For these reasons, preserved foods also benefit from cool or cold storage. For example, the storage life of canned foods can be doubled; dried foods can be stored 4- 6 times longer.

When storing and handling food; it is necessary to specify the optimum conditions of temperature and the relative humidity. The optimum relative humidity arrived at is often a trade-off between those conditions which cause excessive drying, and those which favour the development of micro-organisms.

Chilled/Frozen Storage (-30 to 0 C)

In general terms, fresh foods of high moisture content have a freezing point 0 to 5 C. However, with certain foods such as milk powders and some dry foods, the moisture content will not freeze. During the freezing process, ice crystals are formed within food. This may have damaging effects on its texture and appearance; it is to this extent therefore possible to forecast the effect of sub-zero storage temperatures by considering the freezing point of the particular foodstuff. However, the rate at which heat is removed during freezing also affects the extent of possible damage.

Whilst chilled storage, does not provide indefinite protection against microbial spoilage, it does give a degree of rigidity to say animal carcasses which aids handling and also, avoids tissue disruption. With frozen storage, food materials may dry out unless protected by packaging. Drying in the frozen state causes a porous "corky" appearance. This condition is known as "freezer burn" and it is caused when food is stored very close to the cooling surfaces.

Storage Conditions

Both temperature controlled vehicles and warehouses are very expensive to build and to maintain. The cost of building a cold store, for example, being about three times that of an ambient store. Additionally the storage temperatures required, considerably affects the running costs of the distribution system. These running costs need to be balanced against the need to preserve the product.

Handling Conditions
It is critical upon first receiving products into the system, to establish fully the required storage conditions under which the product is to be handled.

Next, it is critical to establish the match of the "required" condition, with the current condition of the product. The highest possible standards of quality control are needed.

This is done by visual checking and by test probing and/or sampling the condition of the goods. Where a mismatch occurs, appropriate remedial action will be needed and must be fully documented. At each step within a distribution system, matching the condition between the actual and required states is a necessary and a critical job function. For example, reliance on the fridge vehicle to pull down temperature in transit is a hazard to avoid.

A product being stored need to be handled in such a way as to ensure adequate air circulation occurs around the product. Accordingly product stacking methods and procedures need to be identified and followed.

Monitoring of the temperature conditions during storage and transport need to be undertaken at regular intervals. This monitoring becomes especially important during the transportation as products are typically solely in the care of an individual - the vehicle driver. The driver needs to regularly monitor and take remedial manual defrosting and frosting as required. Within the very narrow temperature bands for chilled and cold cargos this is not a task that can be easily dismissed. So the vehicle driver is a crucial resource and one which, by UK transport industry standards, is generally acknowledged as not being adequately rewarded, as compared to say the wage levels of fuel tanker drivers.

Condensation Damage
When goods are exchanged between low temperature and ambient conditions, it is likely for moisture to condense on the exposed surface. For example vehicle loading in ambient conditions of frozen or chilled loads can cause condensation to form on the product. Four courses of action are possible to prevent excessive condensation:

1. Ensure distribution from the refrigerated storage is in small lots for immediate consumption.

2. Provide a series of "tempering chambers" in which goods can be brought back to ambient temperatures in stages under conditions of low relative humidity.

3. Arrange immediate protection by moisture proof covers.

4. Ensure removal from cold stores is at night when ambient temperatures are low. The best course of action will depend upon actual circumstances and the specific requirements involved.

Service Levels

As varying types of products are often handled in a temperature controlled distribution system, these products will likely require varying rates of delivery into retail outlets. These varying delivery rates are due to the mix of service levels required, related to the product life cycle. For example the following requirements may be required:

Type	Examples	Typical Deliveries
Frozen	Meat	2/3 times a week. 48 hour cycle
Chilled	Fresh Meat	Daily/3 times a week. 24/48 hour cycle.
Cold Cool	Dairy Produce, Citrus	2/3 times a week. 48 hour cycle.

Goods with a short shelf life may be moved in and out of a chill store in hours, whereas with a frozen store, the time scale may be weeks or years. The middle ranges of chilled and cold products are the most critical and therefore requiring stricter operational controls.

Vehicle Design

Vehicles need to conform to design standards and ideally comply with the international ATP agreement - established in 1970 by a UN agency (ATP - Accord Transports Perishables). The ATP agreement recognises that perishable foodstuffs need special skills to maintain commodities in an adequate condition and to ensure that appropriate equipment is used. The agreement covers foodstuffs for human consumption only and specifically lays down technical standards for vehicle equipment. It does not cover hygiene standards which are determined by individual national regulations. (For example in the U.K. the Food Hygiene General Regulations 811970 No 1172 requires cleanliness in food handling and articles which could contaminate food must not be carried in a food carrying vehicle).

Exercise: Fish-n-chips

Fish-n-chips is an old established UK Company that is proud of its northern roots. They have 65 fish and chip restaurants in the UK; some are fully owned and some are franchised.

They are committed to serving products of high quality and low price. They have been well able to understand and satisfy their customers, and recently gained a Quality Award. While they specialise in fish and chips, they also sell salads, hamburgers, and fried chicken (branded as Northern Fried Chicken).

They have a key competitive advantage from their products and ingredient supply network. They use only high quality suppliers and have a rigorous monitoring process. Their supply and distribution strategy to the shops/restaurants is the envy of the competition.

They are now thinking of expanding its operations worldwide.

Task
What do you feel are the logistics and supply chain issues for market entry to:
- USA?
- Western Europe?
- Japan?

2: Transport Modes

Freight transport is the method by which goods are moved from one location to another. As industrial society relies on trade, mode selection involves finding the appropriate method of transport to undertake the movement of goods from where they are found, to processing plants and then to a market.

One of the main responsibilities of those involved in transport management is that of selecting the most appropriate means of transporting the goods for the organisation, whether this is direct from the company to the customer, or from the company to other locations such as depots and warehouses. Transport management must constantly seek to improve the service provided to the organisation; one of the important ways is in the selection of the method of transport employed.

Essential features of Transport

The essential features of transport are as follows:

Movement
It provides for the movement between the suppliers and customers. This movement can be for raw materials, sub-assemblies/work in progress, or for the finished goods.

Distance
It can take place over shorter distances on a national basis, or can be involved over longer distances and on a global basis.

Cost
Transport costs increase with distance, and are affected by the size of load. On a unit basis (for example, per tonne), the cost per unit decreases when using larger transport vehicles, as economy is directly proportional to the size of the load.

Speed
Time is often critical in the managing of supply chains. Generally, the faster the method of transport, the more expensive the transport costs. Transport cost must however be looked at holistically across the supply chain. This can mean perhaps paying more for the transport element, for a saving in the overall supply chain cost; for example, high stock holding costs may be cancelled, because the speed of transport enables the goods to be received quicker and stockholding levels are then reduced.

Accessibility
The transport system should be convenient for those who use it to send and receive goods. The system should also enable ease of loading and unloading so that the transport vehicle is not kept waiting. All types of transport vehicles (trucks, planes, ships) do incur high fixed costs, so all delays are expensive. Reducing the standing time during the loading/unloading of transport vehicles makes great improvements in transport productivity and is a reason behind many transport and goods handling developments.

Reliability

To manage supply chains effectively, reliability is an important aspect. Without this reliability, uncertainty occurs, meaning knock-on effects to other activities can occur. For example, late arrival of raw materials can mean the production stage is affected, resulting in a future decision to carry stocks to cover against unreliability.

Transport Methods/Modes

In selecting the method of transport to use, various criteria are involved; these include the following:

- Relative cost of different transport methods
- Past experience, especially on reliability factors
- Frequency, this can be for either the collection times and/or the dispatch times to the destination. For example, a collection may be made on a daily basis, but the goods are held by the transport company before being dispatched on a weekly basis.
- Forced routing for example, the transport decision may have been made by the customer who buys on ex works terms (international trade) or on factory gate pricing terms (domestic UK trade). The customer would then determine the way transport should be organised.
- Operational factors, for example:
  - customer locations
  - deliver point requirements
  - size of orders
  - service level required
  - product characteristics such as size/weight/value/fragility/hazard
- Strategic factors, for example:
  - Manufacturing locations, where are goods produced?
  - Warehousing locations, where are goods stored?
  - Marketing/Customer, where are products sold?
  - Financial situation, what can we afford, do we buy, rent, lease, contract the transport?

There are various methods of transport available. These include Road, Rail, Air, or Sea-based transport methods, and each of these methods of transport has its own particular advantages and disadvantages.

The Main Modes of Transport

The mode decision can be thought of as a hierarchy, as shown below. This hierarchy also summarises some of the varied terms and the "jargon" used with different modes. Assuming a decision has been made to use a scheduled service, the following further decisions are involved (see diagram opposite):

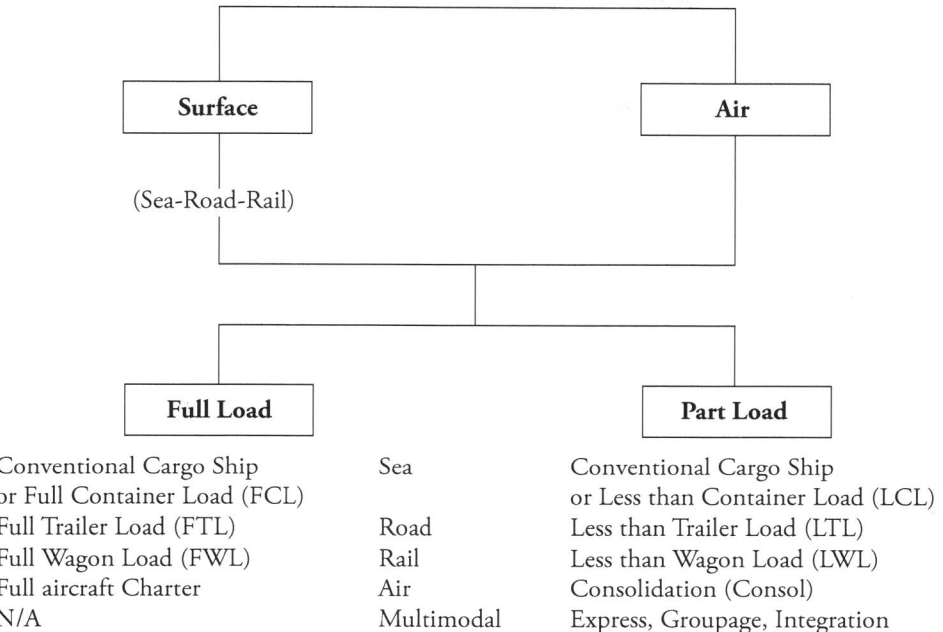

Full Load	Sea	Part Load
Conventional Cargo Ship or Full Container Load (FCL)	Sea	Conventional Cargo Ship or Less than Container Load (LCL)
Full Trailer Load (FTL)	Road	Less than Trailer Load (LTL)
Full Wagon Load (FWL)	Rail	Less than Wagon Load (LWL)
Full aircraft Charter	Air	Consolidation (Consol)
N/A	Multimodal	Express, Groupage, Integration

I shall explain some of this jargon below by looking further into the main modes of transport.

Road Transport

Road transport is the main method used for national freight transport in all European countries. It operates at low to medium cost with flexible service transit times on a door-to-door basis. The largest vehicle in the UK for normal use (excluding therefore, specialised heavy load movements) can carry around 29 tonnes and up to 130 cubic metres.

Many organisations find the convenience of road transport so great that it outweighs any cost factors. In a distribution system, the larger heavier capacity vehicles are used to transport the goods in bulk to warehouses, and smaller delivery vans are used to make the final delivery to the customer. In many cases, the level of stock damage is reduced when using road transport, as the handling can be minimised with direct door-to-door journeys.

Road transport is flexible because of its door-to-door capabilities. For intra- and inter-European Community movements, the usual type of vehicle is the semi-trailer. This has its own road wheels at the rear with let-down legs at the front to support the trailer when it is not attached to its tractor unit.

Trailer sizes can vary enormously. There are no international standards, as are found with international standards organisation (ISO) shipping freight containers, but, as we will see later, national legislation does exist for the external dimensions and gross vehicle weights. The largest general cargo road vehicle is the road train or wagon and drawbar trailer; the trailer can be left and parked like the semi-trailer. Both semi-trailers and road vehicles can also be shipped on

Roll On/Roll Off (RO/RO) sea ferry vessels or via the Channel Tunnel "Shuttle"; semi-trailers, in this case, being sent either accompanied by the tractor unit or unaccompanied, in which case a tractor unit is needed at both ends of the "across-the-sea" movement.

Many different types of bodies are found such as:
- Box Van, these have a rigid closed body with access through doors, usually at the rear
- Curtainsider, these have sliding opening curtains to allow side access
- Tipper, used for products like aggregates held in a rigid open top, for loading, body; the body then rises/tips allowing "sliding off" unloading
- Tanker, used for bulk liquids

Typical Road Trailer Weights/Dimensions

Trailer	Length	Width	Height	CBM	Tonnes
Semi trailers	13.50	2.46	3.0	100	27
Drawbar units	15.65	2.46	3.0	115.5	27

Note: these are internal dimensions for the general EC maximum external height of 4 metres. In the UK for domestic transport, a maximum external height does not exist in the legislation and for example double deck trailers to an external height of 4.9 metres are found in specialist applications.

Advantages of road transport
- All parts of the country are accessible by lorry and by combining with ferries; road transport deliveries can also reach other countries and can, therefore, offer a door-to-door service.
- For short journeys, road transport is the fastest.
- Enhanced security as the driver is in "direct control."
- Marginal costing/pricing for return loads.
- Physical handling is reduced on full vehicle loads, because of the need to load and unload only once.
- Transportation by road in the UK can be undertaken, 24 hours a day, 7 days a week.
- The flexibility of road transport allows changes can be made relatively easily.
- Image and PR possibilities from vehicle liveries that are noticed by many other road users.

Disadvantages of road transport
- The speed and reliability of deliveries can be slowed down considerably because of traffic congestion.
- Large lorries cannot use narrow access places.
- Low bridges can often cause diversions.
- Environmental damage to old buildings
- Pollution levels from diesel engines.
- Image problems when "things go wrong" due to the visibility from other road users.

Rail Transport

In the UK, the privatised rail system has an average freight length of journey of 125 miles (200 kilometres) and is used for moving full trainloads only. Therefore, the rail option is only really accessible to those companies who can provide such loads. This train load may be from one company, or a company which buys the trainload service, and then re-sells space on a wagonload basis.

Trainloads can be, for example, a quarry company moving aggregate from a quarry to a road re-distribution depot with a 3300 tonne payload trainload. Whatever method of rail transport is used, the system cannot flexibly deliver door-to-door, unless a rail connection is directly available.

Rail, therefore, only generally carries cargo on a terminal-to-terminal basis, with the Channel Tunnel spreading the development of UK Inland Terminals with direct train service links to many European destinations (the Tunnel is covered more fully in a later chapter). So the opportunity for more rail movement is available; however, there remains a route limitation on many important rail trunk lines due to insufficient clearance for full-scale train piggyback operations (these are explained shortly in the inter-modal transport section).

Whilst most UK rail movements are currently of rail wagons, they also include carrying "swap bodies", a type of shipping ISO container with a road trailer curtained body (a picture of a swap body is shown in the forthcoming intermodal section). Rail also carries standard ISO containers on flat rail wagons, especially in the UK between seaports and inland container depots.

Advantages of rail transport
- Rail transport is usually used on national freight transport for the longer distance journeys. The maximum general freight rail wagon carrying 63 tonnes, 129 cubic meters or, two twenty foot containers.
- Speed over longer distances.
- More energy efficient than road transport.
- Lower air pollution than from road transport.
- Large consignments can be handled very easily.
- More environmentally friendly than road transport.

Disadvantages of rail transport
- There may be a long distance between the collection and delivery points and the rail freight terminal; it may be very inconvenient to bring the goods to it.
- Trains operate only at specified times.
- Not every town is served by rail so the train will only bring the goods to the nearest town.
- It is expensive for short journeys.
- Quality and capacity of the rail infrastructure.

Sea/Water Transport

The UK, as an island, has a tradition for seaborne trade and has the ports, docks, and infrastructure to accommodate a very large volume of trade. The UK-registered fleet has however declined substantially since the 1980s due to the differences in taxation levels, by registering ships in more taxation friendly countries, and now has only around 1% of the world's registered fleet. Seaborne transport has the advantage of being relatively inexpensive in relation to bulk loads. However, it is a slow form of delivery between port terminals and most of the goods moved also have to be collected at the port terminal and then delivered to the customers.

Sea is normally chosen because of cost and it moves up to 95% by weight and 60% by value of all world international trade cargo. Examples of such cargo are general consumer goods, automotive vehicles, chemicals, iron and steel, ores, oil, and other bulk products and any product that is not time sensitive and where demand can be forecast in advance, to allow for the relatively slow transit time. Whilst it is, therefore, the slowest mode of transport, sea transport benefits from economies of scale as very large volumes of cargo are moved by the one unit, i.e. the ship or vessel. Vessels up to 550 000 tonnes are found carrying bulk cargo, and since the 1960s, container services dominate general cargo shipping, with scheduled services operating between all the world's main trade centres. These regular liner ocean services are relatively frequent and reliable in operation.

Advantages of sea transport
• Reliable transit between terminals with regular frequent timetabled service frequencies between all major trading countries.
• Suitable for transporting bulky goods.
• Cheap.
• The main mode used for companies who trade globally.

Disadvantages of sea transport
• Slow form of transport, although potential developments of "Fast Ship" 1400 TEU vessels using gas turbines/water jet propulsion could mean halving the transit times against current more conventionally powered and designed vessels. Originally scheduled for 2006 and currently scheduled to be operational in 2011, it advertises a five-day, port-to-port time-definite express freight service between Europe and the US and is forecast to enable door-to-door services comparable to standard airfreight, at half the price. The website www.fastshipatlantic.com will carry updates.
• Insurance costs for transporting goods by sea are higher than those for air transport, as the goods spend longer in transit.
• More packing is needed than when using air freight.

Water transport is also found with inland waterways. There is a network of over 3000 miles of navigable inland waterways in the UK, used mainly for pleasure purposes. Freight loads have been falling for many years with less than one per cent of domestic UK freight moved on inland waterways. Traditional markets are in bulk products that have a high volume and a low value like aggregates, scrap, waste, grains, timber and animal feeds.

Containerisation

A subset of sea transport involves containerisation. This involves the movement of cargo where, instead of packages being handled individually at each stage of their journey, they are stowed in a large container, which is then transported as a single unit to the overseas destination. This reduces the ship turnaround time in ports and improves the cargo security.

Containerisation is dominant on sea trades and the inland transport of shipping lines containers is also a common feature on UK roads. Containers are usually built to International Standards Organisation (ISO) specifications. Originally built to imperial external measurements of 20/30/40 ft length by 8 ft width and height, these 1960s original dimensions have been subsequently increased. For example, up to 8ft 6 inches height is now very common worldwide, with a 9ft 6-inch height on some trades. On length, some 45 foot containers are used on European trades and on the width, also in Europe it is not uncommon to find 2.5 metres (8.202 ft).

The following features of containerisation should be noted:
- The containers are of standard sizes with corner twist locks to facilitate universal worldwide handling.
- Special cellular ships are provided to accommodate the containers.
- There are also special types of crane and other handling equipment to load/unload the containers.
- Ideally road or rail trailers are used that have twist locks that fasten and engage the container to the carrying trailers/bodies.

There are several types of container in use. In particular, the following ones should be noted:
- General purpose. This is the standard type of container, which is used for most types of cargo. It is fully enclosed, with doors at one end for access.
- Reefer. A refrigerated container, for perishable cargoes (such as food, pharmaceuticals etc.) which must be transported at low and constant temperatures.
- Open top. Designed for cargoes which are over ordinary height, and so the cargo cannot be loaded into a general-purpose container through the end doors.
- Flat rack. This consists of a base with panelled-in ends, and is used for oversize pieces, which cannot be stowed in any other type of container.
- Open sided. Used when it is more practical to load the container from the side rather than the ends.
- Half height. Suitable for dense cargoes, such as lead, where the weight is high in relation to the volume. As there are design weight limitations for each container, a considerable amount of space would be wasted if such cargoes were stowed in full size containers.
- There are also special types of container for the conveyance of bulk commodities such as liquids, grain, etc.

Two basic types of container Sea/Ocean Services are provided:
- FCL (Full Container Load). This is suitable for the shipper who has sufficient cargo to fill a complete container, or who prefer to load the container themselves. The container will be loaded at the shipper's premises, and after the shipper has stowed

and sealed it, they will hand the container over to the carrier. On arrival at the port destination the consignees can arrange for the container to be delivered to their premises and unpack it themselves.

- LCL (Less than Container Load). This service is most suitable for a shipper who does not have sufficient cargo to fill a complete container. They will arrange for the cargo to be delivered to the carrier, who will stow it into a container together with the cargo of other shippers. On arrival at the carrier's depot, the carrier will unpack the container and the relevant consignees will collect the cargo from the depot/warehouse.

The following four terms are used on container transport:
- FCL/FCL: The container is packed by the shipper to be unpacked by the consignee.
- FCL/LCL: The container is packed by the shipper and will be unpacked by the carrier.
- LCL/FCL: The container is packed by the carrier and will be unpacked by the consignee.
- LCL/LCL: The container is both packed and unpacked by the carrier.

Advantages of containerisation
- The main feature of containerisation is that it can provide a door-to-door service, with no intermediate handling en route of the goods packed inside.
- This, in turn, results in lower risk of pilferage, which can mean lower insurance premiums for FCL/FCL freight.
- In the case of FCL consignments, less packing is required, and often the goods can be stowed unpacked in the container itself.
- Containerisation can enable faster transit times, and allows the carriers to provide through documentation and rates to and from inland origins/destinations.
- From the ship owners' point of view, it is possible to rationalise the fleet and the ports of call, with the cargo being 'fed' by smaller vessels between the main ports of call and the smaller out ports. Ship turnaround time is also minimised, for example it is estimated a 40 000 tonne container ship can discharge or load in 750 worker hours whereas a conventional cargo ship would require 24 000 worker hours. Another telling statistic is from the first large UK container vessel in 1969. In its first year's operation between the UK/Australia, it spent 82% of the year at sea with 18% spent in port; this compared to a modern conventional ship on the same trade, of 59% at sea and 41 % in port.

Disadvantages of containerisation
- Not all cargo can be containerised, and exceptionally large and heavy pieces can only be dispatched by the traditional break-bulk methods.
- Some kinds of cargo cannot be stowed together in the same containers, a problem which applies particularly to certain types of dangerous cargo.
- From the ship-owning carrier's point of view, containerisation is capital-intensive and needs investment and management in the container fleet and in using specialised port terminal facilities.

Length	Internal Width	Internal Height	Cubic metres	Tonnes
20 foot external =5.89 metres internal	2.34	2.4	33.00	28.2
40 foot external =12.00 metres internal	2.34	2.4	67.00	28.8

Note: Door openings slightly reduce the width and height.
Note: Tonne capacity is the design build specification. The effective payload will usually be reduced by national vehicle weight legislation.

The flexibility of the inter-modal container enables easy transhipment, not only between primary and secondary feeder vessels, but also between ship and land modes of transport. Container ships, also known as lift on-lift off [LOLO] vessels, are complimented on ocean liner routes by other general cargo vessels. Whilst some conventional ships remain (these move cargo from land into ship holds by conventional cranes, either on the shore or on the vessels themselves), the growth of Roll On, Roll Off [RORO] vessels is noticeable, especially on shorter sea and inter European trade routes. Roll On, Roll Off vessels on these shorter haul routes generally carry between 50 up to a maximum of 210 x 12/15 metre trailers. These RORO vessels allow for a speedy transfer shore/ship of wheeled freight, for example, road trailers, with Dover being the main UK RORO port, handling around 2.4 million units per annum, around 33% of the total UK RORO traffic of 7.2 million units, with Grimsby/ Immingham and Liverpool being the second and third placed RORO ports respectively.

Container ships on longer haul routes generally carry between 3000 to 4000 x 20 ft containers (or 3/4000 TEU - twenty foot equivalent units). Medium sized (Panamax) vessels go up to a maximum of 4200 TEU so they can fit through the Panama Canal that has a maximum width of 32 metres and a draught of 12 metres. With the Canal expansion expected to be finished in 2014, then the new Panamax II standard will effectively enable 12000 TEU vessels. Larger so-called Post Panama vessels (these cannot fit the Panama Canal) of 8000 TEU are being regularly used on Asia/Europe services operating via the Suez Canal. A new container ship size, reflecting the Malacca straights (near Singapore), gives rise to the Malaccamax vessel size of dimensions of 470 m in length and 60 m wide with a 20 m draught carrying around 18 000 TEU.

Meanwhile, the current (2009) longest ship and largest container freight carrier in the world went into service in 2006; at 397 metres long and carrying up to 15000 TEU by some classifications; (although the company concerned, Maersk Line, classifies it as 11000 TEU). This is one of 8 identical vessels for operation on Asia/European services. Larger vessels have also pushed developments towards main "mega" ports with subsequent increased transhipping. The UK is somewhat behind in the global container port position with Far Eastern ports dominating; Singapore being the world's busiest with around 28 million TEU per annum, with China and South Korea occupying the world ranking positions of 2 to 5. The largest UK port of Felixstowe is ranked 28th in the world and handles 3.3 million TEU per annum. This is

37% of the UK's 8.9 million TEU container movements per year, with Southampton the UK's second container port. UK figures are somewhat behind other European ports, with Rotterdam ranked number 6 in the world, Hamburg 9th, Antwerp 14th and Bremen 20th.

Air transport

Air transport is a global industry and is very often regarded as an important strategic part and a "figurehead" of many countries' transport services. It operates under strong controls, not only by national government legislation, but also through international liaison with IATA (the International Air Transport Association). Governments are often involved as investors, besides being regulators, and from an investment point of view the returns are often below normal commercial business criteria, meaning, in effect, government subsidy can be involved.

Airfreight transport involves the use of both commercial passenger aircraft carrying extra freight, and aircraft used entirely for the transport of freight. Improved aircraft technology, including wide body aircraft, gives an increased availability for "under passenger" space capacity in the lower/under decks. Specialist services have also developed with all cargo aircraft and convertible combined passenger/cargo configurations. The largest freight cargo aircraft (the Russian-built AN 225) carries 254 tonnes, 1130 cubic metres, or space for 25 twenty-foot containers with the smaller AN 124 carrying 120 tonnes, 750 cubic metres or space for 12 twenty foot containers.

Air transport is very expensive, but it is also the quickest method of transport over long distances. It is usually used where the goods involved are small, light and expensive, so that the cost of transport is only a fraction of the total cost of the item itself. Cargo that is regularly carried by airfreight is pharmaceuticals, high tech products, spare parts, documents and fashion goods. These have characteristics of having a high value with possible time sensitivity, therefore needing a quick response and a high value to density ratio; indeed air carries around 40% of world trade in value terms but less than 5% by weight.

Air transport is also often chosen because of the speed needed for freight such as perishables, fashion goods and emergency supplies. For certain types of freight and volumes, air can also give an overall cost effective solution to global supply chain operations. This will usually mean considerations beyond the basic airfreight cost; for example, financial issues such as the cost of money tied up in stocks, the time to market etc.

Advantages of air transport
- Air transport is very reliable.
- It is the speediest form of transport available (between airport terminals).
- Can be used where surface transport is not viable or easily possible, for example, helicopters flying over jungles, high mountain ranges etc.
- Low security risk (between airport terminals) and reduced risk of damage or pilferage; therefore insurance costs are low.
- Less packaging is required.

Disadvantages of air transport
- It is the most expensive method of transport on a cost per mile basis, especially in comparison with road and rail costs.
- Aircraft may be delayed/diverted because of weather conditions preventing landing/takeoff. The mode is the most susceptible to weather delays.
- There are limits to the amount of heavy and large freight that a plane can carry.
- It is necessary to transport the goods from the factory to the airport and this increases the transport costs, especially if the factory is a long distance from the airport.
- Ground handling at airports can be slow.
- Ground security pilferage risks as airfreight handles high valued cargo.

Airfreight has its own type of containerisation but these containers are made of a much lighter construction than the sea transport ISO containers. The airfreight containers are of three types; air cargo pallets, lower deck containers and box type containers and all tend to go under the name of "Unit Load Devices" (ULDs). Like the shipping ISO containers, ULDs can be loaned to shippers/consignees for loading/unloading. As will be seen below, ULDs have unusual sizes, as these have to be compatible with aircraft types/stowage arrangements, and are designed to make the best use of the aircraft cube space.

The air cargo ULD pallet is designed mainly for terminal-to-terminal use, with the conveyor systems in both terminals and in aircraft; the pallet being fitted with lashing points for securing the pallet to the aircraft deck. Cargo is normally secured to the metal pallet by cargo nets, which are then tightened by tensioned straps. Contoured semi-structural covers called "igloos", "hula-huts" or "cocoons" can be used with pallets to provide cargo protection and also to keep cargo within the appropriate dimensions for loading onto an aircraft.

Lower deck (LD) containers are mainly for terminal-to-terminal use and fit in the lower/under decks of high capacity passenger aircraft like the A330, A340, A380, B747, B767, B777 and MD11. They are fully structured and completely enclosed with doors made from metal, fabric or a combination of these. LD containers can be closed and sealed - a common use is for passenger luggage. They lock directly into aircraft restraint systems.

Box type ULD containers were developed in standard sizes to facilitate fixed freight charges, and to be used on a door-to-door basis. They can be purchased by users or loaned from an airline. They must be constructed to IATA specifications from wood, plastic, plywood, fibreboard, metal or combinations of these. Contoured box containers (igloos) are also handled and loaded in the same way as pallet ULD igloos.

Type	Height	Length	Width	Weight	Cubic feet
LD 1	64"	61.5"	64"	1588 kilos	60
LD 8	64"	125"	60"	2449 kilos	254

Intermodal Transport

Intermodal transport is characterised by two basic elements:

- The use of more than one mode of transport for the various component legs of a journey from origin to destination.
- Goods remain in the same load-carrying unit (container, trailer or swap body), throughout the journey with the transfers of the unit between the modes, taking place in terminals or ports.

Whilst we have looked at the relative advantages and disadvantages of the various methods of transport, intermodal transport is the combination of different methods, for example, transport across and beyond national boundaries with a movement from China to Europe, which could involve road transport, sea transport, rail transport, and road transport. The following diagram illustrates this:

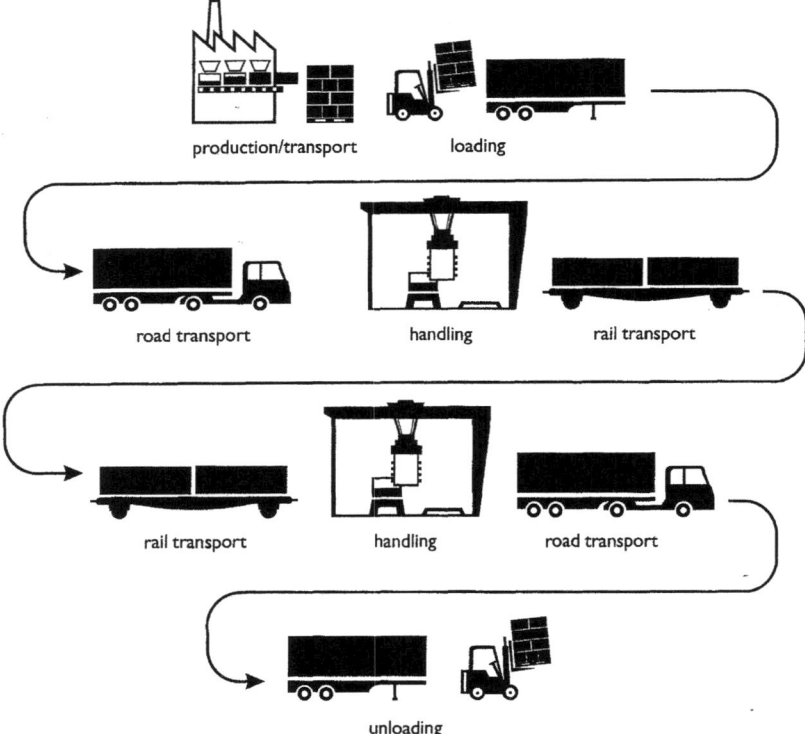

Inter-modal Container transport
(Reproduced with permission Cheltenham Tutorial College)

Intermodal transport is capable of giving a door/door service between senders and receivers. The receiver finally unloads the freight from the freight container; the consignment being untouched/unhandled since being loaded by the sender.

32

Other combinations of modes include the only use of rail/road transport. This method is receiving strong support in the EU as it is seen as an environmentally sensitive transport method. How far these services will remain commercial, and remain competitive with other modes, and whether legislation will "force" their use remains to be seen. In these mode combinations, the complete tractor/trailer or wagon/drawbar road vehicles or just the road vehicle trailer or a swap body from a road vehicle, are loaded onto rail transport. The following diagram shows these three types:

A – Truck and Trailer; tractor and semi-trailer (complete combinations)
The driver steers his vehicle forward over a ramp
on to a very low special wagon

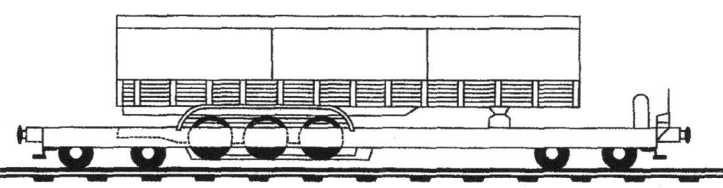

B – Semi-Trailer
Transhipment using (gantry) cranes or by driving
backwards over a ramp on to the wagons

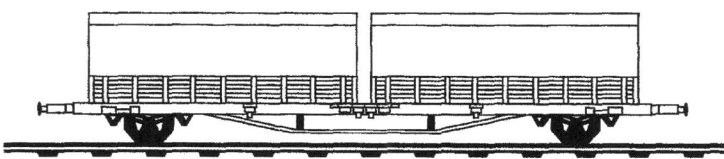

C – Swop-Bodies
(Length of 6m, 7m, 8m or 12m)
Transhipment by (gantry) cranes

Piggyback system
(Reproduced with permission from Cheltenham Tutorial College)

This piggyback system is more widely used in Europe, where the distance freight is moved is greater. Additionally it can also compensate for any travel time restrictions placed on road journeys; for example, during weekends/public holidays in France and the bans on road transit through Switzerland.

In the UK, there are no such travel time restrictions and the journey distances are lower, so there is limited commercial application for some systems. Trails were made using semi-trailers between south England and central Scotland in the 1980s, but commercially they failed. Meanwhile a small service started again the early 2000s and received much environment-friendly publicity.

Advantages of Intermodal transport
- On long journeys, lower costs can be found by combining modes
- Potentially, it can be faster than using just one mode, for example, by using road/sea/air combinations instead of just sea
- Reduces road congestion, for example, when rail combinations are used in the UK
- Lower negative environmental effects than when using only road transport

Disadvantages of Intermodal transport
- Not widely available for many applications/trades.
- Needs specialised equipments e.g. trailers.
- Non-coordinated information/transfers between modes/different operators involved.
- Needs specialised terminals for the interchange to take place between modes.
- Road legs are still needed for the start and destination journeys.

Other Modes

Parcels/Post Office Transport

The cost is low with varied speed of service levels available. Reliability is varied, as this is dependent on the specific national origin/destination office or the other postal authorities for international traffics, and on any available track/trace systems in the national postal authorities. There are capacities issues with post as there are size restrictions. This is mainly 15 kilos, with some countries having a limit of 10 kilos.

Couriers/Express Transport

Courier transport is "hand-held", with express transport for up to 30kg packages. Both offer flexible door-to-door services with medium to high cost levels. Speed is fast with guaranteed services available, for example, Next Day, 48 hours, 3 days or Deferred. Reliability is good as operators often use dedicated "own" networks, and with couriers, one person hand-carrying the package(s).

Forwarders/Agents for Transport

A forwarding agent is an intermediary who buys freight on behalf of the principal. They are "experts" who should continually monitor the "best" options, and then give impartial advice.

A forwarder - a subtle change in name - is a freight specialist/operator of services using their own or hired equipment. They are specific route specialists and service operators in their own right. As such, they cannot be expected to give impartial advice. Both, however, will often give useful advice on customs and prepare documentation.

The distinction between forwarders and forwarding agents is often blurred, but the difference is fundamental when making a selection; forwarding agents should be impartial, whereas forwarders can prefer to use only their own services.

Forwarders and agents can vary in size:

Base	Size	Facilities
Local agent	1-2 offices	Offices only
National forwarder	Major ports and inland towns	Possibly with road vehicles and warehouses
International forwarder	World wide	Possibly with owned ships and aircraft

Forwarders can have a strong and a dominant role. For example with airfreight, over 90% of freight is handled by forwarders/agents, and 70% of this freight is handled by forwarder consolidations. In sea freight, the percentages are lower.

Channel Tunnel

The Channel Tunnel is a more recent mode of transport which started fully moving freight in May 1994 from the UK under the English Channel to France. It offers competition to ferry operators on a terminal-to-terminal basis, and also to road transport/road-based forwarding companies by offering through-rail services that operate to/from inland destinations.

Before the Channel Tunnel, terminal-to-terminal sea ferry traffic comprised approximately of 40% accompanied RORO road trailer traffic, 35% unaccompanied RORO, 20% LOLO container traffic and 5% train ferry. These were the major freight targets for the Tunnel operators. The Tunnel's planned offering was 50% terminal/terminal traffic (Le Shuttle) catering for accompanied vehicles and 50% of the capacity was planned for direct services from inland destinations. The terminal-to-terminal Shuttle, besides carrying passenger cars/occupants, carries up to 28 articulated vehicles up to 44tonnes GVW and a maximum of 18.5x2.6x4.2 metres (LxWxH) with up to four trains per hour in peak times. With no advance booking, turn-up-and-go availability gives under one hour transit time and offers around 25 per cent of the total capacity for UK/North East, near continent and channel RORO terminal-to-terminal sea ferry traffic.

The Tunnel development also gave rail a major and unique opportunity to compete once and for all with road traffic over the long distances where rail is able to effectively to do this. This represented a threat to the road hauliers and forwarders, but offered an opportunity for users who could only gain in the ensuing competition. To support this move, nine dedicated rail terminals were opened in Glasgow (Mossend), Middlesbrough, Wakefield, Liverpool (Seaforth), Manchester (Trafford Park), Birmingham, Cardiff and London (Stratford and Willesden). These terminals were also supplemented by ones at Doncaster and Daventry and were able to handle swap bodies/containers, and also roadrailer and piggyback road trainers.

Through-trains were foreseen from these terminals to varied European destinations, and up to 35 freight trains per day (over 200 per week) could be scheduled through the tunnel. However, in mid-1996, only 45 services were timetabled per week:

- France, Paris and Lille; 8 times per week
- Germany, Duisburg: 5 times per week
- Spain, Silla; 10 times per week
- Italy, Milan and Oleggio; 22 times per week

In addition to these new intermodal opportunities, conventional train ferry traffic was cancelled and now "diverted" by the Tunnel. 40 trains per week were planned for this existing traffic, being fed by over twenty existing ferry wagon terminals/company private sidings and three automotive distribution centres; these train ferry services carrying products like steel and aluminium (Outward) and sugar, zinc ingots, paper, car parts and Evian/Volvic mineral water (Inward).

The new intermodal train services were made available to "aggregators", a wholesaler who would find the traffic and buy space from the train company. As there was little existing traffic of trainload terminal-to-terminal size, this traffic would have to be taken from other modes in the competitive marketplace, where cost and service variables are the important determinants of choice.

Within ten years of the opening, history has, however, written a lesson of the failure to do this effectively. With planned traffic estimates widely over-optimistic and operations beset by perceived transit time reliability problems, coupled with the failure to compete with road traffic, this perceived "lack of intermodal freight" problem was further magnified in 2001. Illegal immigrants using the Tunnel as a point of entry to the UK caused the complete closures of the Tunnel for two-week periods and the consequent "walking" of already frustrated customers. Intermodal services were to resume on a much-reduced basis, for example, to Italy 12 times per week from only four UK terminals (Manchester, Daventry, Birmingham, and Willesden).

A disappointing and embarrassing consequence of the unique opportunity rail was given, is that the actual network is one that falls far short of the original network, which envisaged over 200 intermodal trains per week to over 10 specialist UK terminals. The "jury" is still out for the future intermodal success from the Channel Tunnel opportunity given in 1994. Finally, on this transport modes section, a summary can be found in Appendix one.

International transport liability conventions

Whilst we shall cover insurance provision later, it is important to realise that the different transport modes have variable liability provisions; it is a reality that most users are not aware of these different carrier liability regimes.

With international transport, conflicts between differing legal systems can arise. To standardise this, conventions have developed. This means that all parties involved - shippers, operators, and consignees - are represented at an international convention. A set of rules is then worked upon at this convention and then agreed between the parties. They go back to their home country where they attempt to persuade authorities and governments to enact the rules into domestic law. Once this has been done by the majority of countries, conflicts of law are prevented.

There are five basic conventions which cover international transports and these are as follows:
- Sea: The Hague/Visby Rules, replaced by the Hamburg Rules
- Air: The Warsaw Rules, replaced by the Montreal Rules
- Road: CMR Rules (The Carriage of Merchandise by Road Hauliers)
- Rail: CIM Rules and the COTIF convention (Organisation for International Carriage by Railway)
- Multimodal: ICC298 The International Chamber of Commerce Uniform Rules for Combined Transport Documents

The following table gives a comparison between those conventions:

Mode	Liability	Limits	Document used	Time Limit to claim
Sea	Liable if no due diligence, goods not loaded properly, handled or stowed Not liable if errors in navigation, firs, perils and some other factors	666.67 SDR units per package, or 2.0. SDR units per kilo; whichever is the greater (Hague/Visby) 835 SDR Units per package or 2.5 units a kilo; whichever is the greater (Hamburg)	Bill of lading	Normally one year
Air	Liable if loss or damage or delay. Not liable if the carrier took necessary measures or due to fault of claimant	250 gold francs per kilos (Warsaw) 17 SDR units per kilo (Montreal)	Air way bill	Two years
Road	Liable if loss or damage or delays. Not liable if faults of claimant, inherent vice or circumstances beyond carriers control	8.33 SDR units per kilo (The average value of cargo is approx.1600 Euros per 1000 kilos according to EU sources on road freight).	CMR consignment note	Normally one year
Rail	As road	7 SDR units per kilo	CIM consignment note	Normally one year
Multi modal	Liable for lass or delay	30 Gold Frances per kilo	Combined Transport Document	9 months

These different liabilities are what the international carriers maintain. Users will need to be aware of these differences so they can take informed decisions on arranging appropriate insurance cover. Meanwhile, for pure domestic transport, liability will be subject to the standard terms and conditions of the carrier used, or subject to agreed terms and conditions between users and carriers.

Reasons why organisations switch transport modes

The transport manager may be prompted to search for new modes of transport by the following:
- Improve customer satisfaction in terms of time, method of materials handling, degree of security.
- Deterioration of service provided by the existing mode.
- Reduce costs.
- Reduce transit time.
- Changing needs of the organisation and/or the customer.
- Development of new products which require different modes of transport.

Information concerning modes of transport

During the process of selecting modes of transport, the manager has to examine a number of considerations before making an effective decision. The sources of information available are as follows:
- Past experience of the transport manager. They will have dealt with a number of organisations and modes and will have a high degree of 'market' knowledge to refer to in the decision-making process.
- Marketing/commercial departments of the transport organisations.
- Trade directories and route maps.
- Trade magazines and journals.
- Specialist consultants who will advise on the various modes of transport and the relative advantages and disadvantages of each.
- Other transport managers. If the transport or fleet manager is a member of the Chartered Institute of Logistics and Transport, then information from fellow professionals is available.

Exercise: Appliance Universal (AUPLC)

AUPLC is a medium-size U.K. manufacturer of refrigerators and electric products. During the past fifteen years, they have increased their share of the refrigerator and electric range market from less than two percent to twenty percent. Part of the reason for this tremendous growth was that they offer high-quality products at low prices. In addition AUPLC believe that quality products resulted from actually owning and managing key component vendors and that quality marketing and sales efforts resulted from directly managing distributors and retail appliance outlets.

Alan Brown, Logistics Manager for AUPLC, has had an extensive discussion with his Supply Chain Director. AUPLC had just acquired an appliance distributor located in New York USA and the logistics department has to quickly develop an operating process to support this American distributor with AUPLC products.

Purchasing the New York distributor was the first major international business venture and AUPLC have very limited international experience.

Given the emphasis on quality products and service, top management has mandated consistent, low lead times. AUPLC deliver domestic distributor orders less than five days from the order date. Road transportation, using their own e fleet is the main mode for both inbound and outbound shipments.

Having had little experience in international transportation, Alan Brown felt a little out of his element in developing an international transportation plan.

Distance was going to be a major factor since AUPLC had plants located in Liverpool, Sunderland, and Peterborough. This long distance from the USA market would contribute to two basic problems: high transport costs and long lead times.

Moving the products from the plants to the Felixstowe or Southampton ports would require some new form of transportation. Ocean carrier shipment would be long, and Mr. Read would have to arrange to move the product from the entry port to the distributor.

With the logistics-planning meeting set for the next morning at 0800, Alan Brown prepared the following transportation plan:
1.   Finished products from all three factories would be road transport to the ports
2.   Seafreight by container would be made to New York
3.   Road transport would move from New York to the distributor
4.   From New York the distributor would arrange transport to final customers
5.   An international transport manager would need to be hired
6.   Mr. Read estimated the total transit time would be 4 weeks

Tasks
1.   What are the strengths and weaknesses on Mr. Browns plan
2.   Develop alternatives and provide justifications to support their adaptation

3: The Road Freight Transport Operator

Duties and responsibilities

A transport manager has a vital role to play in relation to the overall product control of the organisation and also to its total profitability. Typical duties and responsibilities of a transport manager are listed below:

- Selection of most appropriate mode of transport, depending upon the materials to be moved and their destinations, whilst balancing/optimising the required cost and service levels.
- Evaluation and control of all the transport services used by the organisation such as recording utilisations, condition reporting, costs etc.
- To work, where appropriate, with warehousing/stores, production, purchasing and marketing to ensure that the transport service provided meets all the requirements of the organisation.
- To ensure the security of goods while in transit and to select modes of transport that minimises the risk of stock loss.
- To ensure that the organisation complies with all appropriate legislation.
- To be aware of changes and developments both internally and externally that will have impact on transport activities.
- To examine and make as appropriate, improvements to transport services and to the organisation as a whole.

I shall concentrate mainly, in this chapter, on fleet management and on road freight transport; the dominant mode of transport in the UK market.

Risk

The freight industry is subject to risk from changes in demand and from changes in contract terms. Changes in transport demand result from transport's dependency on trade. Whilst operators will try to match their own service supply to the customer's demand, there are often difficulties in doing this. The supply of new vehicles, ships and planes does not happen instantly and they are subject to long lead times. Indeed, the ordering of transport capital equipment is used as a useful and practical barometer of the economy, as companies will tend to order when economies are growing. Therefore, if a mistake is made on the timing, new vehicles may be received just as a trade recession happens.

Since the 1980s in the UK, the growth of fixed term "contracts" for UK distribution has been viewed favourably by city analysts, as this represents certainty. When such economic trends become reversed, the city changes its view, and for example, former large operators are no longer seen as "sexy" and appropriate reductions in share values are made.

Another aspect of the freight industry, from a microeconomic theory point of view, is that volume-based discounts are often given on routes where there is a capacity problem. For example, on busy routes from the Far East to Europe, a user/shipper will pay less for high volume movements even when capacity is in high demand. Theory says that where capacity is scarce, rates should be higher, but this does not always happen. Similarly, those who pay the higher rates may not be guaranteed to get the scarce space at the expense of a lower-rated, but earlier-booked shipper.

Marginal costing is often used, a principle where only the extra marginal costs are considered (such as terminals charges for a container ship operator), and therefore any extra revenue that covers these marginal costs is viewed as contributing to the fixed costs of, say, sailing the container ship; after all, "it has to go back anyway". This marginal costing principle, if managed correctly, can certainly give extra revenue that would otherwise not have been received. However if not managed correctly, the risk of all traffics being carried at marginal rates will result in not covering total costs and lead to an eventual business failure. We shall further examine this important aspect of transport costs later in this chapter.

Customer Service

Customer service is fundamentally about satisfying customer needs, and getting this right will enable an organisation to view whether it has a competitive advantage with its customers (who may also be internal).

In the customer-focused marketplace, organisations need a competitive advantage. They must be better than the competition and they can do this by "doing it better" and/or "doing it cheaper." Consider the following table on cost leadership ("doing it cheaper") and service differentiation ("doing it better").

Cost Leadership	Service Differentiation
Standard products produced cheaply	Customer designed products
Production push	Market pull
Flow and mass volume production, with high mechanisation	Job shop production with low mechanisation
Low inventory	Flexible and varied inventory
Focus on productivity	Focus on creativity
Stable planning	Flexible planning
Centralisation	Decentralisation
Standardisation	Bespoke and "one-offs"

As it is "Supply chains that now compete, not individual companies" (after: Prof. Martin Christopher), organisations will need to:
* Segment customers.
* Have good relationships with customers and suppliers and connect "cognitively".
* Use Technology that can "enable" and "connect".
* Recognise there is global competition, meaning a growth of alliances.

However, whether serving internal or external customers, customer service must be a total offering, and some of the most important principles of customer service are as follows:

- Customers have needs and expectations. The magic comes from going beyond the normal customer expectations and going the extra mile to impress the customer.
- Customer service is a source of competitive advantage. But customers may already be using a competitor's products/service; and the question is, "Why?"
- Customer service is always delivered by people, so how we do it is more important, than what the product/service being delivered actually is.
- Customer service has different levels of service, so how do we experiment with different levels so we can better determine the organisations future?
- Organisations must maximise the customer service experience, so that customers will not only return, but will also tell/encourage others to buy from the organisation (repeat business is a cheaper option than having to get new business).

Using customer service this way may require a new style of management; a style that combines hard quantifiable aspects like target setting and measurement, with soft qualitative aspects of communicating and motivating.

Transport physically delivers the service to customers, so asking customers what levels of customer service they actually receive can be revealing. Finding out what the customer really wants will give often a veritable web of similar, different and conflicting requirements; these are important to have knowledge of, so that appropriately required services can be provided. The following is just one example of a way to find this out from customers.

Contact a random sample of customers (10 - 20). Ask them to rate your operation on a scale of 1-10 against varied questions; some question examples are shown below.

Customer Satisfaction Survey

What do you think of the service to you? It would help us if you would rate this on a 1 - 10 scale (1 is poor, 5 is average, 10 is excellent)

Activity	Your Score	Our Target
Response Time		10
Accuracy of orders		10
Complete orders		10
Product Damage		10
On-time Delivery		10

Thank you for your co-operation and in helping us to improve.

It is vital for any business to be aware of just what the customer's perception actually is of the service that is being given. From the supplying organisation's perspective, this level of service provided needs to be not only from the transport point of view, but is the sum of all the operations and activities of the company. Transport is the last link in the chain that started with the customer's order, and can therefore "suffer" from any shortcomings in the company before the transport service is even requested or required.

It is important that companies do have measures in place to reveal their internal activities performance, so that appropriate action can be taken where it is needed. Continual late deliveries from the customer's perspective is nearly always not going to be because transport was delayed somewhere en route with the delivery, but will be due to delays before the transport even left the supplier to make the delivery. Transport managers and operators are often correct in their view that they are made responsible for matters completely outside of their direct control, and will be aware that the provision of the transport service will always be very visible to the customer. However, when an order has been left "sitting" somewhere internally, when no stock is available; then these reasons for late delivery are unlikely to be visible to the customer.

Principles for order fulfilment

Transport has an important part in satisfying customer orders and the following 10 principles contain all the elements that will ensure customer's orders are fulfilled satisfactorily and continuously by a company. It will be seen that transport is just one of the parts involved in doing this and that in fact all the internal and external players of an organisation are involved in fulfilling orders.

Quick throughput - Move it - "Moving not standing"
- Minimised waiting in the supply chain
- Maximised efficiency in the supply chain
- Process integration in the supply chain

Optimised stock - Sort it - "Sorting not storing"
- Replenishment policy
- Stock accuracy
- Minimum holding

Reduced lead time - Time it -"Finding out how long it takes"
- Supply process
- Manufacture process
- Delivery process
- Storage process
- Order processing
- Payment processing

Flexible resources - Use it - "Being able to adapt better and eliminate waste"
- People
- Machinery
- Materials
- Methods
- Processes

Performance ownership - Own it - "Doing what we say we will do"
- Objectives
- Performance measurement
- Taking action

Effective communication - Understand it - "Preventing misunderstanding"
- Appropriate methods
- Effective content
- Openness
- Clarity

Team working environment - Share it - "Working better together"
- Values, vision and objectives
- Understanding each other
- Supporting each other

Education and learning - Change it - "Learning and changing"
- Defining and meeting peoples needs
- Supporting learning
- Reviewing change

Safe secure, working environment - Live it - "Developing a safety culture"
- Personal and equipment safety
- Secure methods and processes
- Knowledge and accountability

Everything in its place - Clean it - "Keeping a clean and tidy work environment"
- Housekeeping
- Workplace layout
- Housekeeping discipline

Operators should always be aware that customers are interested in service performance and that they will be measuring the overall performance to their own customers, for example the following aspects of:
- On time delivery (OT)
- In full order delivery (IF)

Operators can usefully reflect on the role they have with these common OTIF performance measures used by their customers.

Frequency of Service

The longer the journey transit time, the stronger the possibility for a more variable transit time. For example, whilst ships may depart from Hong Kong to the UK every Friday, the week 1 vessel may call *en route* at Singapore and Dubai, the week 2 vessel departure calls at Le Havre, the week 3 vessel is direct. Therefore, a variable transit time can be found with fixed departure frequencies.

On shorter European journeys, similar effects can be noticed. However, there can also be a hidden transit time. For example, cargo is collected in Marseilles on Tuesday for delivery to Manchester. However, it does not leave Calais until Saturday for a Monday delivery. Alternatively, it could have been collected on the Tuesday and have been in Manchester by Friday.

Customer service focus

A company that delivers excellent service will be one that, when compared to competitors, will be preferred by customers. Then the service provider is able to charge a higher price, gain a larger market share and enjoy a higher profit margin than competitors.

This will mean seeing customers as assets that are to be serviced, maintained and nurtured, so that they will appreciate and grow in value over time. Some of the characteristics needed by companies that want to aspire to this are as follows:

- They care about their people: attitude and devotion of all the staff is critical; this will not happen by accident. Subsequent chapters will cover this topic more fully.
- Management is there to help and support: command and control management styles are unlikely to work; again subsequent chapters will cover this topic more fully.
- Service is a way of life to all in the company: this includes all those in the background such as finance, personnel, production, purchasing and depot and administration staff.
- Any failings are quickly recovered: the culture is one of "getting it right" and is not one of covering up mistakes and blaming others.
- Continually looking to add value to the service offered: how for example, can the services be improved and have greater impact on the customer?
- Having knowledge of the customers: understanding customers' businesses and the people in the customers' business is central to being able to serve them better. Customer surveys are helpful here.
- Belief that quality comes before profit: a cost plus orientation of profit will often not succeed, for example as with giving staff bonus payments for reducing costs, when sales are falling and profits tumbling. Quality comes first, and profits follow naturally.
- Carrying out, efficiently and effectively, the basics of the operational service offer: the starting point here being that quality services are undertaken for a fair price and produced at acceptable costs; "wish list" promises and extra "bells and whistles" will never overcome a mediocre service.

To be a customer service focussed organisation, you will need to know:
- Who your customers are.
- What they expect and need from you.
- How well you are meeting these expectations.
- How to provide customer care and follow up.
- What benefits customers have obtained from your service.
- What needs to be done to make improvements.
- What the barriers are to making these improvements.
- How you can remove these barriers.

- How you will know that what you are delivering is exactly what the customer is expecting from you.

The customer service focussed organisation will display the following five key attributes:
- Reliability: Dependable, accurate performance consistently, in all of the details.
- Ownership: Frontline ownership, so that those who receive complaints are also able to sort them out; (it is not unusual that only 5% of complaints are resolved at the first point of contact, thus creating delays with dissatisfied customers).
- Responsiveness: Clear evidence of "willingness to help"; for example, answer letters within 2 days, answer the phone in 5 seconds, answer emails in 24 hours.
- Attitudes: Courtesy, friendly, empathy and caring by employees for the customer's "unique" requirements.
- Appearance: Clean and tidy facilities, equipment, people etc.

Finally, the following benefits from having such a customer focus will make contributions to the survival, well-being and the profitability of any organisation:
- Reliable service is a marketable product with a price difference.
- Market changes (with many fluctuations affecting most organisations) can be better handled and managed.
- Continuous improvement becomes a part of the culture, with innovative and responsive staff; there is a new enthusiasm and support amongst people.
- A positive view of your organisation from shareholders, the community and potential employees, with competitors who "fear" your organisation.
- Customers see the organisation as:
  - responsive and listening
  - collaborative and sharing
  - understanding what is critical to their own success
  - "good people to deal with"

Clearly what is being talked about above is a total culture of delivering service excellence. Posters on the wall will not do this, neither will "pep talks" nor the smoothness of a salesperson; it will require a hearts and minds transformation and a continued effort thereafter. **The Customer Service Toolkit** by Stuart Emmett will be useful in this regard.

Vehicle Types

In the UK, road vehicles will conform to legislation covering the gross vehicle weights and overall lengths. More details on legislation will follow in the next chapter, but meanwhile the following general types of vehicle are found (diagram overleaf):

Vehicle Type	Axles	GVW with RFS
	2	18 tonnes
	3	26 tonnes
	3	26 tonnes
	4	32 tonnes
	4	36tonnes
	4	38 tonnes
	5 (2+3 as shown, or 3+2)	40 tonnes
	5	40 tonnes
	6	44 tonnes
	6	44 tonnes

RFS (Road Friendly Suspension) is effectively air suspension, and the legislation covers the Gross Vehicle Weight (GVW), which is the maximum weight allowed, on the road, of the vehicle plus its load. On some vehicles types, having no RFS reduces the legal GVW.

The subtracting of the weight of the vehicle will give the maximum load weight that can be carried. Vehicle weights have increased incrementally in recent years. Before the current UK maximum of 44 tonnes GVW on six axles from 1999, the previous limits were 38 tonnes on 5 axles in 1983 and 32 tonnes on four axles in 1964.

Outside of the UK, larger gross vehicle weights are found, for example road trains in Australia with B doubles (an artic tractor with two trailers) at 68 tonne GVW giving a payload of 50 tonnes on 9 axles, or B triples with the tractor towing three semi trailers up to 77 tonne GVW giving a 55 tonne payload on 12 axles. It should be noted these higher weight vehicles are, however, restricted to usage on specific public roads.

Trials were proposed in the UK for similar so-called longer heavier vehicles (LHVs) and proposals were made for varied options as follows:
- a conventional articulated lorry but with a longer trailer (up to 18.75m/44 tonnes).
- a rigid vehicle towing a semi-trailer, with the front of the trailer resting on a dolly (potentially up to 25.25m long/60 tonnes GVW).
- an articulated lorry running full standard length with a further trailer (resting on a dolly) behind it (up to 32m long/80 tonnes GVW).
- an articulated lorry pulling an extra semi-trailer with the front of the second trailer sitting on the rear axle of the first (up to 25.25m/60 tonnes GVW).

Whilst only a small number of advocates of LHVs proposed an overall weight of more than 60 tonnes (60 000kg) or a total length of more than 25.25m, the largest proposal was for 82 tonne GVW/34 metre 11 axle road trains.

However, all of these LHV proposals were rejected by the UK Government in June 2008 on four basic grounds:
- rail would lose traffic, especially shipping containers.
- inadequate parking facilities.
- safety aspects on manoeuvrability, field of view, stability and collision severity.
- larger investment costs.

The road transport industry highlighted four points as follows:
- disagreed completely with the pro-rail lobby viewpoint.
- saw that little changes for parking was needed.
- safety is in fact improved as less vehicles would be on the road.
- operational cost savings would more than compensate for the higher investment costs.

Finally, it was alleged that the proposed trials for limited application on designated routes would be able to provide definitive answers to the above questions. Meanwhile, whilst this trial opportunity has currently been missed in the UK, some LHV trials in other EU countries are underway.

It should be noted that the 44 Tonne weight limit can be exceeded for special types and abnormal loads that are authorised by the Special Types General Order (STGO) regulations. The STGO covers operations of vehicles up to 30metres length and 6.1 metres wide and up to 150tonnes; over this weight involves another type of special order. STGOs cover those heavy and often low loader trailer cargos such as generators, military tanks etc. and are beyond the scope of this book.

Vehicles are therefore limited in legislation by the gross weight. Whilst this is important for those who move heavy cargos such as steel and aggregates, the majority of freight is actually constrained more by volume and therefore the physical size of the vehicle is more important when moving such freight. Indeed, average payloads per trip in the UK are only around 9 tonnes. Therefore, the concern of the majority of vehicle operators is the maximum space available for carrying freight. Vehicles are also subject to size limits set by legislation:
- Width of 2.55 metres (2.6 for refrigerated vehicles).
- Length of 12 metres for rigid vehicles, 16.5 metres for articulated and 18.75 metres for drawbar vehicles.

The technology of vehicle design has a part to play here, and there are, for example, semi-trailers (double deck trailers), up to 4.9 metres height (if a vehicle is under 4.95 metres height they will drive safely under unsigned bridges), and these double deck trailers can carry 52 standard pallets, instead of 26 on a straight frame normal height trailers.

The larger articulated and drawbar vehicles have identical gross weight limits, but the drawbar vehicle allows for a greater load space and is therefore more suitable for low-density high cube payloads. The following represents the differences between these vehicle types:

Feature	Drawbar with normal bodies	Articulated unit/ normal trailers
Length	In two or more parts up to an overall 18.75 metres, with a maximum load length of 15.65 metres	Unbroken up to an overall 16.50 metres, with a normal load length of 13.6 metres
Cube space available	More; e.g. 30 pallets of 1x1.2 meters, single decked	Less; e.g. 26 pallets of 1x1.2 metres, single decked
Unladen Weight	More	Less therefore more weight payload available
Operational flexibility	Can run solo as well as drop trailer/body operations	Drop trailer operations
Loading/unloading	Two or more rear doors	One set of rear doors
Manoeuvring	More skilled	Easier
Capital cost	Higher	Lower
Excise Duty	Lower	Higher

Vehicle Selection

It is the job of the fleet manager to select the best total whole life cost-effective vehicles for the needs of the organization. This involves covering such factors as:
- Costs of operation.
- Nature of the goods to be transported.
- Type of work, for example long distance where power/speed are important or local urban delivery where manoeuvrability and economy are important.
- Maintenance facilities required.
- Materials handling systems employed by the organization and its customers.
- Finance available for purchase.
- Driver acceptability.

Meanwhile when operating vehicles, then the following aims will apply:
- Maximise: Payload, Reliability, Service ability, Fuel Efficiency, Safety, Productivity, Legality
- Minimise: Vehicle Weight, Cost to operate, Capital spend

It can be seen that these aims can be related to each other, for example, the payload/vehicle weight.

In specifying vehicles, it can be helpful to use the vehicle manufacturers IT systems to help optimise the specification and also to ask the manufacturer for a demonstration vehicle. Published vehicle fuel performance should be confirmed with actual users and alternative manufacturers and specifications should be considered before making a decision. Additionally, the EU Euro emission standards need to be followed and there are two basic engine options available to do this. Some truck manufacturers have taken the view that the engine must be designed to operate in a clean way by using exhaust gas recirculation (EGR), others have meanwhile taken the view that the engine is made more efficient and the pollutants are dealt with later by a selective catalytic reduction (SCR) system.

Bodywork needs to be specified carefully so that it can do the job that is required and does not include unneeded extras (such as internal body height that is never used). Any aerodynamic fittings also, need to be appropriate for the intended vehicle use.

Vehicle acquisition

The fleet manager may be involved in deciding upon the most appropriate method of acquiring a fleet of vehicles or replacement vehicles for the organisation. The method selected will be affected by the following major considerations:
- Finance.
- Operational skills.
- Nature of the business.

The three options regarding equipment acquisition are:
- Hiring.
- Outright purchase.
- Leasing.

We will look at each of these in turn.

Hiring of vehicles
The fee for hiring is normally set according to the type of vehicle, the period of hire and the routes to be covered. The vehicle remains the property of the rental company, which also retains responsibility for maintaining the vehicle at all times.

Advantages of hiring
- The main advantages of hiring are those of its flexibility.
- Hire charges can be planned and budgeted for.
- No capital commitment is required. Once the hire agreement is settled the vehicle can be put to work.
- Flexibility. The vehicle can be exchanged or returned at any time. If, therefore, the needs of the fleet manager change, the hire company can respond to that change and supply the type of vehicle required.
- Maintenance is the responsibility of the hiring company. Should the vehicle break down, the hire company must either repair the vehicle or supply a replacement. The company need have no in-house skills and still be able to operate a fleet of vehicles.
- Hire payments can be entirely set against revenue.

Disadvantages of hiring
- The major disadvantage of hiring is that of cost in the long term.
- Cost. Hire charges will be designed to pay for the vehicle and then earn a return for the hire company. Therefore, the company could find that in terms of hire charges it has 'paid' for the vehicle, yet it remains the property of the hire company.
- High usage premiums. If the vehicle is going to be used for extended periods at a very high rate of usage, then the hire company can impose an extra charge known as a high usage premium.

The option to hire can be summarized as the best method in conditions of high usage, where no in-house skills exist and where a seasonal or innovative environment is the norm.

Outright purchase of the vehicle
This is an established method of vehicle acquisition, although in recent times there has been a shift away from this purchase option towards leasing options.

Advantages of outright purchase
- Depreciation on the total value of the vehicle is deducted from revenue. Therefore, tax advantages can be gained from the purchase option.
- The vehicle belongs to the organisation and is therefore added to its list of assets and total worth. The organisation has complete control over the vehicle and can thus use it as it sees fit.
- Government development areas. These are areas that the government has decided need special financial assistance to help promote growth and attract new industries. If the company operates in one of these areas then loans and grants may be available to assist in the purchase of vehicles.

Disadvantages of outright purchase
- The main disadvantage of outright purchase is that of initial capital outlay. The organisation must offset the 'opportunity costs' of using the cash required to purchase a vehicle in another part of the business. For example, a vehicle may cost £90,000. What if that sum was used to purchase new racking for the warehouse? The new racking could be so efficient as to save enough money to pay the hire charges on a hired vehicle. Therefore, the company would have a new racking system and the use of a new vehicle.
- The purchase option can be summarised as being the best method in conditions of a cash rich company.

Leasing
This is where the fleet manager leases a vehicle from a leasing company, for a set period of time (normally a minimum of three years) at a set fee. The equipment remains the property of the lessor, but the responsibility for its maintenance is the duty of the lessee.

Advantages of leasing
There are several advantages to the leasing method and it is an increasingly popular option.
- No capital commitment. The organisation will not have to find large sums of money

to acquire the vehicle. The vehicle will, however, immediately begin to generate profit for the organisation.

- The fees for the lease of the vehicle can be offset against tax and, therefore, the net cost of leasing the vehicle is reduced.
- Low cost. This method of acquiring a vehicle is the lowest of the three options and this is its main advantage.

Disadvantages of leasing

- The lessee has to maintain the vehicle. This can be very expensive, especially if the lessee does not have in-house maintenance skills.
- Fixed-term contract. The vehicle cannot be returned to the lessor in the event of changes in the lessee's business needs.

Lease Options

There are various options available when leasing:

	(1) Not Buy the vehicle Operating Lease	(2) Maybe will buy the vehicle Finance Lease	(3) Buy the vehicle Hire Purchase
Ownership	Finance Co.	Finance Co.	Finance Co. (during the lease)
Maintenance	Contract Hire Hirer Op. Lease -Finance Co.	Optional Hirer/Finance Co.	Optional Hirer/Finance Co.
Depreciation Risk	Finance Co.	Hirer	Hirer
Capex Allowance	Finance Co.	Finance Co.	Hirer
Balance Sheet	"Off", not an asset, part of Profit & Loss	"On", as an asset	"On", as an asset

Lease option notes:

(1) Long Term Hire, with no responsibility for ownership. Fixed payments are usually lower than finance leases. This is a popular method of acquiring vehicles as the vehicles do not appear as an asset on the balance sheet and therefore, return on capital employed ratios are maximised.
Called: Operating Lease, Contract Rental and Contract Hire

(2) Long Term Hire, where Finance Company allows hirer to use the vehicle for payment of rent or cost plus interest. The vehicle maybe purchased at the end of the hire period. Fixed payments can be spread up to 7 years (cash flow). It is usually relatively easy to upgrade/re-new during the period.
Called: Finance Lease

(3)   This is really about ways of borrowing money for a vehicle purchase. Fixed payments, writing down allowances and upgrade facilities exist.
Called: Hire Purchase, Lease Purchase, or Purchase Plan

Maintenance of road vehicles

Vehicles need to be maintained and repaired during their working lives. The fleet manager must devise a system of planned maintenance whereby vehicles available for transportation can be regularly maintained. It is vital that this system enables the maintenance to be carried out without reducing the total effectiveness of the fleet. The advantages of a system of planned maintenance are:
*   Planned maintenance will not disrupt the distribution system, whereas random breakdowns due to lack of maintenance will cause delay and non-delivery of goods.
*   Slack time within the distribution system can be used to complete maintenance work.

The transport manager is also responsible for ensuring that maintenance costs are controlled.

Maintenance Guidelines
Whilst the following chart gives guidelines, clearly there is relationship between the type of work undertaken and the distances travelled. This needs to be reflected in the maintenance scheduling and planning. Frequencies can therefore be increased or decreased, according to the operational conditions. Suffice to note however, that the operator is ultimately the one responsible and any doubts on what interval to choose, should always mean that more, not fewer, checks are made.

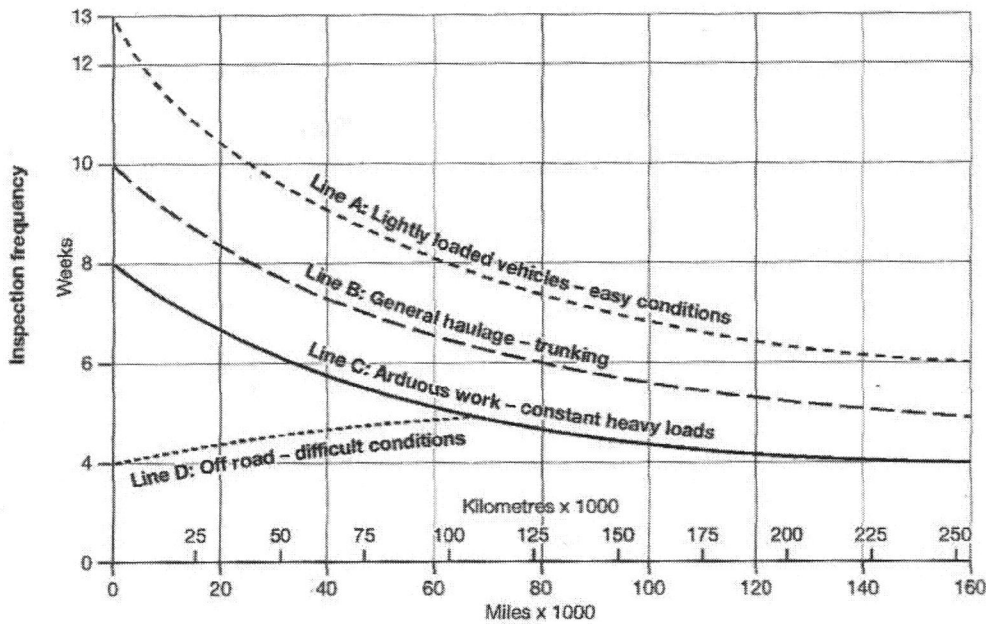

Average on road distance travelled a year

Checklist: A Good Maintenance System

Use these important key points as a guide to help you plan and set up a compliant and effective maintenance system for your vehicles.

1. A responsible person must undertake a daily walk around check, preferably immediately before a vehicle is used.
2. First-use inspections are essential for operators who lease, hire or borrow vehicles. These are especially important where vehicles and trailers have been off the road for some time.
3. Drivers must be able to report promptly any defects or symptoms of defects that could adversely affect the safe operation of vehicles. Reports must be recorded and provision should be made to record details of any rectification work done.
4. Drivers' defect reports, used to record any faults, must be kept for at least 15 months.
5. Operators must ensure that regular checks are carried out on items that may affect roadworthiness,
6. Safety inspections must include those items covered by the appropriate Department for Transport Annual Test.
7. Safety inspections should be pre-planned, preferably using a time-based programme.
8. The system of safety inspections must be regularly monitored, especially in the early stages.
9. Any remedial work carried out as a result of safety inspections must be recorded.
10. The safety inspection record must include:
    - name of owner/operator
    - date of inspection; vehicle identity
    - odometer (mileage recorder) reading, if appropriate
    - a list of all the items to be inspected
    - details of any defects name of inspector
    - details of any remedial/rectification or repair work and by whom it was done
    - statement that any defects have been repaired satisfactorily
11. On some types of vehicles and operations, intermediate safety checks may be necessary.
12. Records of safety inspections must be kept for at least 15 months.
13. Staff carrying out safety inspections must be competent to assess the significance of defects. Assistance must be available to operate the vehicle controls as necessary.
14. There must be an internal system to ensure that unroadworthy vehicles are removed from service.
15. Operators who undertake their own safety inspections must have the correct tools and facilities for the size of the fleet and type of vehicle operated.
16. All operators should have access to a means of measuring brake efficiency and exhaust emissions, and setting headlamp aim.

17. Operators are responsible for the condition of vehicles and trailers that are inspected and/or maintained for them by agents, contractors or hire companies.
18. Operators who have contracted out their safety inspections must draw up a formal written contract with an inspection agency or garage. Such operators should have a means of regularly monitoring the quality of work produced for them.
19. The dates when safety inspections are due must be the subject of forward planning. A maintenance planner or wail chart should be used to identify inspection dates at least six months before they are due. Computer-based systems are equally acceptable.
20. Any system of maintaining roadworthiness of vehicles should be effectively and continually monitored.
21. Any changes by licensed operators to arrangements for safety inspections must be notified to the relevant VOSA office without delay.
22. Drivers must be given dear written instructions about their responsibilities.

Source: Guide to Maintaining Roadworthiness (2007) by Vehicle & Operator Services Agency (VOSA)

Transport Costs and Productivity

Transport cost management can be poorly handled; for many businesses: *"company bosses are in the dark about their transport costs and one fifth of them do not even know which fellow directors take responsibility for it"*. (Motor Transport dated 1 April 1999).

Whilst such comments are probably made mainly in relation to smaller companies, the saying, "if you cannot measure it, then you cannot manage it" is very relevant here.

Knowing existing costs in a meaningful way is the first step to being able to control and then to improve costs, be it in transport or in anything. Improvement needs to be a continual aspect of operational management, and before starting to do this, there is the need to understand the current situation. This is necessary to understand just how things actually work, in measurable terms.

A useful framework to adopt is to use a basic problem solving approach.

Where are we now?
This involves an analysis of the current situation in measurable terms. Measurements can be by quantity, time, or cost. For example, time and quantity measure in road transport, the vehicle miles per gallon. (Please note that miles per gallon are used here, simply because most of the industry still uses these figures rather than litres/kilometre).

Where do we want to be?
This involves setting clear objectives for improvement. For example, on road transport to improve the fleet m.p.g. by 10%.

How are we going to get there?
This involves looking at options and methods available for improvement, making a selection, and then making a plan for implementing improvements.

How do we know we have arrived?
This involves comparing the new situation against the standard expected. For example on the vehicle mpg, this was 6.1 mpg, the improvement objective standard was set at 6.71 mpg, and the actual is currently now 6.52 mpg.

So, by having a clear analytical framework it is possible to work through an improvement programme and measure, objectively, the progress. The plan for the required performance can be represented by the setting of a thermostat, whilst the actual performance can be thought as the thermometer reading.

We will now look at the cost and productivity drivers in road freight transport. It will be seen that these so often centre on time – that four-letter word that we can never get enough of. Whilst concentrating here on UK road freight, it should be noted that the general principles do still apply to all the other modes of transport, for example see the following comparison.

Simplified Cost Comparison: Road Vehicles and Passenger Aircraft

Cost Item	Road Vehicles- UK	Scheduled Service Aircraft- Worldwide
Fixed Costs		
-Wages	44%	33%
-Depreciation and insurance	29%	19% (aircraft have a much longer service life)
-Administration	27%	48% (station costs, ticketing, sales etc)
Total	100%	100%
Variable Costs		
-Fuel	76%	53% (variable worldwide buying power with varied national taxation levels)
-Maintenance/tyres/oil	24%	24%
-Operational expenses (landing, en route costs)	n/a	23%
Total	100%	100%

Transport Cost Drivers

There are a number of costs that have to be budgeted for and examples of these for road freight transport follow. It should be noted that the general principles are the same for all transport modes.

Fixed or standing costs, these have also to be paid when the vehicle is standing and is not working. The standing costs cover the following individual items:

- Labour costs. These cover wages and all associated employment costs, such as pension provision.
- Insurance costs. This covers the costs for the vehicle/equipment and any goods in transit insurance cover.
- Administration costs. This covers management overhead costs; premises and all administration required managing the activity.
- Licence costs. This covers the Government fixed licence charges.
- Depreciation costs. This covers the capital write off, or the finance costing of the vehicle such as lease charges.

Variable or running costs, these costs are only paid when the transport vehicle is working/ moving and running. The running costs cover the following individual items:

- Fuel; this covers the cost of fuel that is used.
- Tyres: this covers all the tyre costs.
- Maintenance; this covers all costs incurred on maintaining vehicles in a reasonable roadworthy condition.

The major cost items with sample percentages of each item are as follows:

Vehicle Costs: Operating Cost Percentages

Vehicle types	Cost item	3.5T Van	7.5T Rigid	18T rigid	26T artic	35T draw bar	40T artic	44T artic
Fixed	Wages	55%	48%	44%	39%	44%	40%	39%
	Insurance	7%	9%	10%	10%	13%	12%	13%
	Administration	27%	26%	27%	25%	26%	26%	26%
	Licences	1%	1%	1%	1%	1%	2%	2%
	Depreciation	11%	16%	18%	25%	16%	20%	20%
		100%						
Variable	Fuel	79%	76%	77%	75%	76%	77%	76%
	Oil	1%	1%	1%	1%	1%	1%	1%
	Tyres	3%	5%	5%	10%	6%	8%	9%
	Maintenance	16%	18%	17%	14%	17%	14%	14%
		100%						

The important aspect to realise with transport costs is that the fixed costs tick away every minute. They have to be paid whether the vehicle is working or not and whether the vehicle is moving or not.

In the different modes of transport, the make up of total costs (from the fixed and variable cost items) is approximately as follows (table overleaf):

Mode	Fixed Costs	Variable Costs	Comments
Road	50%	50%	Wages and fuel are the main costs
Rail	80%	20%	Track and terminal costs are included in the fixed costs (see below)
Air	60%	40%	Fuel and administration are the main costs
Sea	60%	40%	Wages and fuel are the main costs

Clearly the above percentages will vary dependant on the work undertaken, but they do give crude indications. The high fixed costs for rail are explained, traditionally, by the fact the operator also has to pay for the track costs. (In recent times in the UK, the separation of the track costs, from the former nationalised operator through privatisation in 1994, effectively now means that operators only pay for the track when they use it. Therefore in theory at least, this puts them on a more similar variable cost base as the road operators/users).

The question to ask is which of the above costs are controllable on a daily basis? The following may help using the road vehicle example, although similar principles apply for the other modes.

Fixed or standing costs
- Wages are usually determined annually for the basic rate with overtime being a variable element for specific journeys.
- Depreciation is usually determined by finance people and revolves around the vehicle life, a matter of years.
- Administration and Management involves wages/salary costs plus office space/ power/ light/telephones etc. Again usually annually determined items, with power/ light/ telephone usage being a variable dependant on usage.
- Licences are fixed by Government, usually annually.
- Insurance is again an annually controlled cost.

Variable or running costs
- Fuel. The price paid will be determined on a period basis, but the usage will vary on a trip/daily basis.
- Maintenance costs follow usage and take place at specific times (e.g. annual MOT, preventative schedules).
- Tyres and Oil will similarly follow usage rates.

So with road vehicles, there is very little that can be controlled on a daily basis apart from fuel and the other usage costs. As fuel, is the major single cost item then that would seem to be useful to tackle in making any operational improvements as this also concentrates limited time, to that area which will have the largest impact. Is there any real gain for example, by spending precious improvement time on a small cost area like vehicle insurance?

Fuel Economy

It can been seen that fuel is a major cost to be controlled. We are not just talking here about the purchase price, but more about the usage/consumption. The purchase price per gallon/litre certainly has a strong effect on operations and was indeed campaigned strongly about in September 2000, and again in the summer of 2008 when the price of oil per barrel broke records.

However, the usage is something that needs more closer and careful attention of transport management. This is something not done by many transport managers, and whilst they may well be correct to lobby and complain about the price of fuel and the high levels of tax, they are clearly incorrect and, are inefficient, by ignoring the consumption figures.

This is a key management responsibility and is unfortunately a clear failing for those too many transport companies, who do not measure on a vehicle/driver basis what the fuel consumption is. Global fleet consumption is of little use as a control measure, as differences need to be found at the level of the individual vehicle/driver.

At a fleet level, it can however be useful to highlight the impacts of saving fuel, for example a fleet of 1400 vehicles an extra 0.1 MPG on the fleet can save £240000 annually, an extra 1 MPG will saving £2.4 million etc. However, the extra 0.1MPG will only really be found on an individual vehicle/driver basis, control is most certainly needed therefore to this level of detail.

There are many reasons for variances in fuel consumption. Unfortunately this means such divergences can then become a "formula for doing nothing" as handling many variables is not always a straightforward process to manage properly, especially when managing fuel consumption on a vehicle / driver basis. People can become defeated by the variables and can finish up doing nothing. It could be realised however, that, because there are many options, there is always something that can be examined to improve full consumption. Managing fuel consumption is not a "one-off" activity, but should be a continuing part of an effective transport management process.

Meanwhile some of the variances for fuel consumption are commented upon below:

Route/Load factors that have an impact on fuel consumption include aspects such as the gradient, speed of travel, acceleration/braking rates, and the type of road. For example, travelling from Sheffield to Stockport either directly on A-roads across the Snake Pass, or travelling via the M1/M62/M60 represents a "classic" routing decision, not only in terms of the road conditions, but also on the distance and time factors: longer/shorter or quicker/slower?

Additional effects on fuel consumption are from route and load factors as follows:
- day or night time working (vehicles move more freely at night and return better MPG).
- stop/start deliveries or long distance motorway cruising.
- the amount of full or empty running.

- the load containment in the vehicle.
- the climate conditions (vehicles use more fuel in colder weather).

Vehicle factors for fuel consumption include the engine fuel efficiency, the engine rating and the vehicle design for aerodynamics. Maintenance of vehicles is needed, including tuning, to ensure engines run fuel efficient. Travelling/driving speed is affected by speed limiters/ governors which are a UK legal requirement (albeit for accident prevention measures), but speeds do have an impact on fuel consumption. Vehicles also need selecting for the work they undertake and a vehicle geared for long distance motorway cruising is of no use for local stop/ start work.

Aerodynamics fittings can be fitted to reduce the air flow "drag" effect when vehicles are moving and, for example, a vehicle travelling at the speed limiter maximum allowed motorway speed of 56 MPH will have almost half of the engine power being used to overcome drag. Savings from fitting aerodynamic devices to reduce such air resistance can be significant for the appropriate application. Much work has been undertaken on this area and some of the findings of this research are as follows:

Vehicle type	MPG before being fitted	MPG after being fitted	MPG increase
7.5 tonne rigid	17.06	19.23	12.7%
17 tonne rigid	11.43	13.44	17.5%
32 tonne artic	7.60	8.80	15.8%
32 tonne drawbar	7.50	9.35	24.6%

It is worthwhile to point out that these trials were undertaken systematically, using for example regular similar work routes/loads with the same drivers and vehicles, in a before and an after scenario. The 17 tonne rigid vehicles for example, were used on day time deliveries from an RDC to stores, with the Artics and the Drawbars were used on primary trucking work between depots at night. Whilst there is a cost involved in these extra fittings, the payback period can be relatively short and additionally, the savings are effectively "designed into" the vehicle and remain independent some of the other factors such as driving style. Clearly however, constant multi-drop stop/start work in urban areas where average speeds fall below 30 MPH, is unlikely to benefit from having such fittings.

New aerodynamic "teardrop" shaped 13.6 metre trailers entered the market in the mid 2000s with a curved roof giving a variable 3.620 to 4.345 metre height. Independent test track trials showed that fuel economy savings up to 30.3% could be made when travelling at high speeds, with 23.7% for combined speeds from 40 to 54 mph. Normal driving conditions would of course reduce these figures is, but even if this caused a 50% reduction from the trial figures, this would be beneficial.

Driver factors for fuel consumption include the driver's style of driving and the driver's personality and "mood". Drivers are a useful starting point and managers can encourage them to save fuel. The display of fuel consumption figures with targets is of proven use. Not only is this useful as a "motivator" (the DETR reports 5% fuel savings when drivers are aware that fuel costs are being monitored), but it also will highlight any particular problems with specific vehicles.

Additionally, when changing vehicle types, driver training for efficient fuel consumption is useful. A driver who has become used to driving one specific type of vehicle, needs to drive, for example, a more powerful vehicle in a different way. Additionally, standard driver training will also cover not only effective driving for efficient fuel consumption, but also for other reasons like safety, customer service, load care etc.

Correct tyre selection and maintaining correct pressures is needed. Dunlop Tyres estimate for a 5 axle articulated vehicle/trailer at 38 tonne GVW, that fuel costs rise 2.6% when tyre pressures fall by 10%. Added to that, of course, is an earlier-than-intended tyre replacement due to premature wear.

Variations in consumption in fleets amongst identical and consecutively registered vehicles doing identical types of work can be substantial, and here the only main variable left is the driver. Such variations can be substantial and driver training can be one solution, followed by monitoring, and, if needed, to look at other reasons for the variances such as any special vehicle problems, fraud etc.

Fraud factors include billing frauds and direct fuel theft. Fraud can be found when for example, a fuel dispenser charges for 300 litres but only 200 litres is actually dispensed with the difference being divided between the driver and the person undertaking the fuel dispensing. The record of fuel dispensed is meanwhile entered into the system as 300 litres, which will then affect the fuel consumption ratio.

Other possibilities for fuel theft are when fuel is siphoned off for resale or for private use. Fuel is a commodity that has a ready saleable value and is therefore liable to be stolen. A simple fuel cap lock fitting can help. It is only strict control measures on consumption on a vehicle/driver basis that will show any such variances and will then enable further investigations to be conducted.

The reported savings can be very substantial. Anyone who is involved in buying transport can always usefully ask operators what their fuel economy programmes are and what the results have been. This question should always be a part of any reasonable negotiations on price and service levels.

Meanwhile as a summary, the steps to better fuel economy are as follows:

Step One: Measure Fuel Usage, every week. Recognise there are many reasons for variable fuel consumption such as:
- Route/load factors (gradients, climate, road types, full/empty etc.).
- Vehicle factors (engine size, body type, tyres, pressures etc.).
- Driver factors (driver styles, speed, personality etc.).
- Fraud factors.

Step Two: Challenge Variances. Appreciate the above reasons are not "a formula for doing nothing." For example, why is it that identical vehicles on identical work return wide variations in MPG?

Step Three: Examine Improvements. Known and tested improvements are:
- Route selection & planning.
- Preventing theft of diesel.
- Aerodynamic fittings (12 to 25% reported savings).
- Driving training reinforcement (5 to 16% reported fuel saving).
- Vehicle maintenance/tuning (5 to 10% reported savings).
- Fuel efficient vehicle engines (up to 8% reported fuel saving).
- Change the fuel supplier (1.5 to 6% reported fuel saving).

Step Four: Management Control. Reinforce improvements, maintain vigilance with an effective management system and recognise that there is always something that can be done to improve fuel consumption. Only around 15 per cent of vehicles in the UK are estimated to be subject to some kind of fleet fuel efficiency management programme, even though such savings are well documented. Fuel is the major controllable cost; it has been shown that improvements in excess of 25% or more are achievable.

Summary

Whilst Step Three has many of the known and tested improvements, in the late 1990s, respondents to a survey reported that the implementations that had been tried were: aerodynamics' 48%, driver training 40%, monitoring fuel consumption 33%, vehicle selection 32% and maintenance 28%. This shows the many remaining areas that are still available for fuel savings, but also that the majority of those surveyed have actually done nothing.

More details on this critical subject of proactive fuel economy will be found on www. freightbestpractice.org.uk (part of the Department of Transport.) Government has undertaken some excellent work in this area and the information is freely available. This website is a critical one that all transport managers and operators should regularly visit.

Transport Productivity Drivers

All companies need to measure and control their cost expenditure. But cost measurement is only one side of the coin of measurement. There is also need to measure the utilisation productivity and performance. These non-financial terms must have meaning and be able to be identified by those directly involved. It should be appreciated here, that the financial measures are always post-event, whereas productivity measures are virtually pre-event in examining the way resources are used on a daily basis. In turn, these then actually determine the financial output.

It should also be appreciated that the data for measurement (by quantity, time, and cost) will already exist within the operation – it needs 'digging' out and making into useable information. Then, with constant monitoring of the productivity drivers (or Key Performance Indicators, KPIs), an ongoing health check and early warning of problems is available.

In transport, and at the risk of stating the obvious, vehicles are expensive and only earn money when they are working. So, an analysis of this working time is important. Simply, we can see three key measures of time:

- The Time Vehicles are Used working/ Time Available (Time Availability)
- The Percentage of Time Used Working on Journey Time (Time Utilisation)
- The Percentage of Time Used Working on Turnaround Time

In the UK – a small place – the Journey Times are relatively low. So, the Turnaround Time is often the critical item of the time a vehicle is working.

Average UK National figures indicate that with a vehicle 8.2 hours working day the Moving Time is 42% and Non-Moving Time is 58%. When a vehicle is working but not moving, then it is either stood in traffic or stood whilst being loaded /unloaded. The excellent study by Alan McKinnon (*The Effect of Traffic Congestion on the Efficiency of Logistical Operations* in **International Journal of Logistics Research and Applications Volume 2**, July 1999) showed that 65% of delivery delays were due to problems at collection/delivery points, with only 18% of delivery delay due to traffic congestion.

Now, which of these productivity time drivers are controllable on a daily basis by operational people? The following may help:

Time Working/Time Available
This is controllable, but other parties are involved on the origin and availability of work.

Time Working/Journey Time
Journey times can be looked at through re-routings, avoiding known congestion points etc. The need also here is to ensure maximising the use of the driver's working time is just that; the driving time. Having a key cost element sitting or waiting around is not efficient practice. Options to help on this are; sharing drivers on vehicles, 2 drivers keeping a vehicle working seven days a week, 3 shift systems over 24hours, vehicle/trailer interchanges. All of these are options for specific operations that will ensure maximising use of the drivers working time. Practically, however, options may be limited.

Time Working/Turnaround Time
This is an important one to examine fully. It has a major impact on vehicle productivity, as it is so often the major use of time.

The first thing to do then is to measure turnaround time; the vehicle taco graph will do this. Next is to put a cost on the time. Then, once the 'hot spots' are identified, a visit is necessary to discuss ways to avoid delays. This is unlikely to be straightforward, but by knowing objectively the time and the cost involved, suitable monitoring can be made and more effective decision-making will occur.

It is generally the case that, left to normal transport operations, the popular times for delivery are first thing in the morning (for those vehicles running overnight) and first thing after lunch (for those vehicles leaving their origin depots in the morning). These times may not, of course, suit customers/receivers and clearly large receivers will usually need to stagger arrivals, by using book in times to optimise their warehouse operations.

In addition to the above time measures, utilisation of transport is also involved with measuring the following:

- Vehicle fill: by weight or space (the cube or number of unit loads such as pallets and roll cages). A UK government-sponsored survey in late 2003 reported 51% utilisation of available cube, 54% utilisation of weight capacity, and 74% of deck length capacity being used by a sample of 1879 vehicles over a 48 hour period. For container ships, 62% utilisation of TEU slots is reported to be the industry average, whereas the largest company has a figure reported of just under 90% (Cudahy 2006).
- Empty running: by percentage of full journeys. About 30% of road vehicle journeys are empty, although the figure has fallen down to 25% in more recent years so perhaps there is a downward trend here.

These measures look at how the vehicles are being used. It maybe pointless, for example, having good fuel consumption if, regularly, articulated vehicles are delivering goods that could fit into smaller rigid vehicles. The "whole" needs looking at and such holistic views are needed. This can mean, therefore, looking at how much fuel is used to move goods, for example:

- 7.5 tonne vehicle at 16mpg for 3 tonnes payload = 5.3333 mpg per tonne payload
- 44 tonne vehicle at 6.3mpg for 27tonnes payload = 4.2850 mpg per tonne payload.

Or:

- 7.5 tonne vehicle at 16mpg for 10 pallets load = 1.60mpg per pallet
- 44tonne vehicle at 6.3mpg for 26 pallets load = 0.242mpg per pallet

Evaluation of performance

To enable transport managers to effectively control their transport operation, they must be able to evaluate the performance of the system employed.

Consider the following diagram:

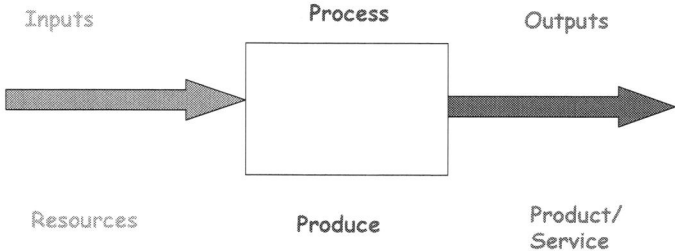

What is critical in this diagram, is that:

- The outputs represent the performance of the product or service.
- In turn, the performance comes from what the process has produced.
- In turn, the process will have used resources: for example, the usage of money, time, equipment, materials, methods of working and the people (as individuals, groups and teams).

It follows, therefore, that we need to have inputs of resources into a process, before we can have a performance output.

As all of the input/process/output aspects are related, we cannot improve performance without considering the process and methods used, and the resources used in the process.

The following feedback loop is another view of the relationships involved here:

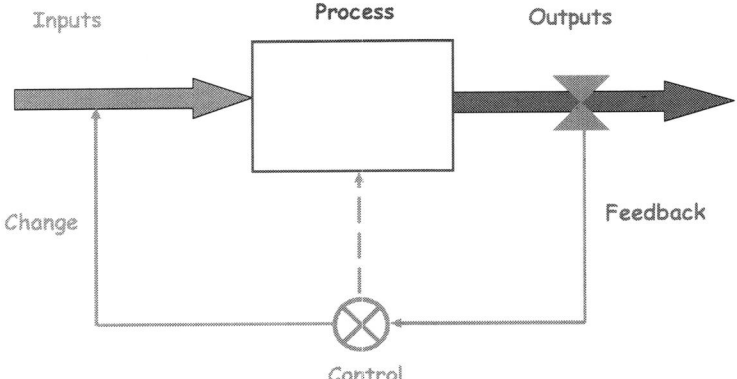

In measuring and checking what has happened, then the output, or the performance, is looked at to compare what has happened, against what we expected to happen. If it does not match, then we can generate feedback to change the process and /or the inputs, so that we can get the exact output wanted.

To summarise, therefore, the aim here is to measure the outputs which represent the performance of the process, so that these may be compared and controlled, which in turn can change the resources or the process being used, so that the required performance is obtained.

To do this, there are many measures, called Key Performance Indicators (KPIs), which can be examined in relation to mode performance:

Customer service-focused KPIs
- Analysis of on-time deliveries over a period of time, destinations and goods.
- Analysis of on-time collections.
- Analysis of 'customer' complaints, in relation to such factors as damage, loss, delivery, materials handling and level of overall service.

Operations-focused KPIs
- Costs of transportation as indicated above (on fixed and variable costs) and compared with budgeted costs.
- Productivity KPIs as indicated above (on working times and vehicle fill and empty running) and the "actual" compared with the expected standard.
- Analysis of claims for damages and losses over a period of time/materials/routes.
- Accident analysis (we will refer to this later)

The costs involved in transportation are very high and, therefore, every effort must be made to ensure that the most effective mode/sub-mode of transport is employed.

Checklist Productivity Measures: some examples

Utilisation measures, calculated by the ratio of used/available:
- Drivers shift time used/available
- Driving hours used/available
- Vehicle time used/available
- Vehicle space used/available
- Vehicle weight use/available

Performance measures, calculated by the ratio of output (or what has been done)/the standard expected:
- Turnaround time actual/standard
- Miles actually driven/expected
- Fuel consumption actual/standard expected
- Number of deliveries actual/standard expected
- Weight delivered actual/standard expected
- Drops undertaken actual/standard expected

Vehicle drivers

A large cost item is the labour cost of employing drivers. It is useful to ensure they are productive. The following series of questions focus on this area:
- What is the driver selection process?
    - Knowledge, personality testing
    - Full checking on past performance
    - Eyesight/medical examination
- How are driver licences checked?
    - At interview
    - Every month when employed
- What is the company policy on:
    - Age/experience?
    - Endorsements?
    - Disqualification's?
    - Uniforms?
    - Safety equipment?
- Are drivers fully trained, including on:
    - Driver hours/taco graphs?
    - Vehicle "defensive" driving?
    - Fuel efficiency?
    - Safety?
    - Customer service?
- How is it ensured that drivers are working within the law, relating to:
    - Hours?

- Rest periods?
- Record keeping?
- Tachographs?
- How often does management:
  - Meet drivers during their delivery operations?
  - Ensure drivers are punctual?
  - Give drivers positive feedback?
  - Hold driver meetings?
- How is it ensured drivers show a good customer service attitude?

In addition to the above points on employing drivers, often operators use agency drivers to cover for sickness, holidays, peak volumes etc. This means additionally verifying the Agency Company and the questions to ask the Agency Company is as follows:

- What is the driver selection process? Does it contain:
  - Knowledge, personality and attitude tests
  - A comprehensive application from
  - An eyesight and medical assessment
- Are references checked?
- Are driver's licences regularly examined?
- What is the age and experience policy for drivers?
- What is the company policy on endorsements and disqualification?
- How closely do you work with others to screen "problem" drivers?
- Are drivers fully trained on driver hours/tachographs, vehicle sympathy, fuel efficiency, safety, customer serve?
- Do drivers need a uniform and safety equipment?
- How will you ensure driver work with the law?
- How will you ensure drivers are flexible and punctual with a good positive attitude?
- What is the employment status of the agency drivers? (Holiday pay, full timers with the agency, their contact details)
- What will be the driver's reactions if they are asked to break the law?
- What happens if drivers do not meet our required standards on skills, integrity and reliability?
- What examples have you of quality customer service and long term relationships?
- What is your liability cover?
- Do you have 24 hours service?
- What quality schemes are you in? (IIP, BS5750/IS9002 etc)
- Do all drivers have photo identify cards?
- What are you problem solving techniques?
- Do your drivers sign a declaration saying they will operate within the law?
- What is your system for tachograph returns/reconciliation?

(Source: Motor Transport 7 January 1999)

Once the agency driver is there, then the following "How to make the most of your agency drivers" gives useful guidelines to ensure agency drivers do a good job; agency drivers do need to be given clear and concise instructions on what is expected when they report for work:

- Vehicle registration number and instructions.

- Instruction regarding diesel.
- Vehicle defect reporting procedures.
- Any special equipment required.
- Arrangements for the return of tachograph charts.
- Trailer numbers etc., if applicable and instructions regarding lights and couplings.
- Details of the journey, timed deliveries and reporting procedure.
- Night out and break requirements.
- Anticipated length of time required.
- Accident and emergency procedure, e.g. tell driver not to accept any liability for any damage etc.
- Driver and load instructions, giving details of planned work and special load instructions where applicable, including routing, timed deliveries, CODs, ferry connections, pallets, vouchers, refrigeration requirements etc. In addition "contact from" telephone instructions.
- Policy on passengers/dogs/use of mobile phones and smoking.
- The company subscribes to the "good lorry code" where appropriate.

(Source: News Link Autumn edition 2000 from Driver Hire Nationwide at www.driver-hire.co.uk)

Determining transport rates

There are many options available for transport Operators   to determine rate pricing strategies. From a marketing point of view, pricing may be made low to enable gaining a market share, pricing may be made towards "what the market will bear", or cost-plus pricing may be the favoured option. Whatever method is used, a fundamental point is to first determine the base line costs that are involved in operating, and we have already looked at this for road transport vehicles.

Costing a transport service can be very simple or can be very complex. Costing is usually done before a job is undertaken; it is therefore important to have a systematic procedure to determine the costs so that the "before" and "after" events can be checked and verified. Costing also helps third party companies to determine the base line on which profit and the revenue can be determined.

A procedure that can be used is as follows:
1. Specify clearly what the service is.
2. Identify what method is being used.
3. Estimate the resources that will be used in terms of the labour, equipment and miles.

This procedure can be explained further by looking at some road freight transport examples. Please note that these financial figures are for illustration purposes and do not represent real and current figures; these will need to be applied as appropriate in a "real" situation.

Service: Secondary/Local Transport (simple method)
Method: local delivery from a DC.

Annual deliveries: 2000 drops
1000 tonnes
£800,000 product value

Resources: one driver and one 18 tonne rigid vehicle, 30000 miles per year.

Costs per annum

Driver	15000
Holiday cover for driver	1500
Standing/Fixed costs	5000
Running/Variable cost 30000 miles @25p	7500
Total	29000

Cost of Service

Average cost per drop (29000/2000) = 14.50 per drop
Average cost per tonne (29000/1000) = 29.00 per tonne
Cost as % of sales value (29000/800000) = 3.635%

This simple approach may be misleading as costing on averages when, for example, drop sizes and distance of delivery will vary over a wide range, means that costs are not being truly allocated; it therefore gives a crude indication only.

Service: Secondary/Local Transport (complex method)

Method: local delivery from a DC.
Resources: one driver and one 18 tonne rigid vehicle; stem mileage speed 45 mph; delivery area speed 5mph; delivery area miles per drop 5 miles; delivery time per drop of fixed time of 12 minutes, plus 12 minutes per tonne; average time DC-deliveries-DC 8 hours; average payload 7.5 tonnes.

Costs per annum:

Driver	13500
Standing/Fixed costs	6000
Running/Variable cost	@25p mile

Therefore:
Driver cost per day (225 days) 13500/225 = £60 per day
Standing cost per day (240 days) 6000/240 = £25 per day
Driver and standing costs = £85 per day

It should be noted that 52 weeks work cannot be assumed, and the vehicle standing cost is therefore calculated here at 240 days per year, effectively 48 x 5 day weeks; the driver working for 225 days, due to taking 15 days holiday. We have also assumed there are no driver sick/absent days.

Delivery cost

Cost per hour: 85/8 x 100 = 1062.5 pence per hour

Stem miles cost per mile: 1062.5p/45mph + running costs@25p = 48.67 p per mile
Stem miles out and back: 2 x 48.67p/7.5 tonnes = 12.98 p per tonne mile
Delivery mileage cost: 5 miles x 1062.5/25p + 5 x 25p = 337.5p
Drop cost: (12 min x 1062.5/60) + (12 x 1062.5/60) = 212.5p plus 212.5 p per tonne

Total Delivery cost:
Stem miles = 12.98 pence per tonne mile
Delivery mile = 337.5 pence
Drop cost = 212.5p plus 212.5p per tonne

Therefore the delivery cost is:
£5.50 (337.5+212.5) plus £2.125 per tonne plus 12.98pence per tonne

All the costs have been detailed here and applied and allocated to the exact method and the resources that are used. So the cost, for example, of moving 1 tonne for 50 miles is (£5.50) plus (£2.125) plus (50 miles @ 12.98pence = £6.49) = £14.12

Primary/Full Load Transport (round trip, empty return)

Service: Full trailer load from Birmingham to Middlesbrough
Method: Artic 38 tonne 13 metre Curtainsider trailer, returning empty
Resources: One driver; single journey distance 210 miles, single journey driving time 3.9 hours; loading and unloading time 2 hours; one day allowed for the roundtrip (7.8 hours driving, plus 2 hours load/unload).

Costs per annum:

Driver	18000
Standing/Fixed costs	15600
Running/Variable cost	@35p mile

Therefore:
Driver cost per day (225 days) 18000/225   = £80
Standing cost per day (240 days) 15600/240   = £65
Running cost 420 miles @35p   = £147
Total cost   = £292

It can be seen that the empty running is substantial, indeed around one quarter of UK road freight vehicle journeys run empty. If, therefore, a return load is found, the cost structure is altered dramatically and the concept (important in transport) of marginal costs may also be used. Marginal pricing allows for the recovery of all fixed costs, with the extra (marginal) cost being that of only the variable costs that are associated with service being offered. In transport operations, marginal costing can be the source of "extra" profit or loss: the following example shows this.

Primary/Full Load Transport (round trip, loaded both ways)

Service: Full trailer load from Birmingham to Middlesbrough, with a return load for Wolverhampton from Durham
Method: Artic 38 tonne 13 metre curtainsider trailer.
Resources: as below

Journey	Miles	Driving time	Loading & unloading time	Total time
Birmingham to Middlesbrough	210	3.9	2.0	5.9
Durham empty	50	1.0	-	1.0
Durham to Wolverhampton	180	3.7	2.0	5.7
Wolverhampton to Birmingham	45	0.9	-	0.9
TOTAL	485	9.5	4.0	13.5

Assessment of 4 round trips in one weeks work or 1.25 days per trip

Costs per annum:

Driver	18000
Standing/Fixed costs	15600
Running/Variable cost	@35p mile

Therefore:

Driver (1.25 days)	£100
Overnight	£15
Standing (1.25 days)	£81.25
Running(485 miles)	£169.75
TOTAL	£366.00

A comparison with the earlier empty return journey is interesting. The cost including empty return is £292.00, therefore the marginal cost Durham to Wolverhampton is £74.00.
It will be seen that, the extra/marginal cost, of undertaking the journey from Durham to Wolverhampton, is substantially less then the cost when returning empty.

The operator, if determining pricing/revenue, now has important decisions to make. Assuming, for example, the revenue market rate is based on return empty running, then the price for the load to Middlesbrough is £292 plus a profit margin, and the price for the load from Durham is very similar, plus a profit. So for, say, revenue of £584, plus profit, the cost is £366. In reality, though, given market pressures, the return load from Durham could be undertaken at a rate of around £200; a still reasonable "mark up" on the costs.

There is good source of "extra" profit here from having effective operations that allow for such return loading. Of course, the converse can also be true, and large losses can occur from marginal costing. For example, imagine that the loads are costed out as above, however, after only a few months, the loads to Middlesbrough are not as frequent. Meanwhile, to serve the Durham customer, vehicles are sent there empty from Birmingham to bring the loads back to the Midlands. Operations and customer service are at the forefront, however the reader is left to calculate the financial consequences. This reflects important issues of management control between the pricing system and the actual operations undertaken.

Road transport routing & scheduling

Transport Management is involved in serving customers, and maybe also collecting raw materials from suppliers. This means that the vehicles used will have to be routed correctly to enable the deliveries/collections to be made; the operations are load planned and scheduled effectively (for example, by one vehicle/one driver) with all this being undertaken in accordance with the legal requirements (such as driver's hours).

The following conflicting objectives will need to be met:
- Maximising vehicle driver's time.
- Maximising the vehicles carrying capacity (weight and/or cube).
- Minimising the distance travelled.
- Minimising the fleet size.
- Whilst satisfying cost and service parameters.

This will involve looking at the following; not in any specific order:
- What is the main scheduling objective, such as maximise payload/utilisation of vehicles, minimise distance, minimise time?
- Can collections and deliveries be grouped together?
- Fully aware of the effect of time/distances on journey times?
- Fully aware of the fixed and variable times of turnaround times?
- How many journeys are/could be made per vehicle shift?
- Are customers served on a fixed day or a fixed interval delivery system?
- Are routes fixed because demand is stable?
- Do deliveries have to be made in reverse order of loading?
- How are delivery restrictions allowed for?
- When last were the computers scheduling programme parameters checked?
- What is it that delays vehicles?
- How are such delays recorded?
- How are such delays analysed?
- What action is taken on repetitive delays?
- Who has responsibility for checking the vehicle schedules?
- Who authorises the schedules?
- Who can override schedules and arrange special deliveries?
- What delay is there between receiving the order and delivery of the goods?

In determining routes, calculations are needed on the time and distances travelled. Routings may be on a fixed day basis, inasmuch as a customer receives deliveries on a dedicated time/day basis, but the quantity is variable. Alternatively, deliveries are only made at an interval basis, for example, when they are economical in transport terms. If vehicles are able to make more than one journey per day, it will also be necessary to select and allocate vehicles across the daily demand.

73

The critical factors affecting routing and scheduling are as follows and it will be seen that many of the variables are to be considered:

Manpower factors
- Availability?
- Licence held?
- Trained?
- Legal hours?
- Shift patterns?

Vehicle factors
- Availability?
- Fleet type & mix?
- Maintenance requirements?
- Payload capacity?
- Ability to preload?
- Ability to "drop the trailer" at customers?

Product factors
- Size/weight/value?
- Packaging?
- Fragility?
- Hazards?
- Special handling?

Throughput factors
- Frequency?
- Seasonality?
- "Usual"?
- Changes?

Collection/Delivery Point factors
- Locations?
- "Features"
- Specified times
- Access restrictions

Company Policy factors
- Service level?
- "Returns"?
- Order size?

Infrastructure/ Environment factors
- Road patterns?
- Legal restrictions?
- Climate?

Each of these factors will, at some time, need to be considered. For many operations however of a repeat nature, that these may be known and fixed in advance. Take, for example, a full load delivery from RDCs to stores on a fixed day basis, where the variables of manpower and vehicle factors are the main ones to be considered on a daily basis.

There are also operational differences found in separating between Primary (trunking) and Secondary (local) transport; or as the Americans describe them: line haul and city transport. The major differences are as follows:

Feature	Primary ("line haul")	Secondary ("city")
Area covered	National/international	Local to each depot
Deliver from	Factories, NDCs	RDCs
Deliver	Large customer orders	Smaller local customers
Vehicle size	Large	Small
Vehicle flexibility	Swap trailers, drop bodies, driver exchanges	Rigid vehicles
Routing problem	"Matching loads"	"Travelling salesman"
Usual loads	Single and large drops	Multiple small drops
Routes	Between fixed points	Recalculate each day
Scheduling	All depots together	One depot at a time
Computer maps	Used at the start then occasionally modified	Use each day and need continual updating
Delivery locations	Limited in number	Variable each day
Network	Diverse	Uniform
Speed	High average speed	Slow average speed
Delivery reliability	More predictable	Less predictable
Environment impact	Less noticed	More noticed

It can be possible to combine primary trunking and secondary local delivery and the following diagram (overleaf), reproduced with permission from Cheltenham Tutorial College, illustrates with the use of drawbar vehicles:

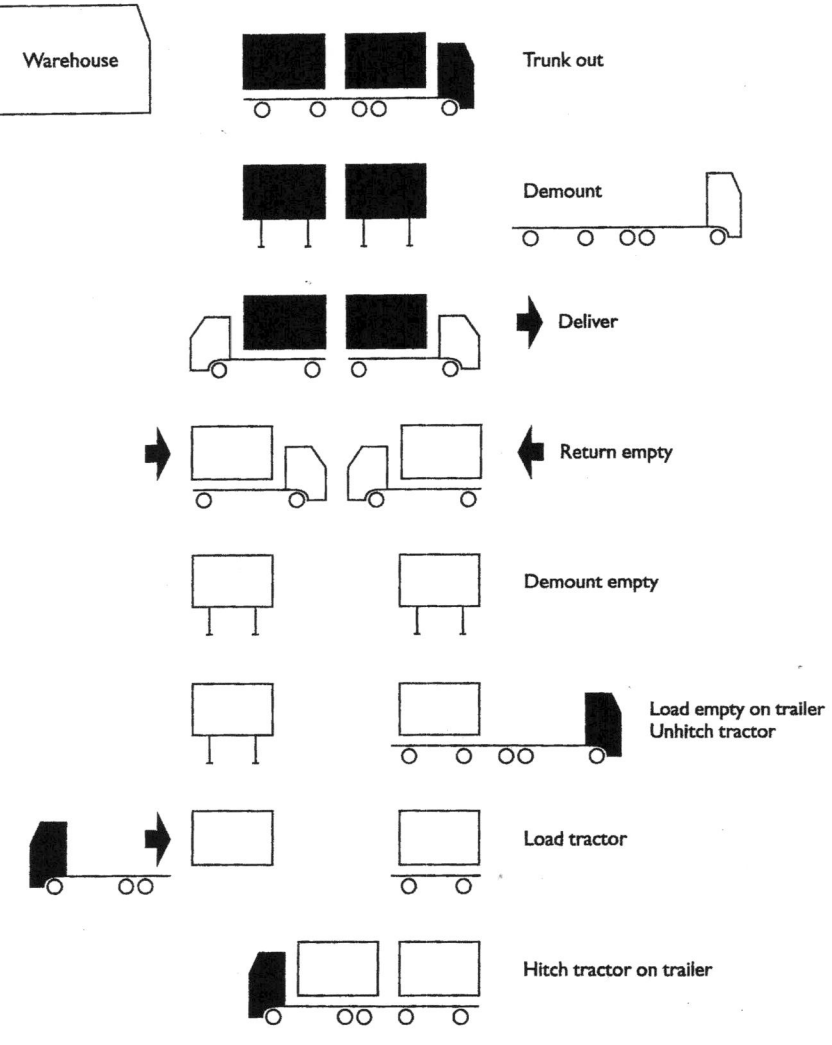

Warehouse

Trunk out

Demount

Deliver

Return empty

Demount empty

Load empty on trailer
Unhitch tractor

Load tractor

Hitch tractor on trailer

There is some overlap between these two extremes, and hybrids are also found. For example, on full loads from RDCs to retail stores, this is secondary for the "area covered/deliver from", but is primary for most of the rest. It will also be seen that the routing problem is different between these two extremes. On primary, matching loads to resources is the basic issue, with secondary; the so called travelling salesman problem is to find the least miles and least vehicles per day, whilst being able to satisfy customer requirements. This is likely being undertaken on a depot basis, but it is also possible to consider this on a network basis using computerised routing and scheduling software, as we shall shortly see.

When routing and scheduling vehicles, the following "ideals" may be useful:
- Arrange stops in close proximity.
- Cluster stops more tightly.

- Always use the largest vehicle available that can be filled.
- Arrange any pick ups/collections with drops/deliveries.
- Avoid time window deliveries/collections.
- Avoid diverting off the main journey pattern/route.
- Travel on m-way/trunk roads as much as possible.
- On Local/multi drop journeys, start at the furthest point, and work back.
- On Trunking/Long distance journeys, consider vehicle and/or driver swap over/exchanges.

Journey planning in routing and scheduling

This considers the time and distance elements in journeys. Each vehicle journey involves two basic operations:
1. Moving Time when travelling on the journey, i.e. Journey Time (JT)
2. Standing Time when loading/unloading, i.e. Turnaround Time (TRT)

These can be calculated as follows:

Moving Time (JT)
This is the distance travelled, divided by the speed. Even simple computer programmes like AutoRoute will quickly calculate this. But do be careful when using computer programme speeds, test them and ensure using realistic ones are being used.

Standing Time (TRT)
There are two parts to this; first, a fixed time to cover the vehicle positioning, opening/closing the vehicle and the paperwork; second, the variable time to cover the loading/unloading. This is varied because of the volume being handled and because of the operational method used. For example:

Fixed Time	e.g. 10 minutes per stop
Variable Time	e.g. per Pallet by Forklift/Dock
	e.g. Per Pallet by Forklift/Floor
	e.g. Per Pallet by Hand Pallet Truck/Tail - Lift
	e.g. Per Package by Handball

Times for such variable operations are available from Work Study or Synthetic Data. If using synthetic data, the following variable times may be used:

Operation	Activity	Timing
Manual Pick up /put down	Small package	10 seconds (0.1666 minutes)
	Up to 18 Kilos	20 seconds (0.3333 minutes)
Manual Travel	Empty handed	61 metres per minute
	With hand pallet truck	30.5 metres per minute
Forklift Pick up/put down		65 seconds (1.08333 minutes)
Fork Lift Travel	Travel	120 metres per minute
	Hoist up/down	20 seconds per metre
Tail Lift	Hoist up/down	20 seconds per metre

A full worked example using all these moving / journey and standing / turnaround time variables follows:

Given Load:	24 Pallets			
Given Distance:	100 miles			
Given Time:	220 minutes			

Operation			Time (mins)	Distance (miles)
TRT	Loading	Fixed time	10	0
TRT	Loading by FLT on Dock PU/PD	20 mins. out/ 20 mins. back	34	
JT	Out		220	100
TRT	Unloading (Assume no queuing delay)	Fixed Time	10	
TRT	Unloading by HPT/ Tail-lift PU/PD, HU/HD, Travel same		70	
JT	Back		220	100
	TOTAL		**564**	**200**

NOTE: TRT has a variable element and is often an ignored variable in planning and in the above example, the division is as follows:

JT	220 + 220	= 440 mins. (78%)
TRT	44 + 80 mins.	= 124 mins. (22%)
TOTAL		= 564 mins.

When multi-drop loads are involved, additional journey times and turnaround times will need to be added and calculated.

Computerised Vehicle and Routing Scheduling (CVRS)

It is possible and indeed, is largely used to undertake some form of computerised vehicle scheduling. This can be possible when the following conditions are satisfied:
• How many vehicles are operated?
- Under 6 vehicles, highly unlikely to be needed

- - Over 10 vehicles, it could be useful
  - Over 50 vehicles, should be using
- How often are loads planned?
  - The time taken is important, as this can be a cost saving.
  - For example, full loads planned once per week, takes less time than with multi drop planning every day.
- Is their access to the computer file containing orders?
  - Sales Order Processing downloads are very successful
- What types of customers are being delivered to?
  - The delivery point details must be accurate
  - For example, "in house" retail store deliveries are different to home delivery. The former is regular and known, the latter place maybe only served once.
- What software suppliers are there?
  - Check the Chartered Institute of Logistics & Transport Supply Chain Integration Technology Forum (access via www.ciltuk.org.uk)
- Important questions to verify with software Suppliers are the following:
  - Where is the software written?
  - Was it written for Windows?
  - How often are maps updated?
  - What benefits do the suppliers expect?
  - Where have the systems been used?
  - Which users can you talk to/visit?
  - How easy is the package to use?
  - How easy will it import data?
  - What does it cost?
  - How much does support cost?
  - What level of training is required?

There are two basic types of computerised vehicle routing scheduling packages; journey planners and vehicle scheduling. Journey planners are more used in manual scheduling of single routes where the calls are allocated to each journey, whereas, vehicle scheduling processes information about all the variables of customer locations, goods and vehicle characteristics and matches all these to produce the routes. The comparative benefits of both types are shown below:

Journey Planning	Vehicle Scheduling
Reduces mileage and fuel use	Same but fewer vehicles, fewer drivers, less manual entry and more economic routes
Slight reduction in planning time	Substantial reduction in planning time
Concentrates on distance and lowest time/cost	Concentrates on all variables to produce overall best fleet routes
Suggests collection and delivery times with best sequences	More predictable and consistent accuracy
Some efficiency improvements	General improvements in efficiency

Meanwhile, the following article provides a useful CVRS overview and also gives information on related vehicle-tracking systems.

Case Study: Computerised Transport Scheduling and Tracking

(Source: Logistics Europe July 2000, Tracking: the Load Down)

Over 20 per cent of vehicles on the road are empty; of those that aren't; only half of their space is likely to be filled. And if these figures, published in a report by Prof. Alan McKinnon of Heriot-Watt University commissioned by the DETR, aren't shocking enough, read on.

Freight-related congestion costs amount to Euros 1.8 Billion - 17 percent of total outlay - according to the report. In the food supply chain, congestion-related delays cost around Euros 1,650 per vehicle per annum. A quarter of all journey legs are reported to have an unscheduled delivery and 23 per cent are held up by traffic congestion. To make matters worse, freight traffic is forecast to increase by 13 per cent within the UK and 26 per cent across Europe by 2005. It is no surprise that the market for real-time, dynamic routing and scheduling is expected to grow by 26 per cent over the same period, with automatic positioning and navigation systems due to increase by 67 per cent and in-cab mobile data communications by 54 per cent.

The need to minimise congestion delays and the costs associated with them are not the only reason why fleet Operators turn to computer technology for help. Growing customer demand, both from home delivery consumers and business-to-business customers, fuelled by the growth of e-commerce and increased emphasis on customer service, mean that orders must be delivered efficiently and on time, and visibility of the order and its status must be available at all times.

While technology cannot eliminate traffic jams or repair flat tyres, it can go a long way towards optimising the quickest, most efficient and/or cost effective delivery route. It can also provide real-time, instant identification of where vehicles are and where they are going.

Systems can work in two ways

Basically, there are two types of vehicle management and tracking software: route planning and scheduling and automatic vehicle location (AVL) and tracking. Planning and scheduling systems can work in two ways. Some systems, like Fleetstar, the new product from Traffic Master, are primarily tracking systems with some route planning capability. They plan a route for each driver, using details of allocated drops or pick-ups in conjunction with maps of the area - but they do not allocate loads, schedule an entire fleet or optimise a route.

The dedicated planning and scheduling systems do all of this, and more. Order details, including drop and collection addresses, are either input into the system or fed automatically from sales order processing or other applications. Details of vehicles and drivers available are also keyed in, along with any constraints, such as customer delivery windows, road closures, urgent orders, etc. Using a map incorporated into the software, the system works out which is the fastest or cheapest route. Human intervention can change the result. For example, if the cheapest route is not the fastest because it avoids a toll road, but the user doesn't mind paying the toll, or because the fourth drop on the route has to be moved to first because of a delivery promise, the planning manager can either add the new criteria or adjust the route manually.

The best systems can cope with multi-site planning and compartmentalised vehicles - say one that has chilled and frozen sections or one that accommodates different types of grain or chemicals. Exel and Tibbet and Britten worked together to create a delivery product for 16 Marks & Spencer's depots using Manugistics' Networks Transport linked to an Isotrak tracking system.

Central planning spreads capacity
'One of the trends is for companies to plan centrally,' comments David Holmes, managing director of software vendor Paragon. 'This could be regionally or nationally. Depot boundaries may be flexible so that, for example, an Oxford depot can take on some of the Bristol depot's business if Bristol lacks capacity. Companies are finding that if depots plan individually, they may have spare capacity in every depot - but no capacity on certain routes.'

MFI transformed the way it delivered furniture to home consumers when it created 14 delivery centres to serve its 190-odd stores five years ago. 'Previously, each store delivered furniture, unless the customer collected their purchase themselves,' explains Shane Webb, general manager routing and planning. 'Now we have four PCs running Roadshow, from Descartes, at our Northampton site. We have around 400 vehicles with demountable boxes and another 100 or so transit vans. All our drivers are sub-contracted but are under our control, as we would not want someone else to be responsible for our deliveries.

'Vehicles call in certain areas on certain days of the week and all route planning is done three days in advance. Each vehicle does two separate delivery schedules per day, with 10-12 drops morning and afternoon. One of Roadshow's draw-backs is that it cannot schedule multi-routes together, which means we have to schedule a separate route for am and p.m.; there is also no database of vehicle capacity or weight.'

However, MFI has gained tremendous benefits from central planning. 'We don't order from our supplier unless our customers order from us,' explains Webb. 'We order in pallet size, which means we may have some stock left over, but each delivery centre now turns stock around 50 times a year, where-as before all stores always held some stock. The new system has led to massive savings for the company. Two third party operators are looking at central planning. BOC Distribution uses both Paragon, which is, says John Burkill, general manager logistics, 'good for radial distribution', and an in-house written package, Cirrus, to reflect fixed delivery times and product availability. But it plans to introduce national scheduling, using Manugistics software, by September this year.

Flexibility required

'We have a number of networks adjacent to each other,' explains Burkill- 'If we schedule nationally, we can integrate some of these networks and produce more efficient, cost effective solutions We need a flexible system to recognise different types of operation, different constraints. Manugistics can deal with multiple sites, multi-modal transport, cross docking and so on...," adds Burkill.

TNT Logistics currently has a separate transport management centre for each country in Europe, using around five systems throughout. But it, too, intends to bring its route planning to a more European level'. Although it has only just begun a review of its planning system and options available, it wants to standardise more on software. 'We want a package that can plan on a tactical level as well as carry out real day-to-day route optimisation,' explains Teun Rilkin, business technology manager. 'We want one that can automatically transfer routes to a despatch system and that can communicate with an in-cab system, too.'

The rise of collaborative planning

If being able to plan on a pan-European basis is becoming increasingly important, so is shared, or collaborative planning. As companies begin to work together to fulfil contracts (e.g. Exel and Tibbet and Britten), planning needs become more complex. The move towards on-line trading and, especially, industry exchanges is leading to more collaborative planning, too. As Graham Newland, director virtual service provision for Manugistics, points out, 'smaller hauliers are banding together to meet transport needs of exchanges and to get more business; this makes planning more complex and track and trace more important'.

To provide track and trace capability, some sort of in-cab device needs to be installed. Although many companies rely on mobile phones for drivers, this system is not 100 per cent reliable because it depends on drivers phoning in or answering the phone and networks to keep working; in addition, unscrupulous drivers don't have to tell the truth. In-cab communications, like planning systems, can take different forms. The most basic AVL is a black box in the cab, which sends signals back to base. This is overlaid with a map so the depot knows where the vehicle is and at what time the signal is sent out. The system can be set up to send signals at varying intervals - 30 seconds, five minutes, and 10 minutes and so on. Most suppliers' recommend 'exception reporting' that alerts the depot only if something out of the ordinary occurs. The AVL system can also be set up to notify base if the vehicles enter a particular zone. For example, when the vehicle is a certain distance from a customer it can signal the depot, which then notifies the customer that the load will arrive within 30 minutes. The best AVLs can also zone by time, rather than distance, since it can take longer to move 10 km if there is a railway or river in the way than if there is a direct line to destination - an important consideration.

Historic reports prove their worth

Data collected from AVL devices provides good management reports. 'Historic reports are very useful,' says Richard Gilbert, general manager of Ken Thomas Ltd, a third party distributor. 'Sometimes a client says a delivery was late - but we can prove where the driver was at what time and for how long with our Securicor Datatrak system. Tracking information can also be used to identify any problem areas - where vehicles are always held up, for instance, or customers that always hold up the schedule by not being ready for collection or pick up. Slow or inefficient drivers can also be identified. By placing sensors in appropriate spots, AVL users can also monitor temperature or fuel usage and see what doors were opened when, and for how long. To gain the full benefits from AVLs, it may be best to integrate them with routing and planning software so that real-time planning 'on the fly' becomes possible. By comparing real to planned routes, users can identify if a driver is late and can notify the customers - or re-schedule the vehicle in order to meet a delivery window of a drop scheduled for later in the day, if necessary.

'Customers are interested in where a vehicle is, what it's doing, and when it's finished with any particular activity,' points out Tim Pigden, managing director of Optrak, a scheduling software vendor that links with AVL suppliers. 'Our next major release will enable users to take the real-time position and re-schedule on the fly. If each vehicle makes more than one trip, a delayed vehicle's second load can be re-allocated to another vehicle; if a driver is 40 minutes late, the route can be re-optimised, if the need arises. Not everyone feels the benefits of integration are worth the cost, which can be high. Ken Thomas Ltd uses Securicor Datatrack separately from its Haulmark planning package to identify the position of vehicles and to record information on the vehicle's movements. As well as finding this information essential in its food distribution business, the tracking system brought additional benefits early this year, as Richard Gilbert explains: 'We had a vehicle stolen from our Middlewich depot in February, some time between 00.40 and 02.30 on a Monday morning. The driver called headquarters, which used Datatrack to find the vehicle 150 miles away in the West Midlands.

Fighting crime
'We then called the police, who called off a chase because of safety issues. We were able to continue following the vehicle's movements and locate its position when it was dumped. We recovered the vehicle at 9.30 am - and were able to tell the police where it ad been, allowing them to find the load stored in an old farm building. 'Datatrak certainly earned its keep! But tracking vehicles, even when integrated with planning, isn't always enough: many companies want two-way communications with the driver, MFI's system has two buttons on an in-cab Vodafone – one to say a drop has been carried out okay, the other to say there's a problem. The phone can then be used for voice communication in order to explain the problem.

Getting the message across
A number of users opt for an AVL with phone attached so that two-way voice communications is possible, although some prefer data communications. Exel's in-cab device has a small printer to print out a message for drivers, so that they can read it at a convenient moment. "We felt this was the best system because we are not distracting

the driver and because on-screen messages can be affected by bright sunlight or other conditions," says Paul Ryan, general manger European transport at Exel.
"Data is more reliable and does not distract the driver," agrees Rilkin. "And a high speed mobile data network is being rolled out in Europe that is a quarter of the price of GPS in capital investment and also offers usage savings."

The new network, explains Richard Horsman, commercial director of Global Telematics, is GPRS, a successor to GSM. It offers wider bandwidth at high transaction speeds, allowing much larger blocks of data to be transmitted in seconds. The move of most systems to internet versions also helps to reduce costs, as well as improve efficiency since data can be made available to anyone the user wishes, and that includes customers.

The costs revealed
Obtaining costs of planning or tracking systems is difficult, as vendor's point out it depends on number of vehicles and type of use. 'Usage varies according to the market,' says Pigden. 'If users only want confirmation a driver is at a certain point, they can use WAP phones for Euros 45 per vehicle, although messaging costs are a big issue. Julian Longson, vp marketing of Pole Star, disagrees. 'It can cost just seven UK pence for a position report via satellite communications,' he says and sat coms are considered the most expensive communications method. Add up the cost over a 10-hour day, though, and five-minute position reports will cost Euro 12.6 per vehicle - and that does not include the relay of other information that may occur.

Capital investment can cost from Euros 1200 per vehicle for an in-cab device, although some companies, such as Trafficmaster and Crossland, offer rental at Euros 45 and 67 per vehicle, respectively. Planning and scheduling packages can be as little as Euros 15, 000 for a basic single-site system, but the average appears to be a lot higher, say Euros 50, 000 upwards to a six figure sum that Manugistics says is 'justifiable' for any multi-site system.

Whatever the cost, there can be real paybacks from routing and tracking systems. Indeed, with the customer now King, the company that cannot warn clients of delays or prove the driver was doing his job correctly may lose important business contracts altogether.

(Source: Logistics Europe July 2000, Tracking: the Load Down)

The arrival of dynamic 'real time' routing and scheduling software offers significant savings in both time and money. The rapid growth in un-metered broadband and ADSL connections now makes it possible for smaller companies, that do not have the luxury of a large IT department or the expertise, to use inexpensive 'plug and go' web packages. Such systems offer online or integrated booking and tracking of deliveries via any computer with a web browser. Job details are retrieved automatically with subsequent status updates such as accepted, allocated and proof of delivery. In addition, bookings taken in the traditional way over the telephone are also logged into the system so that all orders can be tracked irrespective of the original booking method.

Computerised packages allow for modelling and asking "what of" questions. For example, fixed route secondary distribution networks can evolve over a period of years. Re-modelling such regular delivery routes involves calculating improved routes and schedules, and also transport resource requirements, drivers' hours, mileages, vehicle utilisation and the overall cost. Saving made can be substantial for example, a national 600 small van fleet delivering pharmaceuticals to chemists twice daily found an immediate transport cost saving of £1 million. This equated to a ten per cent reduction in fleet size whilst maintaining the existing requirements for the twice daily delivery. These types of savings, also demonstrate one of the greatest strengths of routing and scheduling software; the ability to maximise co-ordination across networks whether at countywide or local levels.

Exercise: Raleigh and Transport Scheduling Software

In a highly competitive market, Raleigh is reaping the rewards of improved customer service and a more efficient transport operation having introduced Paragon software for daily route planning in a delivery operation that involves 400,000 bicycles being transported to 1,100 retail outlets each year. With an implementation that took only two months and a payback period of less than a year, Raleigh is benefiting from an order cycle that has been reduced by one day, a 50% reduction in transport planning resources, a 9% increase in units per vehicle and a string of additional benefits.

Raleigh, the Nottingham-based bicycle company and own account distribution operator, previously used a manual planning system to schedule 150-200 daily deliveries from two depots to destinations throughout the UK. With the bicycle market becoming increasingly competitive Raleigh recognised the importance of reducing lead times to improve customer service. The answer was to implement a vehicle routing and scheduling solution to enable faster planning that would reduce the order cycle by 24 hours. Having tested several systems using live data, Raleigh found that only Paragon's software could produce more efficient routes than their manual planners.

Paragon's compatibility with Raleigh's SOP system enables delivery information to be automatically downloaded to the PC operating the Paragon system. The Paragon software typically takes just two minutes to process the information, calculating a delivery schedule that takes account of order quantities, delivery addresses, vehicle capacities, promised delivery time windows, driver time constraints and driver work standards. Paragon produced routes are then passed to the planning team for a final check before being automatically uploaded to the Warehouse Management system to drive the picking and loading processes - replacing a manual data-entry task that previously took two hours per day.

With planning time dramatically reduced, orders are processed more quickly and the overall delivery cycle has been cut from three days to two, representing a significant customer service improvement. In addition, Raleigh has also reported several sources of cost savings, including a 9% increase in vehicle utilisation, and reductions in spot hire transport, warehouse overtime, stock-holding cost and administration resource. Consequently, Raleigh achieved a pay-back period of less than 12 months.

"We needed to install a routing system in order to reduce our lead times, but we weren't prepared to compromise the efficiency of our manual planning," comments Steve Wigley, Distribution Centre Manager. "Paragon was the only system that could produce more efficient routes than our manual ones. As a direct result of implementing the software our delivery operation is now more efficient than ever before. Vehicle utilisation has increased and the reduced order cycle has both improved customer service and led to a whole series of additional improvements. We hold a day's less stock and on average we can invoice a day earlier -both of which give us a cash flow benefit. The shorter order cycle means our previous two day pre-weekend peak is now spread across an extra day, leading to less warehouse overtime and less use of costly emergency carriers. Our planners are happier too because there is less tedious administration activity - the implementation has been a resounding success"

Question:
What benefits were gained from the software?

Source: Case study from Warehouse News late 2002 ("Paragon software enables Raleigh to reduce order cycle and increase fleet efficiency").

Computer Applications and Controls

Computers can also be used to monitor and control activities, either directly or indirectly by remote devices. The direct applications such as routing and scheduling are commented upon above, the indirect applications are commented upon here.

Use of such systems enables more efficient and effective management leading to better productivity and lower costs; a win/win situation from the use of the following devices that can be fitted to vehicles:
- Vehicle and driver data
- Vehicle/equipment tracking
- Paperless documents
- Traffic information
- On board navigation

These are amplified further opposite:

Device	Some Features	Some Benefits
Vehicle and driver data	Largely on performance, and often provided as OEM by manufacturers, however after market producers are often more up to date	Lower costs and increased productivity which can also compliment driver training
Vehicle/equipment tracking	Position can be viewed on the internet or on bespoke system. Running costs can be high but fixed cost systems are available.	Improved visibility of activity. Provides customers with up to date information. Provide data for actual versus plan routing and scheduling. Increased security. Increased productivity. Remote temperature checking when temperature controlled goods are being carried
Paperless documents	Manifests loaded up and accessed during route delivery as needed. Electronic signature recognition. In cab terminals enabling real time interaction with base.	Reduced paperwork and errors. Improved order status information.
Traffic information	In-cab information on the route ahead. Links to navigation systems.	Finding alternative routes. Improved customer information. Reduced delays
On board navigation	Driver guidance to postcodes. Can be dynamic if linked into routing systems.	Journey times reduced. Reduced driver stress.

Some Transport Companies do need to think differently when looking at ICT applications. Some years ago they had operations that were totally internal and no integration was needed with any other systems. Today, this is not the case and sharing information and moving it fast with access and integration to the customer's/supplier's ICT technology, are key competitive differentiators, and are also the source of cost savings and productivity gains. Information reaches everywhere, and companies who ignore such ICT applications can themselves, eventually, reach nowhere.

Meanwhile a summary of the centrality of ICT for Road Freight Transport follows, some of these legislative aspects, such as road user charging, may not be welcomed by the industry:

Digital Tachographs
- Law from August 2005.
- "Stand alone" or integrative into other ICT applications.

Road user charging
- Road tooling tracking/plotting vehicles using GPS.
- Such schemes look likely to be progressively introduced, especially in large conurbations (as is already found in central London).

On-board management systems
- Fuel monitoring.
- Driver performance.
- Driver information(safety, engine diagnostics).
- Overloads.
- Manoeuvrability aids.

Fleet management
- Tracking for maintenance.
- Messaging and communications.

Network performance
- Traffic flows.
- Alternative routes.
- Journey time predictions.

Security and Safety

The transport manager is responsible for the security and safety of the vehicles within the fleet and also for the goods that are being transported. This task broadly involves the following:
- Ensuring that vehicles are safe and secure when not being used. Here organisations can have a 'vehicle compound', into which the vehicles are driven and stored when not being used.
- Ensuring that goods are properly checked during loading, so that discrepancies due to faulty counting can be corrected.
- Ensuring that vehicles are properly 'sealed' so as to indicate any unauthorized entry between destinations.
- Training of staff, including the drivers, to ensure that safety and security procedures are carried out properly.

Load Safety

Vehicles must be loaded safely. Believing loads will automatically stay secure, is not realistic. The danger en route from acceleration and deceleration of the vehicle causes stress/strain to the load and to the load securing fixtures. The following load restraint requirements are found:

Restraint	Requirement
Anchor points	a) Standardised at a constant Safe working load (SWL), for example: -500 kilos, or -1000 kilos, or -2000 kilos b) Are provided in relation to the vehicle length, for example: -if payload is 20000 kilos = 40x500 kilos or 20x1000 kilos or 10 x 2000 kilos
Headboards	Can withstand a force: -forward of not less than the total weight of the load (100%). -backwards/sideward, then half of the weight (50%).

88

Load safety should be one part of the health and safety risk assessments. It should be detailed in standard operational procedures and customised to cover specific activities and operations. Some guidelines are as follows:

- Check the weight of the load being carried and make sure the vehicle is safely capable, of carrying it.
- Ensure safe systems of work exist and that risk assessments are carried out on the loading/unloading activities.
- Do no overload vehicle axles or load too high; ensure a balanced load including making allowances for load re-distribution when undertaking, multi drop deliveries.
- Load restraining devices are needed for all vehicles; the curtains on curtain sided vehicles/trailers are not "automatic" load restraints.
- Loads must be packed tightly before applying the restraint system.
- Loads need to be checked and the lashings tightened, after vehicles have moved a few miles, and then again at regular points of the journey.
- Restraints and lashings must be attached to anchorage points; (see above for the requirements).
- If roping and sheeting loads on platform vehicles, then the rear sheet should be placed first, with the following ones progressively towards the front of the vehicle.
- After such sheeting, ensure, all loose rope ends are tied up and that any vehicles lights, signs etc. are not obscured.
- The overall width of the vehicle should not exceed 2.9 metres, and for projections in excess of .305 metres, special markers are required.
- Special markers are also required for loads that project more 2 metres in front or back of the vehicle, with police permission needed for more than 3.05 metres front/back projections.

The Road Traffic Act 1991 covers load safety. Around 4000 prosecutions occur each year for unsafe loads. A person, if guilty of using a vehicle in a dangerous condition, faces a maximum penalty of £5000 plus 3 penalty points, and if dangerous driving is also proven, then the maximum penalty is 2 years imprisonment. If causing death by dangerous driving, then the maximum penalty is determined by the relatively new corporate manslaughter charges (discussed later).

Both loading and unloading should be subject to Risk Assessment under the Health and Safety Regulations (covered later in this book) and need to cover the following:

- Risks of people falling from the vehicle.
- Risks of being struck by other vehicles (such as fork lift trucks).
- Risks of loads falling of vehicles.
- Risks from straps under tension, breaking.
- Risks from load moving.
- Risks from trips, slips and falls on vehicles.

Risk control measures to be adopted include:

- Safe loading/unloading plans.
- Proper instructions to all staff involved.
- Competent supervision.

- Proper instruction and training.
- Regular checking of equipment.
- Restricting access to vehicles to authorised persons.

The Government publication "Code of Practice: Safety of loads on Vehicles" is a useful guide and contains the following checklist:

Checklist: Safety of loads on vehicles

- DO check the weight of the load to be carried.
- DO make sure that the vehicle is capable of carrying the size and type of load.
- DO remember that the size, type and weight of the load will affect the handling of the vehicle.
- DO check the load before moving of and whenever items are added or removed.
- DO remember that loads can settle and shift during a journey causing lashings to slacken.
- DO check the load at regular intervals and after heavy braking or sudden changes of direction.
- DO make sure safe systems of work are devised and followed when loading and unloading vehicles.
- DON'T overload the vehicle or the axles.
- DON'T load the vehicle too high.
- DON'T reduce the load on the steered axles by positioning the load too far back.
- DON'T move the vehicle with any part of the load not restrained.
- DON'T climb onto the vehicle or its load unless it's essential and there is a safe means of access.
- DON'T take any chances; there are better things to do than have an accident!!

Source: Code of practice: Safety of Loads on Vehicles, Third edition 2002, from www.dft.gov.uk

The safety tasks for transport managers means ensuring operations are conducted in accordance with all appropriate legislation, but also that vehicle safety is maintained when they are "away" on the road. On average on UK roads, 9 people per day are killed, 110 people per day are seriously injured and over 730 people per day are less seriously injured. This death rate is equivalent to a passenger air liner jet crashing and killing everyone on board every month. Such an air crash event receives enormous publicity, whereas road deaths do not.

These death and accident figure cover all road users, but clearly the physical impact on large freight vehicles can be significant, especially as most accidents happen on A roads and Motorways where not only the speeds are higher, but also where larger freight vehicles are concentrated.

The transport operator therefore can ask the following questions about vehicle safety:
- The Driver - how long since the training was upgraded?
- Driver Management - how long is it since management undertook any training & development?

- Vehicle Maintenance - is it up to date and is maintenance carried out in accordance to a good plan?
- Delivery Times - are they realistic? Are drivers expected to do too much?
- Mobile Phones - Mobile phones are a major distraction and are illegal unless they are used hands free. Is usage limited?
- Smoking - Banned whilst driving? Smoking is a distraction.
- Eating/Drinking - Banned whilst driving? Both are distractions.
- Vision - Seat position? A good clear view is important.
- Are vehicles and pedestrians kept safely apart in depots and warehouses?
- Are internal traffic routes free from obstructions?
- Penalties are enforced when safe working practices are not followed.
- Reversing manoeuvres are minimised and are always supervised.

The 'Pledge to Drive Safely' campaign has noted the following:
- Belt up, use safety belts.
- Back up, keep distance from the vehicle in front.
- Wake up, take regular breaks.
- Wise up, by driving in accordance with road conditions.
- Move up, headrests to no lower than the tops of your ears.
- Sober up, no to alcohol if driving.
- Shut up, mobile phones distract.
- Check up, daily and report defects (see below).
- Slow up, abide by speed limits.
- Buck up, and concentrate on driving and not being angry, excited or "stressed".
- Look up for other road users.
- Sharpen up eyesight if needed.

Meanwhile, safe driving is recognised as that which is:

Patient	not	Arrogant
Self Disciplined	not	Aggressive
Concentration	not	Risk Taking
Responsible	not	Irresponsible
Respectful of others	not	Disrespectful

Safe drivers are:

Structured	not	Negative to Authority
Honest	not	Dishonest
Self Reliant	not	Impulsive
in Stable relationships	not	in Chaotic relationships
Mature	not	Immature
Observant of others: "We"	not	"Macho I"

(Source: "Getting Personal" Motor Transport; August 3rd October 2000)

Safety and accidents at work are an important management responsibility, which will be returned to in Chapter Six.

To assist in maintaining vehicle safety, the following defect reporting sheet should be completed every time a driver uses a new vehicle or starts a shift:

Driver Reporting Vehicle Defect Sheet

Driver Name: Date:
Vehicle No: *Trailer No:
Odometer reading:

There is a legal obligation to report defects daily or at the start of a shift. Please complete the following by placing a CROSS against the item found faulty. If NO CROSS then it is understood there is no defect.

Item		Item		Item	
Fuel leaks	☐	Horn	☐	Coupling security*	☐
Oil leaks	☐	Wipers	☐	Electrical connections*	☐
Tyre pressures	☐	Washers	☐	Brake lines*	☐
Tyre defect	☐	Mirrors	☐	Glass	☐
Hoses/connectors	☐	Steering	☐	Markers	☐
Lights	☐	Secure body	☐	Excessive exhaust smoke	☐
Indicators	☐	Secure wings	☐	Reflectors	☐
Load security	☐	Spray suppression	☐	Other	☐

If you have placed a CROSS then please write details of the defect below and hand this form to your supervising manager.

Driver signature: Date:
Action by: Signature:Date:

Security

The value of vehicles stolen in the UK is very difficult to know, but conservative estimates are that over £100 million per annum is stolen, with knocks on effects to the economy estimated at £800 million per annum. In just one day (16 April 2003) a police campaign, called Operation Coppergold, involved 13 police forces with 63 fixed roadblocks, and resulted in the arrest of 37 people and recovery of £600,000 worth of stolen loads. If this one day was representative, then at least £3 million worth of loads are being stolen every 5-day week, around £150 million per year. These figures are for what was definitely found on the one day; the true figures, which would involve what "got way" on this day, are virtually impossible to know.

Unfortunately, however, what is recognised, if not universally accepted by management, is that most theft results not from external thieves, but from employees. Such internal theft is the most hidden and the most prevalent. This is not easy to accept and is not a pleasant business. But the evidence is very clear and for example, for the "average" theft, five people are involved and thefts have been taking place for six months. Internal theft is reckoned to be valued at ten times more than all "external" street crimes.

Employers often model a culture of acceptance on employee theft; those caught are rarely prosecuted. This is seemingly due to fears over bad publicity and also the fear of not being able to prove the theft, therefore being unable to ensure a correct summary dismissal (which is allowed for proven theft). As an example of the continued failure in detecting and preventing theft, the theft of alcohol loads rises fourfold in the months before Christmas. Yet these "statistics" happen year after year.

Meanwhile, some employees see theft as providing informal "perks of the job", as besides goods, cash and time are all commonly pilfered. Cash and time theft, for example, can happen when an employee that is fit and well makes sure that sickness entitlement with pay is taken fully year, they see it as a "holiday perk". The goods that are regularly stolen include "mundane" items like fuel and wooden pallets. In excess of £100 million per annum is one estimate of the value of wooden pallets that go "missing;" these are commonly not reported or regarded as theft, with the loss being sometimes largely due to poor control systems.

Management must therefore recognise that any potential thief (internal and external) needs to have knowledge of the load, access, opportunity, time and a market to sell to. Clearly, the internal employee is well placed for many of these points. Ways to prevent internal thefts include the following:
- Install security systems and internal controls for all people entering/leaving premises, including all grades of management, and every visitor, including customers and suppliers.
- In recruitment and selection, use valid integrity tests.
- Conduct background checks as thoroughly as is allowed by legal requirements.
- Review and revise information that is made available to employees.
- Stress the importance of honesty, integrity and the costs and consequences of being caught stealing.
- Model honesty in the company.
- Counsel "troubled employees" out of the company.
- Know your people and create bonds between employees and the company; (people management will be covered fully in Chapter Six).

Most "external" theft of vehicles in the UK happens near to Port areas, so areas like Greater London, Essex, Kent and Suffolk are especially at risk. To counteract such types of vehicle theft, a driver and management need to:
- Randomly vary routes/break places.
- Stop/park in busy places.
- Keep any unattended vehicle in sight.
- Not talk about the load.

- Fuel fully on site before leaving depots.
- Park overnight in secure, well-lit lorry parks.
- Park with door/side access against other vehicles.
- Not allow passengers to be carried.
- Protect documents.
- Use roof markings to help police air units spot vehicles more easily.
- Use alarm systems and immobilisers (category one in the Thatcham approvals/insurance standards).
- Use satellite tracking for vehicles and equipment.
- Use electronic or electro-mechanical immobilisers including a coded fuel valve (category two).
- Use mechanical immobilisers (category three).
- Ensure staff/management risk awareness training is undertaken and is continued.

Case Study: Crime & Punishment

Companies which fail to tackle theft or fraud by employees could find that the costs to the business go far beyond just the financial, warns Jo Pawley, a partner in the law firm Wed lake Bell, and formerly the senior employment lawyer at British Airways. According to Royal and Sun Alliance, corporate fraud alone costs UK business an estimated £10 billion per year. A survey among members of the British Chambers of Commerce found that 16% of businesses have been hit by employee theft.

Jo Pawley comments: "Prevention is certainly better than cure as far as employee theft is concerned, but if it is happening, it needs to be tackled as soon as it becomes apparent." Employers are often reluctant to take action, particularly at the out set, fearing that they could make a bad situation worse. They don't want to put at risk the trust between them and their customers or staff or create bureaucratic problems for themselves. However, burying their heads in the sand is not the answer."

"Businesses may take the view that attempting to identify the source of the problem will be very difficult and is likely to adversely affect its competitiveness, reputation and industrial and/or employee relations without any guarantee of a successful outcome."

Business costs
Financial theft or theft of material goods could have huge cost implications. However, employers should also ensure their intellectual property and confidential or proprietary information, such as customer databases, are safe guarded. Failure to do so could undermine an organisation's competitiveness. For instance, in a high profile case in the mid 1 990,s, a senior executive at General Motors, subsidiary Opel was investigated for taking crucial new product information and supplier lists with him when he moved to rivals Volkswagen. This, it was alleged, gave Volkswagen a significant competitive advantage.

Reputation costs
"All companies want to avoid negative publicity. But failure to act adequately or at all, either to prevent theft or fraud or to deal with it one committed, could do more harm

to a companies reputation than taking decisive steps," says Pawley. "You only have to look at the recent Channel 4 documentary alleging widespread, increasingly organised theft of mail by employees of Royal Mail to see the damage this can do."

Pawley adds that this is not only true in cases where employees are stealing from customers. Theft from the company can also impact negatively on shareholder or client confidence.

Employee relations costs

"Shareholders and clients are not the only stakeholders," adds Pawley. "If there are any other employees who may be dishonest, lack of action against thieves may seem like an open invitation to them to follow suit. In addition, honest staff may feel de-motivated and frustrated that nothing is being done to check such activities by their colleagues."

Tips for employers

1. Carefully vet potential new employees to reduce the risk of taking on dishonest staff. Some industries will be obliged to carry out criminal records checks. Even if not actually required, employers are entitled to specifically ask employees as part of the recruitment pro cess whether they have any previous criminal convictions and if so, what they are. Any failure to pro vide details of previous convictions (other than spent convictions) would amount to misrepresentation and if discovered could be treated as such and/or dishonesty, and the employee dismissed as a result.

2. Ensure that internal procedures are in place which makes theft difficult to carry out but easy to spot; also check regularly that these procedures are being strictly adhered to. Dishonest employees often identify and take advantage of opportunities because of poor procedures or where they know that the procedures are not adequately monitored and enforced.

3. Remind employees of the company's policy in relation to theft — that is, that the employer will not tolerate theft within its business, and that if employees steal from the employer and from customers they will be dealt with in the strongest terms, and if found guilty will be dismissed.

4. Recruit specialist external resources when necessary to establish, audit and enforce the procedures. If a problem is widespread it can be difficult to provide sufficient resources internally to investigate theft properly or combat it. There can be an element of arrogance amongst those involved in planned and systematic theft. They may believe it is worth the risk because companies do not have the man power to deal with the matter. Even if companies have adequate resources internally they may actually lack the expertise which is needed to determine who the culprits appear to be and the best way of investigating it.

5. If theft is uncovered, ensure that the correct dismissal procedures are followed. If not, the employee may successfully bring an unfair dismissal claim, however unjust this may appear.

6. If unfair dismissal claims are brought, wherever possible, to avoid setting a precedent, resist the temptation to make a settlement before an Employment Tribunal hearing, despite the time and cost such a hearing entails. Otherwise, other employees may view it as a reward for dishonesty. A settlement in these circumstances is likely to convey the wrong message about a company's attitude to the relatively small minority of employees who are dishonest and give others a bad name.

Source: SHD August 2004

Exercise: The Yogurt Company and Security

The following is a briefing note given to a security expert by the Yogurt Company who has a warehouse complex of 50000 square feet located in South London next to a railway line. Housing in the area is expensive. The perimeter has a chain fence around the premises and access is through one entrance only. Parking is allowed inside the premises as parking in the local area is not allowed. There are over 100 vehicle movements in and out per day. Goods are packed in cartons and are shrink-wrapped onto standard pallets.

A local small independent company based nearby handles the security. They work 24 hours a day. There is a CCTV system in the premises and the two cameras watch externally. Loads are recorded in and out of the premises by the security company on the gate.

There has been a series of small- scale thefts going on for some time. However, in the months of October and November, the thefts have increased from major supermarkets for short deliveries and also more discarded cartons of yogurt can be seen in the warehouse.

Questions
1. Discuss the security implications.
2. What would you do?

The UK Third Party Sector

From the earlier section on Transport Statistics, it is possible to view the "typical" UK road haulier; A. Haulier Limited as follows:
- A private hire and reward haulier (and therefore in the third party sector).
- 5 vehicles, family run with one depot.
- Under 25 tonne GVW rigid vehicles that are average 5 years old.
- 80% of work is casual, the balance is contract.
- Handles mainly minerals, food/drink and building materials.
- Average haul is 54 miles.

- Average distance travelled is 24000 miles per annum.

The management of our mythical "A. Haulier Limited" has to ensure the operations maximise vehicle utilisation, whilst minimising vehicle miles with effective scheduling and vehicle routing. In order to get the best utilisation it should attempt to minimise vehicle turnaround times whilst maximising vehicle payloads and use standardised equipment. In marketing its services, the company will try to seek long term commitments enabling it to invest in a planned way. Top management will ideally co-ordinate operations with the marketing activities and aims to deliver reliability to its customers.

However, problems will be found in a dispersed cottage industry that needs tight control, but is decentralised in its cottage industry structures. It will usually be very customer-focussed, but the people nearer to the customer on a daily basis, the drivers, are low paid and traditionally enjoyed minimal levels of supervision by being away from the management base "face/face" controls. Management in turn gets deflected into dealing with increased legislation requirements, with can mean its customers and their staffs are neglected. Management structures are typically "ma and pa" companies with family succession, and are traditionally vertical, often meaning some degree of inflexibility, little change and poor communication.

However, as with all averages and such composite views, these hide the ranges. For example, the management process of an owner driver one vehicle operation will differ from a company with over 1000 vehicles, and likely owning/operating many warehouses of behalf of contract clients with global connections and networks. On a UK and European basis, the top turnover companies are very large organisations offering a comprehensive range of services, with companies in the sector being subject to takeover and amalgamations, thus making the big bigger.

Feature	Integrators /couriers e.g. DHL	Contract logistics e.g. Wincanton	Forwarders/ 4PLs e.g. Panalpina	Single Mode operator e.g. A Haulier Limited
Assets	Heavy ownership of assets	Managed but not always owned	Asset light	Owned or leased /rented
Basic business driver	Volume through the network	Long term stable customers	Trading	Personal service
Branding	Important	Not important	Some importance	Possible
Customers	Anyone, from one-off to long term contract	Long term and contractual	Local and possibly Global	Local
Product /service offering	Network Coverage, offer a range of services	Specialised including warehousing	Anything at all, with "extras" such as packing	Full loads and possibly some part loads
Modes used	Road/Air with some rail	Mainly road based	All modes, especially sea and air	Road only

Third Party Structure and Types

Training Topics

It can be useful for a company involved in Transport Management to ensure that all people involved have a common understanding of what is involved.

The following is an example of the contents from one such training programme:

The Role of the Transport
- Objectives, roles and responsibilities
- Definitions and uses of transport

Transport Modes and Methods
- Speed, cost and reliability variables
- Choosing transport modes
- Why is road transport dominant in the UK?

Product Classification
- Supply and Demand Variables
- ABC Analysis
- Product Handling Groups and Classifying for effective operations

Vehicles and Equipment
- Vehicle types
- Body types
- Mechanical handling equipment
- Vehicle specifying

Routing & Scheduling
- The trade off between vehicle fill and customer requirements
- Critical planning elements to cover in every journey
- Scheduling differences dependant on drops and distances
- Use of computerised packages

Legislation overview
- Vehicle, operator and driver legislation
- Vehicle Maintenance and Checklist
- Accident awareness
- Health and Safety legislation

Own or Contract out options
- Alternative methods of vehicle acquisition
- Using third party Operators
- Contracting Out procedures

Security and Loss
- Internal theft

- External theft
- Preventative measures

Productivity, Cost and Service
- Identifying the Typical Costs involved
- Getting costs under control by targeting and measurement
- Checklists on Vehicle Productivity, Vehicle costs and on fuel economy
- Service level analysis

The 8 Step Model for Better Transport Management
- A structured approach to ensure all elements are considered
- Transport Improvements
- Transport Excellence

Exercise: Twinxelock

Twinxelock are a UK manufacturer of office equipment such as files, cabinets, furniture, planners, pencils, staples, shredders etc. They have seven factories each making different products, and to satisfy customers, consolidated deliveries are made through their National Distribution Centre (NDC). So all this can be planned adequately, they do the sales forecasts 24 weeks in advance and the factories receive orders for the next 5/6 weeks.

Own account transport uses drawbar vehicles with a 100 drop body fleet that load 12 pallets each body. 4/8 bodies per day are collected from each factory, (located at Kendal, Crewe, Llangollen, Worcester, Peterborough, High Wycombe and Maidstone) which are trunked to the Birmingham NDC. The NDC is 200000 square feet, with 15000 pallet positions storage and receives around 350 pallets per day; stores and order picks 4000 order lines per day.
Secondary/local delivery uses only the units and one body from the drawbar fleet and National delivery uses drawbars (unit and two bodies). After all deliveries have been made, empty bodies are dropped empty at a factory, and the units return with full bodies to NDC.

Task
1) Map the transport operation.
2) Comment on its effectiveness of the transport operation.
3) Comment on the supply chain.

4: Freight Transport Regulation

Transport has much regulation, and very specific legislation applies to road transport operations. This legislation is additional to the legislation involved in employing people and covering health and safety requirements. Transport operations are also subject to comply with such legislation, however in this chapter we shall be looking at not only UK road transport legislation but also at UK HMRC legislation and regulations, and the affects on conducting export/import trade.

It should be noted that road transport legislation is complex and needs to be understood competently. These notes are only intended to provide a broad view and to give a "taster". Readers may therefore wish to check the specialist publications that cover this topic, such as **Croners Road Transport Operations** (this includes an updating service) and **The Transport Manager Handbook** by David Lowe (published yearly). Additionally, www.roadtransport.com is a useful resource.

Road Freight Transport legislation

The transport manager has to ensure that the organisation's vehicles are being operated in accordance with the national and international regulations that govern commercial transport. Transport legislation is a large subject and covers all aspects of operating a fleet of vehicles. A brief summary of the UK legislation follows:

- Vehicle construction and use involves the aspects of vehicle construction (such as vehicle weights and sizes), the fitting of safety features (such as speed limiters), and vehicle testing requirements. We shall not explore these in any details as some parts were covered when we earlier looked at vehicles.
- Operator licensing involves the requirements for obtaining and keeping the licence for the operator to operate, including obligations for maintenance, operations in accordance to the law, the financial standing of the business and that "correct" people are used in managing the business.
- Driver's licensing involves driver testing and keeping records including the use of tachograph recording, with a driver certificate of professional competence
- Legislation covers many other aspects, such as driving offences, road usage/speeds, load safety, and specialist legislation on abnormal loads, the transport of food (especially on temperatures for chilled and frozen goods), sand and coal. Full coverage of these specialised legislation topics is beyond the scope of this book, but we look at shortly, the legislation for dangerous goods.

Operator's Licences

An Operator's Licence is needed if a business involves the carriage of goods and uses a vehicle above 3.5 tonnes GVW, employs drivers or agents. The vehicle ownership is irrespective of whether or not vehicles are owned or hired, loaned or subject to a hire purchase agreement. An application has to be made to the traffic area where vehicles will be parked when not in use. O-Licences are granted by the local Traffic Commissioner (TC) of each Traffic Area. They have the power to grant or remove an Operator's Licence.

Depending upon the nature of the business there are three types of Operator's Licence. They are:

- "Restricted" is for carrying of own goods and are known as an "Own-Account" Operator.
- "Standard "National" is for carrying own or, other peoples' goods in UK and are known as a "Hire or Reward" haulier.
- "Standard "International" is for carrying own, or other peoples' goods for hire and reward in the UK and in connection with an international journey.

An Operator's Licence, when granted, will authorise the maximum number of trucks and trailers that can be run on that O-Licence and also record the actual number of vehicles currently used or "specified" under it. Thus a "margin" is effectively the remaining "spare capacity" on the O-Licence. If the number of vehicles specified on the O-Licence is less than the number authorised, then the remaining extra vehicles (or "margin") can be used at any time provided:

- The maximum number of vehicles and trailers on the licence is not exceeded.
- That any additional vehicles are specified on the licence by notifying the local Traffic Area. Notification can also now be done by being registered for on-line self service.

When an application is submitted there are a number of undertakings and "conditions" given, which must be fulfilled to avoid action being taken. These undertakings are to make proper arrangements so that:

- The rules on driver's hours and tachographs are observed and proper records kept.
- Trucks and trailers are not overloaded and operate within speed limits.
- Trucks and trailers, including hire vehicles and trailers are kept fit and serviceable.
- Drivers report promptly any defects or symptoms of defects which could prevent the safe operation of any vehicle or trailer and that any defects are promptly recorded in writing.
- Records are kept (for 15 months) of all driver defect reports, or safety inspections, routine maintenance and repairs to vehicles and trailers and these are made available on request.
- In respect of each operating centre specified, that the number of authorised trucks and trailers kept there doesn't exceed the maximum number recorded against the operating centre.

Conditions can also be attached to the O-Licence that could affect it, if they were breached. Normally there's a general condition to notify the Traffic Commissioner (TC) of any convictions, or changes in the statements of intent or facts given in the application form. Breaching a condition is a criminal offence, therefore any subsequent changes to the facts, for example, a change in the directors, must be notified.

The TC can impose additional conditions to prevent or minimise the adverse environmental effects that arise out of the granting of an Operator's Licence in relation to a particular operating centre. Those conditions include:

- The number, type and size of authorised vehicles (and trailers) that can be held at the operating centre for maintenance or parking.

- Parking arrangements for the authorised vehicles (and trailers) in the vicinity of the operating centre.
- Times when the operating centre may be used for maintenance or movement of authorised vehicles.
- How authorised vehicles enter and leave the operating centre.

Good repute is an essential requirement to the keeping of a Standard National and International Operator's Licence, along with requirements covering financial criteria; these not being required for the Restricted own account Operator's licence. The good repute requirement, in effect, is whether or not a person is fit to hold a licence.

When it comes to considering repute, the TC will take into account any previous convictions or information they consider is relevant or material. This will include any convictions or conduct in relation to a previous O-Licence held, and the general fitness to hold a licence. It's important to note that this is a fairly wide criterion. All convictions should therefore be notified when applying for a O-Licence. Existing O-Licence holders should notify their Traffic Commissioner of any convictions within 28 days of conviction. When a company applies for an Operator's Licence the application form requires the notification of all the convictions of the company, the directors, and the partners and transport managers. Failure to notify the TC of any convictions is likely to result in a licence being revoked or an application being refused.

Vehicles and trailers can be hired for the business, provided the business holds an Operator's Licence; has the spare capacity on that licence (a margin) and that the vehicle is not kept for longer than 28 days before being specified. Otherwise, an application for an increase to the authorisation is required which must be granted before it is used. Hired vehicles are not therefore exempt from the Operator Licensing system.

Breaching a condition or undertaking is a disciplinary offence and the Traffic Commissioner can take action against the O-Licence. The TC therefore has the power to:
- Revoke the licence (i.e. take it away with immediate effect).
- Suspend it (i.e. the TC can suspend the permission to use all or some of the vehicles for a specific period of time at their discretion).
- Curtail the licence (where the number of authorised trucks/trailers are reduced for an indefinite period; until the operator makes a fresh application to increase the authorisation back to its pre-curtailment level).

The Traffic Commissioner requires the operator to inform them within 28 days of any event that could affect good repute or financial standing. This includes:
- Convictions against the holder of the licence.
- Convictions against the transport manager.

Therefore, all convictions must be notified to all the Traffic Areas where a O-Licence is held when that condition is imposed on the Licence.

The O-licence holder is responsible for maintenance and must carry out the undertakings given when the licence was granted. Responsibility cannot be passed to an outside contractor. If an outside contractor fails to keep vehicles fit and serviceable or fails to keep proper records, then the O-Licence is still in jeopardy because the maintenance obligation remains with the licence holder.

It is an offence to park an authorised vehicle at a place which is not designated on the licence, even though the place is perfectly suitable. Different O-Licences are also needed for depots in all appropriate and designed areas for that traffic office.

If vehicles are being used for hire and reward, then the operator also has to have a person at each operating centre holding a Certificate of Profession Competence (CPC). This is a government-controlled qualification and can be thought of as a transport manager's licence. Holders have passed an examination involving multi-choice and case study questions on business generally, but also specifically on transport legislation requirement. The CPC is granted for life, but if the company is involved in any serious transport legislation infringements, then the CPC can be withdrawn from that individual CPC holder.

It is worth noting that other activities in Logistics, like warehouse management, have no such CPC requirement, and whilst some believe the duty of care requirement in warehousing is a critical area for management (which it certainly is), the same health and safety duty of care requirements also apply to those involved in transport management.

Driver legislation

Transport vehicle drivers are subject to all the normal road user legislation that all car drivers will be aware of. However, there are some differences and for example, the speed limits vary for goods vehicles, as does the requirement for driving licences.

Speed limits are modified for goods vehicles. The car driver's maximum on derestricted roads of 60 and 70 mph, is reduced to 50 and 60 mph for all goods vehicles. There are currently exceptions on 3.5 to 7.5 GVW, but these are expected to be changed with the fitting of speed limiters to these vehicles, and then this will mean a limit speed to 56 mph on all goods vehicles over 3.5 GVW.

For licensing purposes, vehicles fall into the following categories:

A: Motor cycles
B: Cars and van vehicles up to 3.5 tonnes GVW
C: Vehicles exceeding 3500 kilos GVW
C+E: C vehicles towing a trailer over 750 kilos

A large goods vehicle licence (LGV) is needed for vehicles over 7500 kilos. Drivers have to be over 21 years old and take a theory and a practical driving test. When passed, the licence is valid to 45 years of age or for five years, which ever is the greater. For people from 45 to 65 years old the licence is valid for 5 years until they reach their 66th birthdays. After this, licences have to be renewed annually. Medical reports are needed each time a licence is applied for.

Drivers also will need a Driver Certificate of Professional Competence (CPC). This Driver CPC qualification means that holding the above vocational driving licence will not be sufficient. The Driver CPC came into force across all European Union member states on the 10 September 2008 for lorry drivers. To maintain their Driver CPC, all category C licence holders are required to undertake 35 hours of compulsory approved training every 5 years; the training covering:

- safe and fuel-efficient driving.
- legal requirements.
- health and safety.

The driver CPC also introduced a new requirement for an Initial Qualification for drivers entering the industry after the 10 September 2009.

Work Time Directive (WTD)

The original 1993 WTD covered all sectors of activity except transport, doctors in training and "at sea" activity. In April 2000, the directive was then extended to cover transport workers and the WTD Road Transport Directive (RTD) was implemented on 23 March 2005 and affected some companies' warehousing, distribution, logistics and supply chain strategies. This meant changes to transport operations, for example, such as 2 drivers working a vehicle separately over 7 days, the use of 3 shifts in 24 hours and vehicle/trailer interchanges. The main points of this RTD are:

- A maximum of 48 hours per week working averaged over a four month (17 week) period; but this can be extended to 26 weeks under a relevant agreement with a maximum of 60 hours in any single week. (On average this is estimated to reduce driver productivity in the industry by 10%).
- Opt out clause is available for individuals who wish to work more the average week.
- A minimum daily rest period of 11 consecutive hours a day (for the EU driver's hours, see below).
- A rest break after six hours of working time. (30 minutes for 6-9 hours; 45 minutes for over 9 hours). EU driver's hours rules however take precedence here.
- Night time is between 0000 hours and 0400 for goods. Work done in this period must not exceed 10 hours in a 24 hour period, unless there is a relevant agreement.
- A minimum of one day off per week.
- A statutory right to annual paid holiday of four weeks.

Driving hours

Drivers are restricted in the number of hours they can drive. EU Driver Hours Regulations effectively apply to vehicles exceeding 3.5 tonnes GVW, including any drawn trailer. The regulations can only be deviated from in a genuine emergency, or due to any unavoidable delay that could not be foreseen. Any such deviation is only allowed if road safety is not jeopardised. Additionally they must be clear and objectively proven reasons for any deviation.

The regulations get complicated, but briefly, driving time maximum can be generally thought of as 9 hours a day, with no single driving period over 4.5 hours before a rest is taken. The regulations meanwhile cover daily driving, weekly driving, fortnightly driving, maximum driving before a break, break time from driving, daily rest periods, and weekly rest periods. Fuller explanations of the EU Drivers Hours Regulations follow, based on News Link issue 29 from Driver Hire Nationwide at www.driver-hire.co.uk. It should be noted that changes occur and the following is not meant as a legal or an up-to-date statement.

EU Driver Hours Regulations

Definition	Period	Permissible Variation	Explanation
Driving Time: continuous or aggregate	4.5 hours maximum		After 4.5 hours driving, a break must be taken unless a daily or weekly rest period follows immediately
Break(s) from driving	At least 45 minutes	2 or 3 breaks (minimum break 15 minutes)	The final part of a split break must follow immediately after the aggregate driving reaches 4.5 hours
Daily driving total	9 hours maximum	May be extended to 10 hours not more than twice in a fixed week	These extensions must follow on successive days
Weekly driving total	Non-specified, but effectively 56 hours		4 daily driving periods of 9 hours, plus 2 if 10 hours equals 56 hours in total
Fortnightly driving total	90 hours maximum	If 40 hours are driven in week 1, a max. of 50 hours in week 2,then a max of 40 hours in week 3 etc.	A fortnight is two consecutive fixed weeks
Daily rest (single manned)	11 consecutive uninterrupted hours in 24 hours	May be reduced to not less than 9 hours, 3 times in a fixed week	Any reduction in daily rest, must be made up (compensated) before the end of the following fixed week
Daily rest (double manned*)	8 hours in a period of 30 hours	One driver may take the 45 minute break whilst the vehicle is moving	Daily rest may be taken in a vehicle as long as it fitted with a bunk and is stationery
Daily rest (split)	12 hours	No limit on number of split daily rests in a fixed week	The 12 hour total can be split in to 2 or 3 periods. Periods must be at least 1 hour each. The last period must be at least 8 hours
Weekly rest (after 6 daily driving periods)	A daily rest extended to 45 hours	May be reduced to 36 hours minimum at base, 24 hours minimum away from base	Each reduced weekly rest must be made up by taking the balance en-bloc attached to another daily or weekly rest period before the end of the following third fixed week

* If the vehicle is double manned, the Regulations are different with regard to daily rest only. All other "Driver Hours Regulations" remain unaltered. For double-manned vehicles, the daily rest requirement can be changed from 11 hours of continuous and uninterrupted rest in a period of 24 hours to 8 hours of continuous and uninterrupted rest in a period of 30 hours.

Important Note: For the double-manning option for daily rest to apply, all drivers must be in the vehicle for all journeys during the shift. One driver having second drivers for different periods of the shift would not count as double manning, and the double-manning option would not apply.

Tachograph

To ensure compliance with Driver Hours Regulations, vehicles are fitted with a tachograph, which automatically records the driver's hours. The tachograph records have to be kept by Operators for one year and the tachograph equipment has to be checked every two years at approved calibration centres. Tachographs used to use a card system, but now it is mandatory, since 1st May 2006, that all newly registered commercial vehicles of 3.5 tonnes upwards are equipped with a digital tachograph (unless they have an exemption).

Records are saved on a credit card sized smart card rather than the previous waxed paper chart; the cards being issued on application, for example, for driver or company cards from the DVLA and workshop cards from VOSA. The vehicle unit into which the smart card is inserted will hold data for 12 months, however it is recommended that downloading is undertaken every three months to prevent automatic overwriting when the driver's unit is full. Meanwhile, the driver card should hold around 28 days' data, although again, downloading at least every 21 days is recommended.

Driving without a card is allowed, but the law then requires the vehicle unit to produce printed records. This will make it easier to analyse records, and will also enable key information on journeys to be more easily checked: a most valid and beneficial management tool.

Enforcement

If an operator fails to meet strict requirements on drivers' hours, tachographs, speeding, overloading or maintenance, they are likely to undergo a public inquiry, which could damage the reputation of the business and lead to loss of the 'O' licence. Also, if the operator is seen to have caused a regulation to be breached, the licence would almost certainly be revoked through loss of good repute. Whatever the offence, such a breach of the undertakings on an Operator's licence can have far-reaching consequences, not just for the operator, but also for the directors of a licence holding company, the CPC holder and the employees.

Hauliers are only too aware that they can acquire convictions no matter how well runs their transport operations are. For example, they can be convicted of having a vehicle with a defective tyre, even if the vehicle left the premises with a brand new set. If a tyre then subsequently ran over an object that caused some damage during the journey, both the driver and the operator could then be very likely to be prosecuted if the damage was discovered, for example, at a roadside check. Both would have to plead guilty because the offences are absolute. In other words, it does not matter whether the driver, the operator or neither is to blame. If a tyre is defective on a vehicle they are using, then they are guilty. This would apply to any part of the vehicle, found to be defective, even if it had only become so during the journey.

Similarly, a perfectly professional operator with well-trained drivers could receive a conviction for overloading, even though he was confident that the gross weight of the vehicle would not be exceeded during its trip. If the driver distributed the weight incorrectly on the vehicle, this could result in an axle overload that the operator may not be aware of. If the vehicle was stopped and the overload discovered the driver and the operator would be likely be prosecuted and convicted. The operator could only avoid a fine by proving, with documents, that the driver had been properly instructed and equipped to redistribute loads.

One of the main ways hauliers can avoid and minimise the unwelcome consequences of offences is to make sure they have proper systems in place that will ensure that the operator's undertakings are complied with. If they are accused of offences and do not have documentary evidence to prove they have comprehensive systems and procedures in place, they could find themselves in serious trouble. Both courts and Traffic Commissioners will be a lot more understanding and lenient if the operator is able to prove that there were sufficient systems in place to stop a breach of the regulations from taking place.

It is worth noting, however, that the EU had alleged the UK (and Portugal and Greece) did not arrange for a sufficient number of checks of driver's hours. Accordingly, it was expected that such checks would increase between 2008 and 2010 to meet European Court of Justice requirements.

Transport Health & Safety

The transport and distribution industries are potentially dangerous places in which to work. For example, large vehicles and people come together, working at speed and often under pressure. It is essential, therefore, that management's plan for safety and plan to minimise the risk of accident and injury. Employers must make reasonable steps to ensure the health, safety and welfare of their employees and are required to provide the following:
- A written policy is made available to all employees.
- A workplace that is safely constructed and maintained.
- A safe means of access to the work place.
- Safe systems of work including equipment and supervision.
- Competent fellow workers.
- Protection from the risk of injury.

The law has recognised the key role played by employers in controlling health and safety at work. Important obligations and restrictions have been placed on employers by legislation originating in parliament and in the EU. Managers need to keep them selves updated; for example, the Corporate Manslaughter and Corporate Homicide Act 2007 is a landmark in law enforcement. For the first time, individuals as well as companies and organisations, can now be found guilty of corporate manslaughter as a result of serious management failures resulting in a gross breach of a duty of care.

The Act, which came into force on 6 April 2008, clarifies the criminal liabilities of all companies, where any serious failures in the management of health and safety, results in a fatality. Therefore, individual managers are at risk unless the correct risk assessments, safe working practices and training are all in place. The question "How sure am I, that the organisation is being run safely, and what is my role in this?" must therefore be answered by every manager.

HASWA

The Health and Safety at Work Act 1974 (HASWA) is primary legislation defining principles and objectives. It is very general in its scope, and it places responsibility for the health and safety of workers into three categories, namely:

- the responsibility of the employer.
- the responsibility of the employee.
- the responsibility of manufacturers.

HASWA clearly states that it is the responsibility of employers to maintain the health, safety and welfare of all employees including provision of a statement of health and safety policy, safety equipment and training staff. HASWA also states that employees have an obligation to the employer to undertake the training when provided, to use equipment provided for safety as trained, to report any unsafe practices and not to misuse safety equipment. The manufacturer of equipment has a specific responsibility under HASWA to ensure that the product is safe to use in the environment it was designed for in normal circumstances and is fit for its purpose.

Every manager needs to be aware of their obligations under HASWA, which may mean undertaking specialist training or liaising with an appointed health and safety manager. It is prudent for managers, when assessing any operation or new development, to liaise with a suitably qualified health and safety professional to ensure compliance with the legislation. More specifically to aid managers in their dealings with health and safety issues in the workplace, there is a wealth of supporting approved codes of practices (ACOP) and other regulations which are all legally binding and underpin HASWA.

Management of Health and Safety at Work 1999

This regulation supports managers in fostering a proactive approach towards building a health and safety culture within the organisation. In the past some employers merely responded to unsafe practices in order to limit damage, minimising the impact on production, sales and direct costs. Under this regulation organisations are encouraged to be proactive in their approach to accidents and unsafe practices, which means that the logistics manager must ensure that systems are in place for planning, organising, monitoring and reviewing operations with regard to the health and safety of staff at work.

Display Screen Equipment 1992

This regulation applies to visual display units (VDU) for computers or microfiche, in that the risks associated with the use of VDUs, mainly eyestrain, backache and limb pain, are minimised by providing staff with suitable training and equipment that can be adjusted for each individual at that workstation. This includes the ergonomics of the workstation layout.

Personal Protective Equipment (PPE) 1998

Employers are required to provide PPE to employees where there are risks to their health and safety which can not be controlled by other means, e.g. mechanisation. PPE is described as being any equipment designed to be worn or held by the person to protect them from one or more risks. This could be simply gloves and goggles or warm clothing or heated cabs on MHE for use in temperature controlled warehouses. The wearing of correct PPE should be mandatory in the following circumstances:

- a hard hat should be worn where there is a risk of items falling on the driver, of them being struck or of the driver striking his head against some object; the hard hat should be worn with the chin strap in place to stop the hat from coming off.
- ear and/or eye protection should be worn in designated areas.
- a high-visibility jacket or tabard should be worn at all times when outside the vehicle cab.
- safety gloves should be worn when handling steel, securing straps, ropes or chain slings.
- safety footwear should be worn when taking part in the loading (or unloading) operations.

Provision and Use of Workplace Equipment Regulations 1998 (PUWER)

This regulation requires employers to ensure that equipment provided for use at work complies with the regulations (for example, MHE, staple guns, wrapping or weighing machines). Work equipment must be:

- suitable for intended purpose.
- assessed for risks associated with use.
- subject to a recorded inspection.
- maintained in efficient working order.

Reporting of Injuries, Diseases and Dangerous Occurrences Regulations 1995 (RIDDOR)

This regulation requires employers to notify the Health and Safety Executive of fatal and major workplace accidents and those causing more than three days incapacity, work-related diseases and any dangerous occurrence, whether or not anybody is injured. In the case where an accident occurs to an employee away from the normal place of work, e.g. delivery drivers, the Health and Safety Executive suggests that the occupier of the premises where the incident occurs should advise the person's employer as soon as possible.

Workplace (Health, Safety and Welfare) Regulations 1992

This deals with preventing hazards that result from poor housekeeping and includes cleanliness and waste materials. Waste materials should not accumulate, creating slipping or tripping hazards or obstructions to fire exits and fire doors. In addition, these regulations impose requirements on management for the maintenance of the fabric of the workplace, ventilation, lighting, space planning and provision of washing facilities and changing rooms.

Risk management

For managers, the role of the risk assessment is to assess what is probable, and not what is possible. This means making an informed judgement based on the balance between the needs of the business, the operation and the customer. Risk assessment requires the employer to ensure that assessments are undertaken and the findings acted upon, recorded, and communicated to employees. The control measures introduced as a result of assessment must be monitored and reviewed to ensure that they are effective.

Risks may include:
* slips, trips and falls.
* pedestrian and vehicle movement.
* objects falling.
* fire.
* power failure.
* eating, drinking or smoking in the workplace.

Handling of loads

Handling of loads applies to both mechanical and manual handing (Manual Handling Operations 1992). The Health and Safety Executive publish specific guidance notes for the safe operation of mechanical handling equipment. More recently, employees are turning to litigation for damages as a result of manual handling incidents. Therefore, managers must be confident that all staff members have been adequately trained in the correct lifting and carrying techniques, commensurate with the operation they are working in.

A risk assessment might imply that a manual handling operation should be replaced by mechanical handling. If the logistics manager cannot eliminate the hazard, there is a responsibility to reduce the hazard by providing aids (e.g. scissor lift or hand pallet transporters), to reduce the risk of injury, or reduce employee exposure (for example, by reducing the distance or the frequency the load has to be carried).

Health and Safety Arrangements

The employer must have arrangements in place to cover health and safety. These arrangements must include:
* planning to eliminate risks
* a suitable organisation structure
* control systems to ensure decisions are implemented
* monitoring and review procedures

Health Surveillance

If the risk assessment shows the likelihood of employees etc. being exposed to disease or adverse health condition, the employer must introduce appropriate health surveillance.

Information for Employees
The employer must provide his employees with comprehensive and relevant information on matters such as:
- the risks to health and safety identified in the assessment
- the preventative and protective measures
- the identity of the people nominated to assist in this safety work

Training
All employers must ensure that their employees are provided with adequate health and safety training. This should begin at recruitment, be supplemented whenever an employee is exposed to a new risk, and be "topped-up" by means of refresher training.

Working Environment

The Workplace (Health, Safety, and Welfare) Regulations 1992 replaced many of the requirements previously laid down in the Factories Act 1961 and the Offices, Shops and Railway premises Act 1963. The major provisions contained in the regulations are backed by approved codes of practice and deal with: ventilation, falling objects, temperature, windows and skylights, lighting, toilet and washing facilities, cleanliness, drinking water, room dimensions and space, clothing and changing rooms, workstations and seating, meals and rest, and floors.

Administration and enforcement of health and safety legislation

The Health and Safety at Work Act 1974 set up three bodies:

1) The Health and Safety Commission
This advises the Government on future health and safety policy, and on strategy. It also helps to prepare new regulations.

2) The Health and Safety Executive
This carries out policies and is responsible for the Health and Safety Inspectorate.

3) The Health and Safety Inspectorate
This enforces the regulations. Health and safety inspectors have the right to enter premises to make inspections and at any other time if they have reason to suspect a dangerous situation.

They have wide powers, and two principal weapons are:
- **Improvement notice.** This is issued where the inspector believes that a statutory provision has been breached and that the occurrence is likely to be repeated. The notice will specify the breach and will lay down a period within which the situation must be remedied (minimum 21 days).
- **Prohibition notice.** This is issued when the inspector is of the opinion that an activity involves a serious risk of personal injury. This notice will order the immediate cessation of the specified activity until the situation is remedied.

112

Appeals can be made to employment tribunals, but the employer must comply with the requirements of a prohibition notice until it is withdrawn.

Meanwhile, the following Checklists will help on complying with legislation:

Checklist - Organisation Health and Safety
- Have all health and safety aspects of the transport operation been assessed?
- Has an organisation (and arrangements) for securing such safety been detailed in the safety policy?
- Has a person been appointed to be responsible for transport safety?
- Have safe systems of work been set up?
- What monitoring is carried out to ensure that the systems are followed?
- Have all drivers been adequately trained and tested?
- Is there a satisfactory formal licensing or authorisation system for drivers?
- Have all personnel been trained, informed and instructed about safe working practices where transport is involved?
- Is there sufficient supervision?
- Has an update risk assessment been done on all hazards?
- Are people/vehicles segregated?

Checklist - Workplace transport risks
- Do drivers have a safe place to wait during loading and unloading and can they get there without passing through areas of vehicle movement?
- Are security and loading staff made aware of the dangers of moving vehicles?
- Is reversing minimised? If it is unavoidable, are alternative measures taken, such as use of additional mirrors on vehicles, CCTV or a suitably trained guide?
- Is there a clear one-way system and are there pedestrian/vehicle routes (not a big area of tarmac with people and vehicles everywhere)?
- Would a driver arriving at a site know where to go, where to park safely and how to make contact with someone at the premises?
- Do vehicle routes have sharp or blind bends/corners? Are they wide enough and properly maintained? Who plans all this? Who checks all this?
- Are all FLT drivers trained, certified and regularly monitored?
- Are all FLTs in good condition?
- Do all vehicles and trailers have effective service and parking brakes and are here clear instructions on how and when to apply them?
- Have you considered alarms that sound if the handbrake is left off? Several drivers are killed every year simply because their vehicles move off when the handbrake is left off when parked.
- Are all drivers experienced and do you test them to check their competence?
- Are stabilisers always used when operating lorry-mounted cranes?
- Do drivers always use trailer parking brakes and not rely on disconnecting the red line?
- Are tipping vehicle bodies always propped when people work under them or under tilting cabs?

Checklist - Falls risks
- Are sheeting operations carried out with as little climbing on lorries as possible?
- Are vehicle transporters fitted with guardrails on the upper deck?
- Is there an inspection, maintenance and report procedure for all equipment such as ropes, straps, curtains, sheets, nets etc to ensure they are safe to use?
- Is there safe access to bulk-storage diesel tanks?
- Are steps fitted for access to the bed of all vehicles and are they used rather than drivers jumping down or climbing up?
- Are yards well lit, well maintained with an even surface and free of slipping and tripping hazards?
- Are vehicle, trailer and cab access steps all kept in good condition?

Checklist - Depot Roadways
- Adequate dimensions?
- Of good construction?
- Well maintained?
- Well drained?
- Gritted, sanded etc. when slippery?
- Kept free of debris and obstructions?
- Well illuminated?
- Sufficient and suitable warning signs?
- Speed limits?
- Is there a one-way system (as far as possible)?
- Is there provision for vehicles to reverse when necessary?
- Pedestrian walkways and crossings?
- Barriers by exit doors leading onto roadways?
- Separate vehicle parking area?

Checklist - Drivers
- Does the driver hold a valid driving licence for the vehicle being driven?
- Is the driver covered by appropriate insurance?
- Is the tax disc valid and displayed?
- What steps are taken to ensure the driver follows the Highway Code?
- How do you ensure the driver checks:
    - The vehicle is safely loaded and not overloaded?
    - The vehicle is in a roadworthy condition?
    - The vehicle has a valid annual test certificate?
    - Completes the safety checks before moving off?

Checklist - Vehicles
- Is there a maintenance programme for vehicles?
- Is there a fault reporting system?
- Are there regular checks to ensure that the vehicles are up to an acceptable standard?
- Are keys kept secure when vehicles and mobile plant are not in use?

- Are vehicle and mobile plants adequate and suitable for the work in hand?
- Are there any unfenced mechanical parts on vehicles, e.g. power take offs?
- Are there fittings for earthing vehicles with highly flammable cargoes?
- Are loads correctly labelled (especially hazardous substances)?

Checklist - Loading and unloading

- Do loading positions obstruct other traffic, do pedestrian ways need diverting?
- Are there special hazards, e.g. flammable liquid discharge - do pedestrians need to be kept clear?
- Is there a yard manager to supervise the traffic operation, to control vehicular movement and to act as a banks man during reversing?
- Has he received satisfactory training, does he use recognised signals and has he cover during his absences?
- Are there loading docks? Will the layout prevent trucks falling off or colliding with objects or each other?
- Are there any mechanical hazards caused by dock levellers etc?
- Are methods of loading and unloading assessed? Are loads stable and secured?
- Are safe arrangements made for sheeting?
- Is there a pallet inspection scheme?

Checklist - Manual handling risks

- Have all manual handling tasks been identified and eliminated where possible?
- For those tasks remaining, have mechanical aids been provided and training carried out?
- Are there safe means of opening and closing trailer curtains?
- Are there systems for checking whether a load has shifted in transit and for dealing with bulging loads on curtain-sided vehicles?
- Are all drivers familiar with safe loading and unloading procedures?
- Do you and your drivers know what hazards they may be exposed to and what rules they should follow at customer sites?

Checklist - Fork Lift Truck Maintenance and Care

- What is on the manufacturer's data plate?
- Are you working within this data?
- Are breaks, lights, warning devices, safety locks, and overhead guards in safe and working order?
- Are all drivers properly trained and attend refresher courses?
- Are trucks maintained daily, weekly, and six monthly, in accordance with the following checks?
- Are drivers defect reports completed daily and acted upon?

Checklist - Fork Lift Truck Daily Checks

- Daily check: At the start of each shift; check by the driver / supervisor:
  - Tyre pressures are correct on pneumatic tyres.
  - Note and advise any tyre damage.

- All brakes are operating efficiently.
- All lights are working correctly.
- Fluid levels, in engine trucks (fuel - water - lubricating oil - hydraulic oil).
- Batteries, where appropriate are adequately charged.
- Lifting and tilting systems are operating correctly.
- At the end of each check - a written report is completed.

- Weekly check (or 50 hours or period recommended): check by the supervisor/maintenance.
  - All daily checks
  - Operation of steering, lifting gear or other working parts.
  - Condition of mast, fork, attachments, lifting mechanisms.
  - Check hydraulic system for leaks/damage.
  - At the end of each check - a written report is completed.
- Six monthly check (or 1000 hours or period recommended): Check by the supervisor/maintenance.
  - All working parts.
  - At the end of each check - a certificate is completed.

Accidents

Road Accidents are often not thought of as coming under Health and Safety at Work. However, in fact, they are, and since 1999, road fatalities are increasingly being subject to prosecution under Health and Safety Legislation. Additionally, as 95% of all road crashes result from human error, corporate governance is an issue that has to be addressed by many companies. The HASAW 1974 and all the above legislation is the method by which this can be done. But how many companies employing drivers for example, have undertaken risk assessments?

One of the common accidents can involve vehicle hitting bridges. This can be expensive because of paying for the damage to the bridge, the damage to the vehicle and any damage to the load or other property. Fines and penalty points on licences are also additional possibilities. "Avoiding Bridge Bashing" in **News Link,** Issue 30 from Driver Hire Nationwide at www. driver-hire.co.uk gives guidelines and the following are some extracts:

- **Know your height:** all vehicles over 9ft 10ins (3 metres) high must display a notice in the cab showing the height of the vehicle. If the vehicle is less than 16ft 3 ins (4.95 metres) will drive safely under unsigned bridges. If a bridge is unsigned and the vehicle is over 4.95 metres, there is not certain way of knowing whether the vehicle can pass safely through it.
- **Know your signs:** red triangles warn, red circles prohibit – if the vehicle is higher that the height on the circular sign, then the legal requirement is to stop and find an alternative route.
- **Know your route:** any route should always be planned and, if engaged in regular transport of high loads, this means investing in special atlas maps; these, however, generally cover only main roads.

A major problem in handling road accident prevention is that there is a greater acceptance of road accidents, whereas for other transport modes, such as rail and air, strict accident investigations and reporting increase awareness. Yet road accidents in the UK average 66000 per day and range from minor scrapes to multiple motorway pile ups. On average on UK roads, 9 people per day are killed, 110 people per day are seriously injured and over 730 people per day are less seriously injured. These figures are for those people directly involved in the accidents; there are of course additional knock on effects to observers, other drivers, and the family and friends of victims. If such figures occurred on rail or air transport, they would make the national headlines, yet with road transport, a culture of acceptance is the norm. However, as mentioned above, this has changed due to road fatalities increasingly being subject to prosecution under Health and Safety Legislation, and "scenes of crime" investigation by the Police with resulting prosecutions on individuals, as well as under corporate manslaughter charges for employed drivers found guilty. It should be appreciated that most accidents are a result of:

- people not being adequately trained.
- people not reporting possible hazards.
- people not reporting 'near misses'.
- people believing accidents always happens to someone else.

Most accidents are a result of human error. This consists of mistakes in cognitive information processing and from unexpected behaviour. The former involves training, improved technical designs and aids to help memory. The latter is all about attitudes and beliefs about safety. All people at work therefore need be able to:

- Define the best methods of carrying out the job.
- Say what is the right equipment to use.
- Know how to operate equipment.
- Know what dangers are associated with its use.
- Know what the safety precautions are.
- Clean equipment safely.
- Know how to report faulty equipment.
- Use the appropriate personal protective equipment.
- Have undertaken formal training on safety hazards.
- Believe "it can happen to me".

Each manager has a duty of care. This means all individuals who report to them are aware of all potential hazards, risks have been assessed, and corrective action has been taken. If a manager fails in these duties, then not only can this result in unsafe working practices with potentially fatal consequences, it can also result in prosecution not only under Government legislation, but increasingly from private prosecutions undertaken by solicitors acting on a no-win, no-fee basis (such as the fictitious company "Compo Direct" of comedian Ken Dodd).

Costs of insurance claims

Vehicle Operators normally focus on vehicle repairs and insurance costs. There are, however, as pointed out by Dr. Will Murray (**The Costs of Truck Insurance Claims,** in the Institute of Logistics and Transport's Transport Forum Newsletter issue 1, 2003): "Many other costs that are more difficult to quantify, but the quantification of these can make the arguments in favour of investing in fleet safety even greater." Safety pays, and as well as bringing business benefits, there are also legal and moral benefits. Simply put, accidents cost money and some examples of these costs are listed below:

Vehicles costs
- Recovery and storages.
- Repair of vehicle.
- Vehicle downtime and replacement vehicle.
- Replacement by new vehicle if Written Off.
- Increased insurance premiums.

Driver costs
- Loss of expertise.
- Personal injury compensation.
- Lost productivity due to injury absence.
- Replacement driver.
- Medical and welfare.
- Counselling.
- Reassessment and training.

Third Party costs
- Vehicle damage.
- Vehicle downtime and loss of earnings.
- Property damage.
- Personal injury compensations.
- Hospital fees.
- Inconvenience.
- Disbursements such as expert witness, police reports, doctor notes.
- Legal, court issues.
- Fines.

Other costs
- Redelivery.
- Missed/late delivery penalties.
- Customer service, good will.
- Damaged/lost stock.
- Own property damage.
- Investigation times.
- Management and administration time.
- Image/reputation/PR.
- Increased congestion.
- Extra tax to cover road safety improvements.

Dr. Murray notes that even if these costs are all recoverable, the continued submission of claims increases annual premium costs and the size of the excess paid on each crash.

118

One of the fastest growing elements of hidden costs is in the personal injury claims by third parties, especially for whiplash injuries. The best way for Operators to avoid spiralling insurance costs, is to be more proactive in transport safety. Culture and management and driver skills and attitudes are fundamental to this. As noted above, most accidents are a result of human error. Managers need to take responsibility and fulfil their duty of care under Health & Safety. The following aspects are specifically noted by Dr. Will Murray:

- senior and local management must champion transport safety with a proactive risk management strategy.
- conduct detailed crash investigations.
- analyse claim statistics to highlight areas and opportunities.
- train managers.
- improve all the journey, vehicle, driver, road, and site risk assessments.

As noted above, how many companies employing drivers for example, have undertaken risk assessments? All too often, this is done after the event following a death or serous injury: too late. Will it take a prosecution to ensure that duties of care are seriously undertaken and become an accepted part of management responsibility? The sooner most managers fully and accurately realise that their position of responsibility also has a cost, the better. It is a pity that others may have to pay the price until then.

Case Study: Driving at Work

The detailed steps below are widely regarded as best practice:
- Identify who the senior managers are, ensuring they accurately reflect the seniority of the role. All senior managers should fully understand their obligations surrounding health and safety at work and their duty of care to improve and enforce it in the workplace. A safe driving committee, comprising operations, HR, OHS, fleet and risk is an effective way to engage senior managers, set up systems, allocate duties to key members of staff and ensure that everything "reasonably practicable" is being done to avoid and reduce risks on the road.
- Formal company risk assessments, audits or health checks (examples shown in further information below) should be carried out on both the fleet and individual employees, to identify potential risks and hazards within the organization. This must include all company car drivers, cash takers, employees driving on company business, contractors and associated agencies. These risks need to be evaluated, and written policies and controls implemented to cover or eliminate them. All employees must be made to understand the health and safety policies, and be updated when changes are made.
- Maintain appropriate records to demonstrate that vehicles used or provided by the business are legal, fit for purpose, regularly serviced and maintained.
- Ensure that the driving licences and insurance arrangements of all employees who drive on business are checked at least annually to assess their eligibility to drive, and identify any potential risk areas.
- Put in place accident management procedures to assess all collisions/incidents (business and private) and appropriate corrective action to reduce future risks.

- Ensure systems are in place for continual reporting, monitoring, measurement, evaluation and improvement.

Source: 'Driving at Work: managing work-related road safety' produced jointly by the Health and Safety Executive and Department of Transport in 2003.

Further information
- Corporate Manslaughter and Corporate Homicide Act 2007 www.opsi.gov.uk/acts/acts2007/20070019.htm
- Fleet News: www.fleetnews.co.uk
- Health and Safety Executive: www.hse.goy.uk/roadsafety
- Driving at Work: managing work-related road safety: www.hse.gov.uk/pubns/mdg382.pdf
- Department for Transport: www.diigov.uk/drivingfbrwork
- Lloyds TSB Autolease Health Check: vww.virtnalriskmanager.net/Itsba/health/index.php
- Fleet safety audit and benchmarking: www.fleetsafetvbenchmarking.net
- Virtual Risk Manager: www.virtualriskmanager.net

Dangerous Goods

All those who convey dangerous goods (over a minimum threshold), by road, rail or inland waterway, are required to appoint safety advisers, known as Dangerous Goods Safety Advisors (DGSA). This applies to senders/consignees, operators and anyone who loads/unloads dangerous goods, including whilst they are in transit. DGSAs need to have been trained, complete a written examination and if successful are issued with a vocational certificate for five years; after which time, re-examination is needed. Their role is essentially to advise and monitor compliance with legalisation and prepare reports to the employees on all dangerous goods activities and when any accidents involving dangerous goods have affected the health and safety of personnel, the environment or property. In times of terrorism, security has also more recently been incorporated in to the auditing and monitoring responsibilities of DGSAs.

With dangerous goods, all the UK regulations for dangerous goods are effectively harmonised with the appropriate UN regulations and are updated and reviewed in the UK every two years e.g. in 2007 and 2009 etc. There are many rules and regulations covering packing, storing, marking and documentation. Enforcement becomes more aggressive and punitive with penalties up to two years imprisonment and unlimited fines. The shipper has specific legal responsibilities where adherence is mandatory and the carrier in turn has to ensure correct handling, stowing and product segregation in suitable transport conveyances.

Each principal mode of transport has its own dangerous goods regulations:
- Sea/IMDG: The International Maritime Dangerous Goods Code.

- Air/ ICAO - IATA: The International Civil Aviation Organisation and The International Air Transport Association.
- Rail/ RID: Reglement International Dangereux.
- Road/ADR Accord Dangereux Routier: In the UK, domestic road carriage by road is covered by the ADR regulations which are the European embodiment of UN regulations.

Whilst each regulation has its own specific and particular aspects, much is common and relates to the following:

- Commodity identification: Accurate description of the article or substance is needed and the shipper must classify what the substance is. For example, by class number where class 1 is explosive, class 9 is miscellaneous. For example, by using proper shipping names (the PSN). For example, by using United Nations (UN) serial numbers. For example, by using Packing Groups.
- Packaging. Details to be given of the capacity and type used.
- Marking/labelling must be in accordance with standard formats. These are not only the products but also for the carrying units/vehicles; e.g. road vehicles fitted with front and rear orange markers.
- Documentation has to be completed by shippers using standardised formats and details that apply for each mode of transport. Ocean freight has a dangerous goods shipping note (DGN), air has a shipper restricted article declaration (SDDG), road has a supportive transport emergency interaction card (Tremcard). A typical declaration would be:

PSN:	"Paint related material"
UN:	UN1263
Class:	Class 3
Packing Group:	III (Flashpoint 40 deg. C)
Package:	1 x 205 litre (IAI) steel drum

An increasing emphasis has been placed on expanding training for any persons whose duties include the carriage of dangerous goods; therefore loaders, packers, operators , drivers, receivers all have responsibilities. Whilst this is an aspect that is overseen by the DGSAs, it is unfortunately a fact that infringements are found daily. These infringements range from vehicles loaded with mixed and incorrectly declared, packed and labelled goods, to an out-of-date fire extinguisher. Lack of awareness from training is a root cause of many such infringements.

Enforcement can mean a liability of up to two years imprisonment and unlimited fines; management is also directly involved as "where the commission by any person is due to the act or default of some other person, that other person shall be guilty of the offence." Whilst penalties such as these are important and do tend to focus the hearts and minds of those involved, we should not forget that the whole purpose and reason for such regulations is that dangerous goods pose a risk to people and the environment. It is people that get injured or killed.

UK HM Revenue and Customs (HMRC)

When considering the movement of freight in and out of the UK, the influence of HMRC is needed; HMRC being the result of the 2005 merger between HM Customs & Excise and the Inland Revenue. In the UK, a strong influence on Customs practices is the European Community Single Market European Act. The single market is defined as: "An area without internal frontiers in which the free movement of goods, persons, services and capital is ensured in accordance with the treaty of Rome."

A watershed was reached in the history of the EU on the 1st May 2004 with the full membership of Cyprus, Czech Republic, Estonia, Hungary, Latvia, Lithuania, Malta, Poland, Slovakia and Slovenia; a single market of over 500 million consumers in 27 countries.

This enlargement effectively means that supply chain management is now influenced by Tax planning such as tax deferrals and tax reductions. Some impacts are:
*   Centralised purchasing.
*   Contract or consignment manufacturing.
*   Regional sales trading companies.
*   Centralised imports.
*   Centralised warehousing.

All goods leaving or brought into the UK are subject to controls from HMRC. They are responsible for protecting "Revenue" and secondly to protect the "State". These responsibilities can be summarised as "State" protection by stopping illegal movements of drugs, arms, pornography and people, and "Revenue" protection by collecting duty and taxes.

To carry out these responsibilities, HMRC effectively controls and enforces the following things:
*   Value Added Tax.
*   All customs duties collected on goods from non-EC countries; the basis for duty being a calculation on the value of the goods.
*   All excise duties on principally tobacco, alcohol and mineral oils; the basis for duty being not value but some measure of volume, weight or unit.

Customs law is not static and is continually evolving. Customs regulations are complex and often very specific. Therefore, up-to-date knowledge of Customs law for a specific business is critical, and also needs to be checked out fully for specific countries to verify what may be applied to individual requirements.

Further information is available from:
*   EU Regimes: www. hmrc.gov.uk; www.berr.gov.uk (this is the former DTI that is now part of the Department for Business, Enterprise & Regulatory Reform); www.export. org.uk; www.businesslink.gov.uk; www. Europe.eu.
*   Non-EU regimes: UK local chamber of commerce; Appropriate UK based Embassy/commercial attachés; Exporters agent in the appropriate country.

The Customs Tariff

This comprises of the following three volumes:

- **Volume 1** contains essential background information for importers and exporters. It covers duty relief schemes and the contact addresses for organisations such as Department for Business, Enterprise & Regulatory Reform (the former DTI, Department of Trade and Industry), Department of Environment, Food and Rural Affairs (formerly MAFF, Ministry of Agriculture and Fish) and Forestry Commission. It also contains an explanation of Excise duty, Tariff Quotas and many similar topics.
- **Volume 2** contains the 16,000 or so Commodity Codes set out on a chapter-by-chapter basis. It lists duty rates and other directions such as import licensing and preferential duty rates. These are explored further below.
- **Volume 3** contains a box-by-box completion guide for import and export entries - the C88 form, the complete list of Customs Procedure Codes (CPCs) for importing and exporting, the Country Codes for the world and lists of UK docks and airports both alphabetically and by their Entry Processing Unit (EPU) numbers, along with further general information about importing or exporting.

The Tariff is the "bible" which covers every type of goods by Nomenclature commodity coding. This coding has worldwide recognition so it is important to know exactly what the coding(s) are that cover ones own goods/products. The classification used is as follows:

- Digits 1-6 is the nomenclature e.g. 530101.
- Digits 7/8 are for EC statistics.
- Digit 9 is for export statistics to non-EC countries.
- Digit 10/11 cover non-EC imports.
- Digits 12-15 cover special imports from non-EC countries.

Preferential Duties

In addition to the permitted duty free movement between EC member states, other preferential duties are found. In outline, these are as follows:

- EC Preferences: these allow duty free or lower duty for goods originating in certain non-EC countries.
- Inward Processing Relief: this allows relief from duty and VAT on non-EC origin goods which are to be exported outside of the EC.
- End Use Relief: this allows for certain non-EC origin goods to be imported at preferential rates for a specific use. VAT is still paid.
- Customs Warehousing: this allows for goods of non-EC origin to be stored without the payment of duty or VAT.
- Free Zones: these are areas which allow goods to be exempt from all customs control.

Single Administration Document (SAD)

This combines export, import and transit documentation within the EU with an eight copy documentation set; where copies 1-3 remain at export and copies 4-8 travel with the goods.

Basic Export Procedures

Export declarations are only needed for goods that are:
- sent within the EU that are not in free circulation in the EU.
- sent outside the EU.

There are two basic ways of making entry:

1) When all details are known at the time of export, Pre-entry is used with SAD, and pre-entry is mandatory for restricted or dutiable goods. Special procedures, however, apply for:
- goods exported from bonded warehouse.
- goods in transit through the UK.
- licensed goods, such as arms.
- some common agricultural policy (CAP) goods.
- goods exported for process, repair or exhibition purposes.

2) When all details are not known at the time of export, a Simplified Clearance Procedure (SCP) can be used, and goods cannot be loaded onto the exporting vessel without customs having been notified. The documents to be used here can be one from:
- copy 2 of SAD.
- standard shipping note.
- CMR consignment note.
- Dangerous goods note.
- Own document.

The important qualifier here is that the export trader has a customs registered number (CRN) with an export identifier (ECI) entered on the above document. After export, 14 days is allowed to match the SCP with the complete post shipment documentation (i.e. as required for pre-entry). As will be seen with basic import procedures (following), various schemes allow local export clearance and period entries to be made, subject to certain terms and conditions

Basic Import Procedures

Every consignment imported must be cleared through customs. Arrangements must be made to pay any duty or tax before they are released. There are various variations in the basic procedures, for example, goods being imported on inward processing relief, and goods for customs warehousing.

Customs clearance and entry documentation is often left with freight forwarders/forwarding agents, who will give advice and undertake the appropriate procedures as agents to the importer. Care needs to be taken as any incorrect procedures by freight forwarders will be undertaken as agents to the importer; therefore any "buck" stays with the importer and any incorrect procedures could not only result in the wrong rates being paid, but also in fines.

Any delays in customs clearance will most certainly result in rent and/or demurrage/detention charges being levied on the goods. These can be very expensive - port and clearance areas are designed mainly for transit and not storage. So, in the event of there being any "undue storage", the charges are often set deliberately high to discourage such storage usage.

Basic documentation import requirements are as follows:
- A clear commercial invoice.
- A packing list or details of individual items in each package.
- Clear instructions on delivery address.
- Transport document such as the document of title bill of lading.
- Documents related to any specialised customs requirements such as certificate of origin, import licence etc.
- Preparation of customs import entry. This involves: determining the correct tariff heading; availability of any appropriate supporting documentation (such as those above); establishing the value for customs purposes, (this principally is the transaction value adjusted to give the price at the first point of entry into the EC); preparing the customs entry; accounting for VAT payment (for example, due now, or for approved importers, deferred to a bank guaranteed facility); checking to ensure insurance covers the delivered value including VAT and duty.

As stated above, preparation of customs entries is a specialist task. A high percentage of errors is found in prepared entries. This not only adds to the administration workload of all involved but also contributes to delay and extra costs.

Checklist: 7 mistakes with customs entries

Incorrect Classification
The customs classification of import is often difficult, especially with mixed or new products because the customs tariff struggles to keep abreast of technological developments. Average duty rate on import to the EU is 4% of the landed costs of the imports, but rates vary from 0 - 217%. Therefore any error can have significant implications to a company's margins with adjustments upwards and downwards.

Failing to make all the necessary adjustments to the purchase invoice price
The customs regulations provide for a number of items that must be added, or may be deducted to the invoice price for customs duty purposes. Each adjustment is subject to various conditions.

Typical additions you may need to make to your customs value include royalties, selling commissions, insurance and freight costs to the EU, tooling and materials supplied to the seller by the buyer free of charge or at a reduced cost. Typical deductions include buying commissions, finance charges, post import support, certain warranty costs. Importers often fail to make the necessary adjustments and your agents may be unaware of their existence.

A clear understanding of your contract and the Incoterms agreed is needed to meet your valuation obligations. Unfortunately, any agents used to submit customs declarations are unlikely to know these key details.

Using an inappropriate method of valuing the goods

The customs regulations set out various methods for determining an acceptable customs value, which must be applied in a prescribed order. However, most of your imports are likely to be valued under method one, using the export sale price. There are a number of instances where it is not possible to use this method, including transfers to branch companies or agents, sub-contract work where the materials are provided free of charge etc. In these circumstances you will need to determine an alternative method of valuation in accordance with the methods set out in the customs regulations.

Incorrect origin on imports

The EU has entered into various trade agreements with overseas countries which allow your qualifying goods can be imported at a reduced or nil rate of duty. Unfortunately, the system is prone to incorrect application by overseas suppliers' authorities. Where errors come to light, the customs authorities in the EU will always look to recover the full rate of duty from you.

Incorrect origin on exports

You may be asked to complete origin certificates by your customers in non-EU countries to enable them to import your goods free from duty. This helps make your goods more competitive or improve your margins.

You may be providing these documents without a clear understanding of the appropriate conditions or the evidence needed to support the legal declaration been made. If your goods are found not to qualify you may be subject to penalties. Furthermore, your customer will also be subject to penalties and additional duty demands, which they will seek to recover from you.

Incorrect application of a duty relief scheme

There are a number of customs duty relief schemes available to you to reduce or even remove the customs duty costs. However, all of these schemes require you to take on additional responsibilities. If you fail to comply with all of these obligations, forgetting to submit returns or gather appropriate evidence then any benefits you enjoy can be removed with retrospective effect.

For example, HM Revenue & Customs are currently seeking to recover duties saved by people using Inward Processing Relief (IPR) where their freight agents have not entered the correct information in one of the 54 boxes of the customs export declaration. This error usually results from your failure to instruct the agents properly.

Inconsistent treatment

The customs authorities will have a schedule of all the information you submitted at import and export when they come to carry out an audit. This schedule will often highlight different classifications applied to the same goods imported across various consignments, the entry of your goods in to duty relief procedures but no matching discharges etc. These errors are usually the result of poor communication between you and your agent or through lack of co-ordination between various different business functions within your business or group. These errors are easily identified by HM Customs and indicate a poor level of control of your customs function, making you more susceptible to lengthy and time consuming investigations. If you are not comfortable with the control of the customs function you should consider carrying out a review to highlight any potential errors, which can then be addressed going forward.

Source www.internationaltrade.co.uk

The Documentation Chain

Accuracy is vital as mistakes are expensive and difficult/timely to correct. The following guidelines need to be followed:

Sender documents
- Invoice to include shipping marks, terms of sale, terms of payment, unit price and invoice total, with the basic consignment details (gross, net weight, dimensions).
- Packing list, if not included on the invoice.
- Certificate of origin, only for some goods/destinations.
- Inspection certificate, only for some importers countries.
- Dangerous goods note, if applicable.
- Shipping note.
- Shipping instruction.
- Export licence for some goods (some drugs, chemicals, arms/ammunition).
- Insurance policy and/or certificate.

Movement Documents
- Carriage document which acts as receipt and evidence of contract of carriage. For sea only, a bill of lading is a legal document of title whereby the goods at destination are only released to the holder of the original bill of lading.
- Customs, for example, to non EC destinations, SAD for post entry, for example, movement certificates to EC trade agreement areas.

Receiver Documents
- Consular if required, for example, certificates of origin, stamped invoices.
- Customs.
- Import licence if needed.

Electronic Customs/Trading

UK Customs (www.hmrc.gov.uk) were pioneers in electronics, and enable customs control to be moved away from the ports, keeping port-based procedures to a minimum. Import entries for non-EC goods have used CHIEF for many years and export entries also have moved to a total electronic submission. Intrastate entries exist electronically for EC goods/movements. ElecTra is a toolkit to transmit trade documentation and replace paper documents. It is based on TOPFORM, which followed the 1960s JLCD system for aligned documents and is managed by SITPRO (www.sitpro.org.uk). In turn, ElecTra has been the basis for the United Nations electronic Trade Documents (UNeDocs), a project sponsored by the United Nations Centre for Trade Facilitation and Electronic Business (UN/CEFACT).

5: Users' Viewpoint

Introduction

Before undertaking transport, the following questions can be asked by any user: the shipper, the consignor, the exporter, the supplier etc. These questions will give an initial analysis of requirements and the answers will start to build up a picture of specific companies' operations.

General
- Why do we need transport?
- Is the labour force stable?
- Are internal communications good?
- Is absenteeism below the national average?
- How do we know operations are efficient?
- How is performance measured?

Operations
- Are all supply & demand requirements known?
- What are any shortcomings of the current methods?
- How is transport movements organised?
- Do operations satisfy effective customer service or only the transport operations?
- When the transport operations were last examined?
- Is there an objective assessment available of all the work content of a driver's task?

Equipment
- What is the size/weight/value and throughput of each product handled?
- What are the limitations at collection/delivery points etc.?
- What is the vehicle payload constraint, weight or cube?
- Would larger vehicles be more efficient?

Supply Chain Impacts on Freight Transport

The supply chain involves far more than managing transport. The supply chain involves processes such as:

- Purchase/supply/buying/trading.
- Manufacturing/production/assembly.
- Distribution/warehouse/transport/shipping.
- Marketing/selling/customer service.
- Finance/accounts/treasury.
- Stock/inventory.

In fact, the whole business process of an organisation must become integrated and co-ordinated, when a supply chain viewpoint is undertaken.

The Distribution Charter for Cask Marque in the following extracts provides a practical example of how the transport activities link to other supply chain activities:

- The objective of the charter is to highlight best practice in the supply chain to ensure that there are the highest standards of service standards, thus ensuring beer is delivered in prime condition.
- The warehouse should have refrigerated areas for storage with temperatures maintained between 12°C-14°C. (Warehousing).
- Operate a first in, first out stock policy (Inventory).
- Goods received from production should be a maximum of 7 days from rack (Production).
- Delivery to outlets must be at least 14 days before the best before date (Transport and Customer Service).
- Load on the day of delivery to ensure no heat build up (Warehouse and Transport).
- Auditable QC procedures (Customer Service).
- All deliveries are made in Health & Safety standards with draymen trained in the handling of cask ale (Transport).

Accordingly, when taking a whole, complete and holistic supply chain view, all the relevant processes must be looked at. Then, what might seem to be the best from one single individual perspective, may not in fact be the best when viewed from a total supply chain perspective. This will result in "trading off" processes and functions to find the right balance in the overall supply chain.

The concept of total acquisition cost (TAC) from purchasing is one way to examine trade offs in the supply chain. Cost is seen not just as the price paid for something, but as the whole cost of a purchase. The essential components of TAC are as follows:

- The price paid for the goods, say on an ex-works basis.
- The costs of quality, for example, defects, errors causing inspection/re-working costs.
- The delivery costs, for example, the transport charges.
- The performance costs, for example, reliability, KPI measures.
- The lead time costs, for example, money investment, delivery frequency issues.
- The packaging costs, for example re-packs.
- The warehousing costs, for example, break bulk handling storage.
- The stock/inventory costs, for example, for raw material, work in progress, finished goods.
- The costs for a new supplier, for example, start up costs, negotiations.
- The administration cost, for example, ordering, payments.

The price paid may well be the largest item, but all other costs will have many variations. If these costs were equal or of little significance, then the price paid would be the determining factor. Rarely, however, are all the other costs equal. So with TAC, the principle is that all relevant costs have to be allowed for.

For example, transports vary by mode and within modes; variations can be related to performance, transit lead times, and packaging and stock/inventory costs, meaning all the variations would need to be examined.

Air versus Sea T.A.C. example

- If Value Ex Works is £15000.
- If delivery costs via sea to CIF is £ 4600, and via Air to CIF is £ 8800.
- Then Value CIF via sea =£19600 and via Air = £23800
  (Note: The difference between transport costs is 1.913 times, nearly 2 times)
- If the stock/inventory costs are accounted for, then, if Annual stock turnover via Sea is 2 times per annum and via Air is 5 times per annum, then the Stock on Hand via Sea is 180 days pa and via Air 72 days pa.
- If the Cost of Holding Stock is 20 per cent of the value, then the cost via Sea =£1960 and via Air = £952.
- Then the total cost via Sea = £21560, Via Air = £24752
  (Note: The difference is 1.148 times)

Clearly, this quick example does not take into account variations such as lead time, order size, frequency of ordering etc., but it does illustrate that transport cost is only one part of the analysis.

Global Logistics

A growing trend in many industries is the extent and reach of supply chains with global trading strategies and operations. Economies of scale with global media contribute to more global business, and with the death of size and distance that global business brings, global trading operations will need to have international transport as a major consideration. As consumers, we are all involved in this global reach of supply chains. Consider the traditional English Sunday roast. The beef may be from Australia, the green beans from Thailand, the carrots from East Africa, the broccoli from Guatemala, the potatoes from Italy, the fruit from Chile; this overall represents a global travel well in excess of 40 000 miles.

A current business driver for UK organisations is the perceived customer expectations for more product complexity/variation, coupled with "I want it now" urgency. This will often result in revising the company objectives for the product value/service offering, and the following wider and potential global issues are likely to be involved:

- Do we need to work more closely with suppliers?
- Do we move manufacturing to offshore or outsource the whole or part of the operation?
- What are the effects of product complexity? For example, shorter product life cycles and increasing product customising of products may mean assemble-to-order manufacturing, instead of make-to-stock methods of manufacturing.
- What are the effects of transport complexity? For example, increasing distances travelled between manufacturing sites and markets; parts may be made in Mexico and Brazil for assembly in Taiwan with the finished products supplied to a world market.

Likely consequences of these wider issues could be:
- Distances change in the supply chain; meaning examination of the total process and associated lead times.

- Improving the visibility; meaning co-ordinating functions with a proactive real-time monitoring of goods and information flows.
- Managing the whole supply chain; meaning integrating the processes whilst effecting trade-off analysis and TAC examinations.
- As is normal for international trade, this involves both imports and exports in the overall trade between countries; meaning attendant threats and opportunities for companies, such as cheap imports of substituting products that are manufactured locally, and/or more export opportunities.

Incoterms

In trading overseas, a major decision needs to be taken on who pays freight charges and when the liability transfers between senders/receivers, shippers/consignees, and suppliers/customers. There are many options available, bringing in different separation points from what many companies will have experienced when they are trading only domestically. In the UK, carriage paid home is a standard accepted term of delivery; in international trade this is not the norm, and it may be that actually the ex works term is used, which means the buyer is responsible from "ex works," e.g. from the sender's/supplier's premises.

It is interesting that, since the early 2000s in UK trade, the major FMCG retailers have rediscovered the ex work terms with their "factory gate pricing" (FGP) concept, whereas "ex works" within standard international trade terms (Incoterms) have been in existence since the 1930s.

Incoterms are grouped as follows:
- "E" Terms: Goods available at seller's own premises (named).
- 'F' Terms : Goods delivered to a named place/carrier appointed by buyer.
- 'C' Terms: Goods carried to named destination, but with no risk to the seller after shipment or despatch.
- 'D' Terms: Goods carried to named destination, with all risks to the seller.

Looking at these in more detail, the following terms can apply to any transport mode:

-	EXW	=	Ex Works
-	FCA	=	Free Carrier
-	CPT	=	Carriage Paid
-	CIP	=	Carriage Insurance Paid
-	DAF	=	Delivered Frontier
-	DDU	=	Delivered Duty Unpaid
-	DDP	=	Delivered Duty Paid

The following terms only apply to sea or inland waterway transport:

-	FAS	=	Free Alongside Ship
-	FOB	=	Free On Board
-	CFR	=	Cost and Freight

-	CIF	=	Cost, Insurance, Freight
-	DES	=	Delivered Ex Ship
-	DEQ	=	Delivered Ex Quay

As mentioned above, the place must be named, e.g. EXW Manchester, CIF Hong Kong. Also, as the current version is Incoterms 2000 (the next is expected as Incoterms 2010) and when using Incoterms, the version must be shown, for example, FOB Felixstowe (Incoterms 2000).

By looking at what is involved when costing international trade, the following costing sheet shows more fully the appropriate break points on freight charges and the liability transfers involved when using Incoterms.

Incoterms Costing Sheet

Customer: ……………......……………   Terms of delivery:……………………….......

Enquiry for: ………………………….   Terms and methods at payment:…………

Enquiry dated: ……………….............   Transport by:…………………………….......

UNIT COST
Percentage profit…………………………………………………………………
Overseas agents commission………………………………………………
Export turnover, levies……………………………………………………
Other costs………………………………………………………………………
TOTAL EXW

Packing …………………………………………………………………………………
Marking……………………………………………………………………………………
Strapping or bundling……………………………………………………………
Transport to Docks/Depot/
Airport………………………………………………………………………………..
Loading charges…………………………………………………………………
Demurrage/Storage………………………………………………………………
Heavy lift charges…………………………………………………………………
Customs clearance (export)……………………………………………
Other charges……………………………………………………………………
TOTAL FOB/FCA

FREIGHT
Weight……………………………………………………………………………………
Volume……………………………………………………………………………………
Ad valorem………………………………………………………………………………
Surcharges…………………………………………………………………………………
Rebates……………………………………………………………………………………

Other charges...

TOTAL CFR/CPT

MARINE INSURANCE
Insurance premium...
....
TOTAL CIF/CIP

UNLOADING...
TOTAL DEQ/DAF

Transport to buyer...
....
Import duties/taxes...
...
Customs clearance (import)...
.....
TOTAL DDP

FINANCING CHARGES
Banking...
ECGD premium...
....
Other Charges...

TOTAL

The choice of Incoterms is central to conducting international business; it also relates to pricing and to control decisions. For example, a company exporting may need to know what the prices of their products are in the destination market; but if for example, ex works pricing is being used then this will not enable a full view to be taken. If they were to use DDP terms then this could mean selling in a market at different prices with a better profit; as they are now able to price at what the "market will stand", rather than using an ex works or FOB pricing with a only "standard" profit margin.

Another example is where a company is importing from, for example, the Far East and may wish to control the movements more closely, so they have the visibility of arrival times. When they buy CIF UK Port or DDP, then this control can be lost. If they were to change to buying on ex works or FOB Far East Port terms, then this will give them the full control of the routing and shipment to the UK.

However, switching existing suppliers/customers over to different terms may not be easy, as they may be reluctant to abandon existing transport arrangements and to reveal different pricing structures. Therefore, normal commercial rules of negotiation will often need to be applied to bring in this change. In the demise of Marks and Spencer in the late 1990s, changing terms to FOB supply severely strained supplier relationships, due to this being imposed without real discussion but with an automatic expectation from Marks and Spencer that the change would be made.

The following Case Study emphasises this aspect more fully:

Case Studies - Changing to buying EXW

A substantial number of goods are imported into the UK every year. With more companies deciding to outsource manufacturing, this trend continues to grow. Indeed, importing is already the norm for many companies, especially those involved in handling FMCG.

Importing involves a more distant supplier with extended transit lead times. As lead times are one the critical components when deciding how much to order from suppliers, knowledge and control of this lead time is necessary. Indeed, fixed reliable lead times are a mandatory component for effective inventory management.

However, what often happens is that many UK buyers decide to import on CIF or C&F Incoterms, and therefore they leave the organisation of the transit with the supplier. Effectively, the associated supplier lead time is also externalised. Importing companies will then often spend and waste time expediting and checking where the goods are, when they will arrive etc.

Delays in transit times can also cause potential product shortages, impact on customer service levels and to not satisfying customer requirements. With regular repeat orders, any delayed transit times will also inevitably lead to increased stock levels, as the buying company will then be holding additional stock as a protection against the uncertainty of the supplier lead time.

Benefits of changing to EXW/FOB terms
It is possible to control imports better by switching to Ex Works (EXW) or Free on Board (FOB) Incoterms. The following benefits can be seen:
- Control and knowledge of exactly what is happening (management needs to recall here that the management cycle not only involves planning, organising, directing but also controlling).
- Visibility and knowledge of exactly where the products are during the transit; simply, the transit is now in your direct control.
- Cheaper freight costs, as you are now directly paying them. Importers and buyers need to appreciate that suppliers have a margin on the freight costs they have paid; after all they are not, over time, going to be losing money.

Two steps on How to Change
1) Starting out
A useful place to start is to understand some of the aspects of total supply chain management, for example:

- What are your costs of holding inventory?
- What supply lead time is required?
- What part of the supply lead time is the transit lead time?
- What would be the effects of reliable and consistent on-time in-full receipts for your business?
- How does the above compare to your current situation?

Answers to these questions are always revealing, and often show how the internal structure is fragmented and disorganised to undertake effective importing.

Answers will also provide the basis for assessing the benefits of changing.

2) The next steps
- Ask for the suppliers EXW price.
- Negotiate freight terms, possibly by going out to tender for a global or regional freight forwarder.
- Check on the track/trace system to be used. This can be a simple key point reporting with spreadsheet recording, or an instant on-demand access to a carrier's system.
- Assess the risk of changing, for example, any extra management costs, the insurance costs and the risks of direct exposure to regular variations in freight rates.
- Compare and contrast the current CIF price against the new EXW price plus the freight, insurance and risk costs. It is important to ensure a like-for-like comparison with the current methods as many of the current costs may well be hidden.
- If deciding to change, and effectively changing the procurement and buying strategy, ensure that the internal structure will support the changes.

What others have done
There is much evidence to support that the changes above are worthwhile, as shown by the following three case studies.

1) A major food retailer was spending £1200 million on imports via third party wholesalers and £500 million on direct imports. For example, home and leisure products were ordered through UK agents who arranged everything to DDP. Meanwhile, beers, wines and spirits were bought EXW works or FOB with freight arranged through various forwarders. A change in management identified that they had:
- no systems.
- no cost visibility.
- no economy of scale.
- poor product availability.
- an internal fragmented structure; for example: Trading on product selection, negotiations, selection of suppliers, and ordering; Finance on letters of credit, payments; Logistics on order quantity and phasing into supply chain.

The company tendered and then outsourced to one forwarder, but maintained and determined carrier selection when appropriate. The reported results were:

- Freight costs fell by 8 per cent.
- Duty charges reduced by 10 per cent.
- Fuller visibility of supply chain.
- Reduced stock levels.
- Centralised the previous fragmented internal control as a new structure followed the new strategy.

2) A major clothing retailer with nearly 200 stores had 70% of products imported, mainly from the Far East. They identified that they had the following problems:

- No accurate data therefore no visibility.
- Orders arrive "unexpectedly".
- 40% time spent of phoning/checking.
- Paid high demurrage/rent port costs.
- Restricted on buying currency forward.
- Poor QC.

The solution was to:

- Change from C&F to FOB and use one UK forwarder.
- Set up a simple database tracking on transfer points. PO, confirmed, tariff heading, cargo booked, authorise shipment, confirm shipment, documents banked, documents received, arrival time, clearance time, arrival at DC, QC checked, released/available.
- Integrated all their internal systems.

The benefits reported were:

- Lower demurrage costs.
- Improved warehouse efficiency due to scheduled arrivals.
- Improved finance due to forward currency buying.
- Quicker customs clearances.
- Better product availability.

3) A supplier of branded and own label cleaning products to major retailers
Cost-cutting initiatives had become a way of life in the face of major supply chain challenges. The company's supply chain manager noted that: "In the past four or five years we have had to work hard at controlling our costs at a time when there have been no price increases from our customers."

The operation therefore changed to buying products ex-works. The challenge of bringing in consignments cost-effectively is made more difficult by the low-value nature of the products, many of which are very light and use up large quantities of space. The company's continued success is seen as directly related to its freight cost management and arrangements.

Training Topics

It can be useful for a company involved in international trade to ensure that all people involved have a common understanding of what is involved. The following is the contents from one such training programme:

International Trade
- Why do people Buy/Sell overseas
- Features of International Trade
- Supply/Demand variables

Terms of Sale and Delivery
- Incoterms
- Payments
- Documents
- Insurance
- Logistics viewpoints

Freight Transport Operations
- What factors are involved in selecting modes
- Mode characteristics and key features
- Full load movements to parcels and use of couriers
- Chartering, liner and Shared/Network services
- Costing operations
- Best practice
- Models for transport planning

Customs Tariffs
- Calculations and Nomenclatures
- Systems and process
- Operational activity

Legal aspects and Liability
- Agent and principal relationships
- Agent and carrier liabilities
- Terms and conditions of treading
- Contract terms used in International Trade

The Total Documentation Chain
- Shipping instructions
- Letters of credit
- Banking procedures
- Movement documents
- Consular
- Invoices
- Packing lists

- Export documents
- Import licences and controls
- Rent and demurrage charges
- Processing

Costing and Controlling

- Freight calculations
- Mode variations
- Fixed and variable costs
- Overhead costing
- Preparing quotations
- Measuring costs for control and budgeting
- Key performance and control indicators

Reverse logistics and customer returns

Transport and distribution operations are not only always concerned with the outward movements to customers. In many operations, a high volume of return traffic has to be managed; for example, clothing catalogue goods have between 18 to 35 per cent of their delivered goods returned, whereas electrical catalogue companies report only 4/5 per cent returns.

This return traffic is often referred to as 'reverse logistics' and can comprise of any of the following traffics:

- Pallets, roll-cages and other unit-load devices making the empty homeward journey
- Unwanted, damaged or defective goods being returned, for credit, replacement, or repair. In catalogue clothing for example, it is well expected that customers do order goods to "try out" and that they have no intention of buying everything that they order (there is at least some degree of planning certainty for these unwanted goods).
- Products recalled due to quality or safety defects. This, however, will be more random and therefore more unpredictable than catalogue clothing.
- Used packaging being returned for re-use, recycling or for disposal as waste.

It is important to know why goods are being returned. Therefore, the customer contact information and supporting technology should be adequate. Whilst some returns may be expected in overall volume terms, returns could arise due to some unexpected event; for example, the contamination of food products. These particular situations may be further complicated by police insistence on secrecy if blackmail is involved. Even if this is not the case, very often the perishable nature of the goods will have ensured that they were distributed very quickly across a large geographical area.

If goods are defective in some way that is not life-threatening, but where the consumers' reactions to the products may tarnish the company's reputation in the marketplace, then a rapid resolution of the matter may even enhance the standing of the company in the consumers' eyes.

Organising the physical return process will include transport and the "re-checking in" operations at the warehouse, ensuring the quality and condition are verified and that action is undertaken as appropriate. Isolating and quarantining returned goods can be necessary to avoid them being inadvertently dispatched again until they have been checked fully. This will be important where the reason for collection is not always immediately obvious.

Finally, there is a requirement to determine the disposition options, for example: repair, reuse, refurbish, and resale, recycle, or scrap/dispose of. There will need to be a definite policy covering these options.

Case Study: Third Party Home Fulfilment (3PHF) and Returns

Rapid changes have taken place in the consumer electrical goods sector as new technology brings a growth in consumer demand. In the past a customer may have visited an electrical retailer to buy a television and then taken it home by car. Now the consumer expects a home delivery service. Will a simple box drop suffice? Probably not, according to a major 3PHF company who believes delivery should go beyond the front door into installation, return and repair, refurbishment or disposal; in other words a 'cradle to grave' solution.

In the brown goods sector, larger and more technically demanding products such as PCs and home networks require two-man home delivery and installation teams. These will also place new demands on repair services and an increasing requirement for a reverse logistics process that will cover returns management for retailers and manufacturers.

Specialist third party companies are needed to cover such operations. Parcel carriers are unable to provide the service due to the weight of the goods, the risk of damage and the requirement often to configure a product at a customer's home. The heart of the new 3PHF network is its e-hub, which provides core system interconnectivity to a website customised to a client's request and business-to-business integration, allowing the 3PHF services to become available within client's own systems.

The 3PHF company's national distribution centre (NDC) located in the Midlands carries stock for clients to enable orders to be fulfilled. Cross docking for stockless operations can also be facilitated. Customer orders are delivered to the NDC via telephone, the web or EPOS, depending upon the point of sale. When an order is generated, product is dispatched to a local distribution centre (LDC) of which around 20 are needed to give national coverage.

Customers are contacted to confirm delivery details and are given a two-hour time slot with deliveries following a predetermined route. Deliveries are two manned involving installation, demonstrations and the removal of packaging and old product. Products are delivered from the LDC in 3.5 tonne vehicles each fitted with a tail lift. On the delivery routes any necessary collections are made for return back to the NDC for repair or refurbishment.

Repairs and returns

The 3PHF service doesn't stop with delivery or installation, as after-sales are where they believe they can make a difference. Call centre expertise is used to ensure appropriate consumer contacts and repairs becoming an important part of the product life-cycle, as new digital technology, whilst becoming more reliable, does make repairs more complicated. The 3PHF sector may well become consolidated around fewer, more specialised centres that can deliver the required quality "there and back" service at an affordable price.

A challenge for the 3PHF sector is when a product cannot be repaired or a customer requests a return. There is a 20% return on electrical products and the 3PHF company needs to include a collection and screening service for both white and brown goods as well as services for repacking and recycling. Returns are taken to the returns centre for inspection and then, depending on requirements, returned to stock, refurbished, recycled or disposed of.

Added Value

This is a growing and important term that suffers from varied definition problems, but can be, potentially, of great benefit to companies. Added Value is simply doing things better by innovating and by improving the "worth" of a product or service. Added value represents an important aspect that companies need to understand and then apply.

When adding value, this goes beyond a standard performance, and moves more towards delivering customer success and excellence. Added value is often seen as "doing that something extra" which others don't do and is therefore increasingly seen as another source for competitive advantage.

The opportunities for Adding Value are varied, and, in conceptual terms, adding value will mean looking at form, at time and at place:
- Form of the product/service offering. This means asking what the current form is, why is it done this way, how can we do it better?
- Time is involved in the total process/processes. How long does the process take, why does it take that time, how can we do it better?
- Place issues. Where do we do it, when do we do it, how can we do it better?

As products have their maximum value when they are with the customer, in the supply chain(s) there are many Added Value opportunities existing before the customer is "reached". Opportunities for Added Value are many, and can be found within and between the processes of buying, making, moving and selling. The following form, time and place opportunities will illustrate just some of these opportunities.

"Form" opportunities will often exist in the following areas:
- Packaging - for example, hanging garments and not flat packs; point of sale - outers and not items packed within bulk outers.

141

- Packing postponements - for example, packing items only when ordered instead of packing in bulk outers.
- Price tagging/labelling - for example, undertaken just before the final delivery.
- Sub-assembly - for example, assemble to order operations and only then customising product when a definite order is received.
- Sequencing - for example, scheduling to a specific and definite assembly/manufacturing "run".

"Time" opportunities

To examine this properly, it is necessary to establish a complete view of the lead-time involved, not just for a "narrow" operation, but more across the broader supply chain. If, for example, when sourcing products from a Hong Kong supplier to a UK wholesaler, the broader supply chain stretches back from Chinese manufacturers to their suppliers and stretches forward to UK and European retailers and consumers.

Within a supply chain, all the lead times involved in the flows of goods, and the flows of information should be examined. This will, in turn, involve looking at individual processes involved in procurement, production, warehousing, transport, stock/inventory, administrating, ordering and payment.

Clearly this examination will also raise issues for "form" and "place" added value opportunities. Meanwhile, for specifically "on time" opportunities, the following examples may be given:
- Shelf-life reductions or improvements.
- Faster response rates.
- Supply to order options.
- Make to order options.
- Inventory reductions.
- Real time proof of delivery provision.
- Quicker performance reporting.
- Faster invoicing and payments.

"Place" opportunities can be found in the following:
- Supplier visits, for example, to examine stock levels and response times.
- Channels used, for example, home shopping, internet buying.
- Stock positioning, for example, managed inventory at customer locations.

To go further into these opportunities again needs an examination of the wider Supply Chain. A simple framework would be to analyse the following:
- Customer wants/needs.
- Internal processes and relationships.
- External processes and relationships.
- Trade-off analysis between and within processes on cost/service balances, on lead time implications and on make to stock/make to order options.

This examination would fully link both the Supply Chain and the Added Value Chain concepts, and give rise to the "Value Chain" expression. Accordingly, in principle, everything will then be considered as a source and an opportunity to add value (and not to add just cost). Some examples follow:

From........Forecasting   to..........   Make to Order

From ....Inventory push   to........   Inventory pull

From ....Storing   to........   Sorting

From ....Handling   to........   Postponement

From ....Manual ordering   to........   Automated ordering

The relationship between cost and value

We defined Added Value as simply doing things better. Cost examination may therefore result in simply doing things cheaper, and cost reductions will certainly be a feature of any examination or analysis. In broad terms, the following cost reductions can be considered:
*   Decrease the spend (by buying cheaper, the same).
*   Increase the throughput for the same fixed costs (sweating the assets).
*   Increase the productivity (getting more output for the same or less input).

What now becomes interesting, is that, by looking at those activities where cost is being added, these are usually going to be non-Added Value activities. Accordingly, these added cost activities could become opportunities for added value.

If we look strategically across the broad supply chain, the following cost adding activities can become added value opportunities:
*   Forecasting: involves effort and cost, whereas an added value opportunity exists in make to order solutions.
*   Inventory involves varied costs, many of which are disguised; added value would encourage more "pull" rather than "push" supply chain strategies.
*   Storing in bulk would be replaced by added value, sorting to order.
*   Multiple handling would be reduced through added value, postponement.
*   Ordering/invoicing manual processes would be replaced by added value electronic transmission processes.

Third Parties and Added Value

The view of a third party logistics service provider will be often be more towards seeing Added Value as providing Break-bulk/consolidation, Pick/pack, Track/trace, Labelling/assembly and Storage. However, storage may not be seen as value added for a client company pursuing JIT, or make-to-order supply chain options of production. But, from the view of a third party provider, they will often view storage as being added value, if for example, they are now going to provide such a service. It is a question of "perception" (and also of the potential confusion that can follow when using such terms).

The following case study illustrates differences in the perceptions of adding value, and also discusses getting the maximum value from a 3PL relationship:

Add Value with 3PL

Warehousing and distribution is complex and tightly regulated, and there is a need to streamline processes, maximise IT capabilities and take cost out. For companies selecting a 3PL service provider, the starting point for getting maximum value out of the tendering process is to be clear about your objectives. If your existing arrangements are working well for you, but you are obliged to review costs regularly, or you wish to benchmark your service, the best option may be to find a formula which is the least time-consuming and stick to it.

If your existing 3PL service provider is failing you in some way, or your business is changing, it is worth setting up a dedicated team to carry out a thorough review of the options available from different suppliers. This will provide you with 'must-have' information in a readily comparable format, and a proportion to allow suppliers to really demonstrate and discuss with you how they could do things differently.

For best results, you should encourage innovation and creativity. Take the time to find out about the different service providers' cultures, their values, management retention record, contract renewal rates and training stance so that you can make an informed judgement about whether they could work alongside your company and meet changing demands over time. In the long term this will be a more cost-effective option. There is little to be gained on either side by a request for an "all singing, all dancing proposal" in an unrealistically short timescale, and you may miss out on valuable insights if you keep your tendering process within too narrow confines.

You needn't necessarily limit yourself to 3PL specialists in your field when considering who to include on the tender list. Experts in logistics may have knowledge and skills from other industries which can be transferred to yours to provide mutual benefit. It is more important that you find a company you can work comfortably with.

Good working relationships and streamlined joint procedures need to be developed over time. There are great benefits to be gained by working in partnership rather than in a culture of 'keeping your service provider on his toes'. Sharing technology, accurate demand forecasting and successful just-in-time delivery, with windows of a few hours rather than a few days, all require open channels of communication and a culture of co-operation between organisations. The right 'chemistry' between staff, trust and cultural affinity are important ingredients in achieving the best solutions.

As trade becomes increasingly global, the logistics market is growing at three times the rate of Gross Domestic Product. This is within the constraints of continual downward pressure on costs, industry consolidation (fewer buyers, ever-changing requirements) and a tendency for purchasers to opt for short term contracts. Service providers are looking to add value to your business and avoid becoming over commoditised.

Investment in the necessary systems to offer the best solutions is best done in partnership with committed end users.

Of course working in partnership requires buy-in throughout the organisation, not just commitment from the procurement team. There will almost certainly be implications relating to culture, strategies for growth, organisational structure, investment in technology and training requirements. There will be a need to understand the need for change and to embrace it on an ongoing basis on both sides to ensure that the relationship remains valuable to both parties.

Key Performance Indicators should be agreed by both parties and used positively to spot trends and develop the service throughout the life of the contract. Enabling a culture of ongoing change management requires joint responsibility, access to decision-makers on both sides; a hands-on style, excellent communication links and a flexible commercial relationship.

If you invest time over cash, people and paper in the process, it is certainly possible to achieve a 'win-win' position and add genuine value to your warehousing and distribution operations through your tender process.

Source: SHD July 2004 Taking the Medicine by Mark Wallace. NYK Logistics

The Third Party Marketplace & outsourcing transport

Users are often confused by who they should deal with. Whilst names are important in defining what people do, so often different names are given to the same things; often, user confusion results. The following, therefore, attempts to give a view on what the varied name definitions are for third party logistics service provider companies (3PLSP).

A few words of explanation first. Fixed terms arrangements, in the following definitions, means a dedicated provision of services for a specified timed/term contract; Ad Hoc arrangements mean common user/shared provision as required/on demand. Clearly, however, a contract negotiation could also take place for the provision of common user/shared services provision.

Contract Distribution/Logistics
This is a fixed term agreement for provision of dedicated vehicles and/or warehouse resources. It is usually offered by large companies with access to capital to support such operations who also will offer a high range of services.

Haulage Companies/Warehouse Companies
These offer fixed or ad hoc arrangements for dedicated but usually, common user/consolidated services. The companies are usually medium to smaller sized operating nationally or regionally, with sometimes, access to a network of other regional companies. They offer personal services.

Integrators
Fixed or ad hoc on demand arrangements, using multi-modal transport. Often these companies are multi-nationals operating worldwide.

145

Express Companies

Fixed or ad hoc on demand arrangements for local/national express next day deliveries. Either will be a large company with an owned network or, smaller companies with access to a network with other companies and often on a franchised basis.

Forwarding agents, Forwarders and 4PL

These mainly offer ad hoc on demand arrangements, perhaps they are a traditional shipping and forwarding agent, with maybe some transport and warehousing resource. Forwarders usually are smaller and local companies, although there a few large companies who operate with owned facilities on a more global basis. In the UK, there are around 3000 forwarders, with fewer than a hundred companies employing over one hundred people.

Forwarders are involved in numerous activities such as the following:
- selection of the carrier/operator/service provider.
- organising/supervising the movement.
- providing documentation and insurance.
- ensuring compliance with regulations (customs, banking, consular etc).
- advising on packing, warehousing, supply chain management etc.

Traditionally, a freight forwarder acts as an agent on behalf of a shipper. They will do anything, anytime, for anyone, to any place in the world, by any means of transport, for a profit. They are perhaps a partial original 4PL (fourth party logistics provider), a term coined in the late 1990s by Anderson Consulting who defined this as: *"a 4PL is a supply chain manager which can combine its own resources, capacities and technologies with those of other service providers to offer companies, complete solutions."*

However some forwarders do also act as principles themselves and are the actual service operators . In this role, for example, the forwarder "buys in bulk" from the freight services carrier/operator on a FTL, FCL, or ULD basis. Then they sell on a groupage/LCL/consolidated/service, which will operate on a terminal to terminal basis with additional optional services being provided such as collection/delivery, documentation.

Shipping Lines & Airlines

Basic terminal-to-terminal providers, who may have expanded into offering door-to-door land-based services; fixed or ad hoc arrangements.

Postal Companies

Formally, these were state-owned nationally based companies with access to other postal authorities' networks. Since privatisations, many have bought into privately-owned contract distribution/integrators/forwarding companies; mainly thought of as being available on ad hoc on demand arrangements, however, fixed term contracts are an important part of their business.

Parcel companies

Mainly ad hoc on-demand arrangements for non-time sensitive consignments; similar sized companies as for Express companies.

146

Couriers

Fixed or Ad hoc on demand arrangements for hand carried/small packages requiring urgent time delivery.

Another view of the 3PL provider market is from an IBM report (**Building value in logistics outsourcing,** IBM 2006) that sees the following types of players:

- Foundation providers
  - Mainly national providers of transport services
- Core service providers
  - Concentrate on specifics and commodity buying, "famous for few things"
- Extended service providers
  - As core but with a wider range of services, "deliver what they advertise"
- Lead logistics providers
  - More global with "mass customization" of service offerings
- Synchronised providers
  - Offering total supply chain management with standard offerings/ "plug and play"

The IBM report notes that customers require greater reliability with less cost consistently. IBM also see that, to give the full value of trade offs from outsourcing, 3PLs must broaden their span e.g. from a transactional, piecemeal and narrow focus towards a more collaborative, larger and wider scope.

The report notes that, whilst some 3PLs have responded when greater integration and higher performance are required, some conformance is needed, and many 3PLs are found to be lacking as they tend to over-promise and under-deliver.

Using Third Parties

Outsourcing does not only apply to transport, or warehousing or distribution and is often a strategic direction that most companies face. The following "secrets" were identified by **Supply Management,** 29th June 2000:

- Concentrate on what is done well, and allow specialists in other areas to handle the non-core services.
- Adapt to new ideas and developments, as what was acceptable in the past, may not be so in the future.
- Choose a provider who understands all your needs.
- It is crucial to fully know your current costs/service level.
- Ensure outsourcing delivers, planned benefits such as cost/service/time targets.
- Acknowledge that information equals power in areas such as service level requirements.
- Develop a strategic partnership with the provider, based on mutual trust.
- Start with a phase controlled service with monitored cost/service levels at all stages.
- Develop the right company culture which supports outsourcing.
- Monitor the outsourced function with performance measurement regularly.

The following also provides a view on whether to use using third parties for distribution:

- Is distribution non-core activity? Whatever the answer, Management control must remain a core activity, as should, customer contact.
- Can we release some capital? The 3rd Party industries have reported low ROCE ratios, typically 10 per cent, probably well below that expected by many other companies/sectors.
- Will we retain some operations in house? It may be useful to do this for cost comparisons and service benchmarking.
- Will we retain Management expertise? This is important to do; companies should never fully sub-contract control.
- What increased monitoring will be needed? This should be the same as is currently done, but there is often a need to especially watch closely the customer service standards.
- What are the risks of committing to one contractor? Flexibility in the contract maybe possible, alternatively multi-sourcing could be the answer.
- Will flexibility be increased? It should be flexible as in theory, as the third party operator can maybe divert non-specialised resources elsewhere, as after all, transport/ distribution is their core business.
- Will costs be reduced, whilst service increased? This is the ideal.
- How will we account for future changes? Presumably the same as without the contractor; but contract term and 'get outs' is the issue to be considered here.
- Are there any Transport of Undertaking Protection of Employees legislation (TUPE) implications? There probably will not be if there is fewer than 5 people, or some direct control is retained of routing for example, or if relocated. There probably will be if the assets or the whole business is being transferred.

The levels of transport and warehousing outsourcing have remained relatively steady throughout in recent decades, with domestic transport outsourcing at around 75/80% of all freight transport activities and warehousing around 30/35% of companies that were surveyed.

Exercise - New Look (retail fashion and distribution)

Maintaining an efficient supply chain is a major priority for women's fashion retailer New Look in its ambitious plans for growth. The company is upgrading its stores and is widening its appeal beyond its traditional 16-24-year-old customers to older age groups, and needs the slickest possible logistics operation to support its strategy. Logistics director Alan Osborne has control of both inbound and outbound movements to maximise the smooth-running of the operation and to allow the company to respond quickly to the volatile fashion market. "That approach is absolutely critical in fashion. Speed to market - from sheep to shop - is fundamental," he says.

The company's main distribution centre, run in-house, is based at its Weymouth headquarters, where it has around 50,000sqm of warehouse space arranged over three floors. New Look is the town's largest employer and, at peak, 700 staff are employed in the distribution centre. "We have no plans to change that. We have a very loyal and reliable set of staff," Osborne says." The distribution centre is next to the buying office which is a great advantage. I am able to have regular contact with the buying and merchandising director, and I am constantly talking to distribution centre staff as well."

However, the geographic shift in the business has made it necessary to use an additional facility in Doncaster to serve the North and Midlands. The warehouse opened last September and is owned and operated by P&O Trans European. Goods are trunked from Weymouth overnight and merged with those at Doncaster and sent out to the stores on New Look's fleet. Around 48% of the company's deliveries to stores are now made through the facility. P&O Trans European also uses the site for a contract with Flymo manufacturer Electrolux Outdoor Products.

As well as benefiting from shared overheads, the two companies have different trading peaks and the, resources they use can be flexed accordingly. "There is a good mix of demand. They have a summer peak whereas we are more winter-based," Osborne says. This part of the operation was outsourced because New Look did not want to invest large amounts of capital in a distribution centre. "It was also a case of P&O having the resource available to allow us to make the move quickly," says Osborne.

As well as distribution to stores, New Look is paying a great deal of attention to inbound logistics. In future it intends to store more stock overseas, where storage costs are cheaper; and use cross-docking when goods arrive in the UK. The company is setting up overseas consolidation centres for this purpose and one of these has opened in Greece, with another planned in Turkey.

IT systems will play a major part in making the inbound operation work more efficiently, and Osborne says that the company will use fourth-party logistics. It is currently talking to the major providers about the work. "We'll be using a company with global representation. We want them to give us one system solution so that we can have visibility of stock movements all around the world," Osborne explains.

Traditionally New Look has owned all its vehicles, mainly Scanias, and has 44 trucks, either 25ft or 30ft long. However, it is currently switching to leasing and has signed up to take 28 demountable Scanias. This followed its decision to lease six Renaults last year. "By the time we are finished we will have ten company-owned vehicles left, all under three years old," says transport manager Paul Bennett. Although there is a full servicing and maintenance contract, all the work will be carried out on site, using New Look's garage but adhering to Scania's servicing schedules.

The drivers at the Weymouth depot are employed directly by New Look and those at Doncaster are contracted from BRS, although no trucks are taken from BRS. Despite the national driver shortage there have been few recruitment problems at Weymouth, where a 48-hour contract was introduced in April to fit in with the Working Time Directive. "Last year we took volunteers from the distribution centre's picking staff and gave them the chance to do Class HGV driver training," Bennett says.

Store deliveries are made at night, a policy brought in some years ago which other fashion chains are beginning to follow. Security risks are reduced because each vehicle is double-manned; where there are local authorities restrictions, deliveries are made before a certain time in the evening or after a certain time in the morning.

"We have to work around those situations but in a large percentage of cases there is no problem at all. Most of our journeys take place on empty roads," Bennett says.

Tasks:
1) What supply chain strategy aspects are covered here?
2) Identify the strengths and weaknesses in the transport, warehousing, outsourcing and supplier aspects.

Based on: Motor Transport 29 August 2002

Exercise - Ikea and UK Distribution

Ikea is a worldwide name, with some 175 stores world-wide in locations as far apart as Singapore and the Czech Republic. It works with approximately 1,800 suppliers in 55 countries, and its range is made up of around 10,000 products.

Swedish furniture retailing giant Ikea's massive newly-opened Peterborough distribution centre is fast becoming a familiar landmark on the city's outskirts. With over 57000sq m of storage space, and boasting an underground geothermal heating system, the £21.3m warehouse will employ some 250 people by the summer — all newly created jobs. It will help the company service its 11 existing British stores, which occupy up to 26,000sq m apiece. Twenty more outlets should be open by 2010, leading to a huge increase on current annual UK sales of almost £750m.

As well as Peterborough, IKEA has distribution centres at Doncaster — a £14m complex opened in 2001 — and at Thrapston in Northamptonshire. Although it's not all that far from Peterborough, there are no plans to shut the smaller Thrapston warehouse and move its activities to the new building. "We'll still need its capacity," says IKEA Distribution deputy wholesale manager, Bjorn Nilsson. "All three sites will have a role to play in our supply chain strategy. One reason why we chose Peterborough is that a lot of the products we sell come in through the East Coast ports," he continues. "In addition it's well-placed to service our three big London area stores, which account for a lot of our turnover."

Although IKEA owns the three warehouses, Christian Salvesen operates Thrapston on its behalf, while Norbert Dentressangle is responsible for Doncaster and Peterborough. Two different companies are used to minimise the risk to IKEA if one of them happens to get into difficulties. "It also gives us the opportunity to compare their performance," Nilsson says. Why not let Salvesen run both Thrapston and Peterborough given that they're so close to one another? "Because we put Peterborough out to tender, and Dentressangle was the successful bidder;' Nilsson replies. "It was competing against Salvesen plus a couple of other companies." IKEA also uses Dentressangle in France and the Netherlands. Salvesen and Dentressangle don't physically deliver goods to the stores. That's the responsibility of Malcolm's, TNT, and Norfolk Line. Each firm handles approximately one-third of the total traffic, and is solely responsible for looking after its own group of shops. "Again, that arrangement is a consequence of our tender process," says Nilsson.

Each shop receives an average of seven deliveries daily. Usually three to four days elapse between the order being created by the store, and the items arriving. Road congestion makes delivery times difficult to achieve. As a consequence the centres have to operate as efficiently as possible to offset the impact of traffic hold-ups, says Nilsson, and long-distance runs from centre to store tend to take place overnight. "We don't do any inter-centre trunking, or trunking between stores," he says. Not everything IKEA retails passes through the warehouses. "About 30% of the goods are delivered directly to our stores by suppliers," he says. "That only happens, however, if the quality of the delivery service they provide is to a high enough standard, and usually only if it's a full load."

While consumers often carry away the items they've bought themselves, bulkier purchases have to be transported to their homes on their behalf. If it's something that's simply too big to get into a family car, then that can be arranged by the store locally. If it's something as bulky and complicated as an entire kitchen, then all the items are picked centrally, and delivery is organised by the customer distribution centre. "It occupies part of the Peterborough site, and is run by Norbert Dentressangle," Nilsson says. "Norfolk Line transports the products to six hubs around the country for onward delivery to people's houses. Two of the hubs are run by Hammond Logistics, Hays runs two more, while Exel and TNT run one apiece."

The company makes use of rail as well as road transport. "Some of the goods that come into Felixstowe go by train to an intermodal terminal not far from Doncaster, then by road to the Doncaster distribution centre," he says. "We also despatch some loads destined for our Scottish stores by rail. "Throughout the company — in Europe as well as in the UK — we prefer to use rail wherever we can, both to beat road congestion and for environmental reasons," he continues. "We've even got our own railway company — IKEA Rail — tasked with ensuring that an increasing percentage of our traffic goes by train. On the Continent we've got our own trains which we use to move goods between Sweden and the rest of Europe. Unfortunately it's not always easy to send goods by rail in Britain."

Tasks
1) Map the UK supply chain
2) Comment of the use of third party contractors
3) What strategic aspects are involved here?

Based on: Motor Transport 10 April 2003

Information needed

When considering using third party suppliers of transport (or distribution and warehousing also), the following questions will need detailed answers. Giving third parties inadequate information can mean inadequate responses and if, for example, comparisons are being looked for, in order to benchmark against incumbent operators , then a distorted picture will surely be found when giving out poor information. Meanwhile the incumbent operator will have knowledge of all the key parameters/details, and will be in a favourable position. Key information must also be made known to the alternative suppliers that are being sought. It is surprising that so often this is just not correctly undertaken, maybe reflecting that the company is no longer fully aware of what is involved or that they are "only go through the motions" of re-tendering and have no real intention to change. (Please see **Excellence in Procurement**, by Stuart Emmett, for more on Tendering.)

Product Format
- What are the product sizes/shapes?
- What is the weight?
- What is the value?
- What is the packaging?
- How is product identified?
- Is there any fragility?
- Is there any perishables?
- Any hazards involved?
- Any special handling needed?

Throughputs
- What is the frequency? e.g. daily, weekly?
- What is the seasonality? e.g. Over the year, in the month, during the week, during the day?
- What are the usual patterns/requirements?
- How often does the "usual" change?

Collection/Delivery Points
- Where are the geographical locations?
- What are the "features:
  - Limited access?
  - Limited "windows"?
  - Loading docks?
  - Side loading?
  - Height?
  - Day/night working?

Company Policy
- What service level is required?
- What is the "returns" policy?
- What is the order size policy?

Infrastructure/Environment
- What are the road congestion places?
- How can these be avoided?
- Any legal restrictions that may affect us?
- Any specific climatic conditions?

Financial Issues
- Is capital released?
- Is off-balance sheet finance needed?
- What is the asset utilisation?
- Are there any economies of scale?
- What are the planned and the known costs
- Has a cost comparison, involving Total Acquisition Cost been used?

Operational Issues
- What is the flexibility in 'spreading' peaks/troughs ;in delivery times; in future changes?
- Will we get response to special requests?
- What are the management role changes on existing management?
- How will we keep control (management control MUST remain a core activity.)

Strategic Issues
- After the decision, what is the ability to change?
- Have we got "all eggs in the one basket?"
- What is the ability brings it back in house?
- Are we able to use another third party?
- What are the full internal Implications?
- Have we spread the risk?
- What will be our customer reactions? (customer contact must remain a core activity)
- Have we completed a fair and complete comparison?
- Will the change assist in any internal change/new strategies/expansion?

Some of the reported advantages and disadvantages from using third party contractors are summarised below. It should be noted that these have come from specific examples of outsourcing transport. They do therefore show a wide range of opinion and the varied views that are found, for example; innovation is seen as both "more" (an advantage) and as "none" (a disadvantage). As is said, "one person's meat is another person's poison."

Advantages

Cost factor advantages	Service factor advantages
Less capital on the balance sheet	Flexibility against future legislation changes
Costs now fully on the profit and loss statement	Flexibility for sickness, holidays
Less depreciation risk	Less risk of IR disruptions
More economies of scale	Less employment risk
Less administration	Improved service levels
Increase business rations e.g. ROCE	More professionalism and expertise
Cash return for sold off assets	More innovation and new thinking
Tax advantages if leasing	
Planned and more fixed cost levels	

Disadvantages

Cost factor disadvantages	Service factor disadvantages
Less cost control as costs "fixed"	Less direct control on service
More hidden costs for unforeseen "extras"	Less feedback from drivers on customers
Long term contracts	Less response to request
Paying a contractor a profit	No innovation

Clearly these listings also have much to say about how outsourcing is not only approached, but also about the work was previously conducted by the companies involved. No "one size fits all", and again, varied views are reflected: let the buyer beware!

Selecting Third Parties

Users will generally look for the following three characteristics from third party companies:
- Cost/price/rates.
- Speed in transit.
- Reliability.

The order and priority of this top three will usually vary dependant on a company's requirements and its specific offerings in a marketplace.

Many different surveys are undertaken in the UK, on principally domestic transport and distribution services, and a summary of these surveys follows:

Important Factors in deciding which 3P to use:
- Service   98%
- Quality of People   94%
- Cost   90%

Important Factors that 3P see they have:
- Quality of Service   100%
- Reputation   100%
- Experience   60%

Why selected a particular 3P operator?
- Cost   58%
- Service   34%
- Reputation   20%

The Benefits obtained:
- Lower Cost
- Focus on Core activity
- More flexibility
- Higher efficiency
- Improved Service

Implementation fears
-         Fall in Service   30%
-         Lack of Control   26%
-         Higher Costs   14%
-         Staff will not approve   12%

Implementation "reality"
-         No Problems   40%
-         Had Problems   60%

Implementation problems reported were:
- 35%, from IT issues
- 22% People issues ('hide', 'fear', changed)
- 11% Service levels were not what expected
- 10% More resource/costs involved
- 8% Initial data found to be suspect
- 14% other reasons were culture clash, no clear agreements before started no planning or thought to implications.

On a European basis (in UK, Benelux, France, Germany, Italy, and Spain) a survey of 700 senior managers/users in the hi-tech, automotive, consumer goods, pharmaceutical and retail sectors revealed the following opinions:

"Not a problem":
- Lack of geographical coverage
- Specific industry knowledge
- Limited service range

"Weak performance in":
- Price
- Tailored solutions
- Reliability (their most important requirement)
- Customer service

"Will lose business if":
- Inferior value for money
- Lack of reliability
- Inferior service quality

"Satisfied with":
- Expertise
- Size
- Geographical coverage

Sector variables:

- Hi-tech outsource the most with retail the lowest.
- Hi-tech and pharmaceuticals use fewer providers than consumer goods who fragment across several providers.
- Germany outsources the most with Italy the least.

(Source: SHD May 2004: Datamonitor "European Logistics Provider End User Survey")

The following survey also illustrates that different views actually exist when choosing third parties, as each party has different views of what the most important criteria are:

	The Buyers Say % Most Important	The 3PLs Say % Most Important
Quality Service	47%	27%
Lowest Price	19%	26%
Sector expertise	15%	25%
Others: Size/Scope,	3%	9%
Geographic experience,	6%	6%
Reputation/references.	10%	5%

(Source: 6th Eyefortransport European 3PL Summit)

Once again, this survey illustrates the view of service over price. Additionally, the survey looked at the reasons for non-renewal of contracts and found that the 3PLs' view was 56% on price, whereas the Clients' perspective was 55% on poor service.

As also noted above, implementation will not always be easy and automatically trouble-free. Implementation will nearly always involve managing change; a topic that is fully introduced in Chapter Six.

Meanwhile a formal contract may be needed. An example covering forwarding requirements, reproduced with permission from Added Value Logistics Consulting Limited, is found in Appendix Two. Meanwhile, an interesting selection method is shown in the following case study:

Case Study - Toyota USA & Freight Provider Selection

A Description of TOYOTA-NAPO
NAPO-North American Parts Operation is responsible for receiving and shipping $2 billion worth of service parts and accessories globally.

The Toyota Way can be called a mindset and an attitude. Toyota says, "It is the way we approach our work and our relationships with others". The Toyota Way is based upon two pillars:

- Continuous Improvement
- Respect for People

Each pillar has five (5) major principles:

- Challenge
- Kaizen
- Genchi Genbutsu (Go look, go see)
- Teamwork
- Respect

NAPO Mission Statement
"To provide our customers with the right parts at the right time in the right place at the lowest cost". Toyota felt compelled to translate this message into one that would be applicable to their carriers. The translation would allow them to effectively convey the right message to their carrier partners, thereby connecting all of the parties, at least, philosophically.

"At NAPO, we wanted our mission statement to convey the following: the Toyota philosophy; the objectives that NAPO strives to achieve; and to lay the foundation for the expectations that will be placed on the carriers".

Carrier Relationships with Toyota
Relationships are based on three (3) principles:
- Mutual Trust
- Respect
- Work together to reduce waste

Toyota only seeks new carriers when:
- A new facility or new geographical responsibility is required.
- A new program such as returnable program is required.
- The existing Carrier is closing down.
- The business objectives change and a carrier is unable to accommodate new requirements.
- Carrier is no longer able to do an effective job and countermeasures have not been successful.

When looking for replacements, the NAPO bid process is initially issued only to those carriers who are current partners, or, if the transportation requires a niche or specialized carrier, then they may bid the business to new carriers.

How Does NAPO Select New Carriers?
By incorporating all of the principals addressed above, Toyota's selection criteria are presented in a manner that tests the viability of their philosophy and principals:
- Can the partners build a successful relationship?
- Will the Toyota Way be realized?
- Will the partnership withstand the long term, 5, 10, or 15 years?
- What are the business drivers?
- What is the legislative environment?
- What issues or challenges may be on the horizon?

What does it mean to be a Toyota NAPO Carrier?
Toyota has established a set of guidelines that will help the partnership prosper.
Through this process the parties reaffirm their principles by employing the following
techniques:

- Continuously seek improvement
  - Can we move this part better?
  - Faster?
  - Cheaper?
  - Most importantly: All three constraints are balanced equally.
- Toyota will not compromise:
  - We will not give up quality to save a buck
  - Do not carry more inventory if it does not make financial sense
- Genchi Genbutsu
  - Who better to tell how we can improve than those actually doing the work! Ask your partners, what can we do to be a better shipper? And listen!
- Teamwork
  - We took for "partners" to achieve Respect, not "vendors & carriers"

Toyota-NAPO has established and maintains a process that defines the organization
and its philosophy in ways that foster the development of strong logistics partnerships.

Source:: www.transportgistics.com

Developing the relationship with third parties

Effective working relationships need to exist in day-to-day contacts and during monthly/
quarterly/annual reviews. Such meetings often requiring more of the "soft" skills than the hard
skills of management. (Soft skills are covered in Chapter Six).

The key to successful long-term relationships between a company and the carrier/forwarder
is that both parties should feel they are obtaining a positive benefit. They need to have
mutual goodwill and the feeling of being "in this together." This involves "a shared destiny"
approach of going for the same goals, the same added value and mutual long-term survival and
profitability.

People relationships need to be right in both of the companies with compatible cultures.
Positive benefits will only be achieved if there is a long-term relationship between the
Company and Contractor based upon trust and understanding at all management levels, but
particularly from the top. Any type of relationship depends upon trust and understanding. This
needs to be at all levels and particularly from the top. To help on this, a statement of principle
can be agreed between parties. This could include an agreement on the following:

- The relationship will be ethical and progressive.
- Both parties will endeavour to deliver benefits and adopt a continuous improvement philosophy.

- Both parties will commit to achieving mutual trust and understanding and an open sharing of ideas.

The first key sign that a relationship is breaking down is when people fail to talk to each on a regular basis. It should be remembered that issues could usually be resolved by:

- Talking ("it's good to talk").
- Not wanting to prove who is right.
- Seeing the other person's viewpoint.
- Not dragging up past matters previously resolved.
- Openly sharing the benefits of the relationship.

If not handled in this way, then the first key sign of potential breakdown in relationships is when the senior management of either the Company or the Contractor fail to talk to each other on a regular basis, leading to a meeting where the Company has a list of minor grievances gathered over time and the Contractor requires an increase in fee to cover unexpected costs. The first sign of unresolved conflict may lead to a breakdown in the relationship if not resolved rapidly by senior management.

A large number of minor grievances incurred by either party may also lead to the company evaluating their position and seeking alternatives.

In the final analysis, a large number of unresolved minor grievances may eventually lead to a re-evaluation by either party. A final resort will be to consult the original contract to determine the term of the Agreement and the conditions that apply for termination.

Meanwhile the following have been proposed as Strategies for 3PLs to ensure they have successful relationships:

- Develop long-term partnership relationships with customers in which both parties challenge each other to establish supply chain advantages.
- Offer cost-effective methods of doing business by stressing productivity and efficiency goals through technological change and work flow redesign.
- Provide value-added service to customers in terms of individual attention, positive communications and caring/courteous service.
- Formal commitments to continuous improvement processes are critical to the encouragement and streamlining of rational changes.
- Provide two-way mobile data communication systems to customers that ensure availability of real time information on all orders or loads to customers.
- Offer specialised services as well as information systems and logistics consulting for customers. This should encompass a thorough examination of customer needs as well as tailoring carrier offerings (placing the right people, equipment, processes and systems to specific customer accounts).

(Source: International Journal of Logistics Research and Applications, Volume three, number three).

Exercise - Dunlop & Goodyear UK tyre distribution

The formation of a global joint venture between tyre manufacturers Goodyear and Dunlop in 1999 has had huge implications for the UK supply chain and has brought significant opportunities to improve performance.

Since it came into being the joint venture has merged deliveries of its different brands to retailers, opened a national distribution centre, rationalised its network of depots, and replaced its fleet through logistics partner Christian Salvesen.

Goodyear Dunlop accounts for around 25-40% of the tyre replacement market in the UK, dependent on the market segment, and sells in excess of seven million tyres to its customers, who include retailers, car manufacturers, small garages and wholesalers. "In all we've got around six or seven supply chains to deal with," says Wayne Kirby, logistics development manager of Goodyear Dunlop.

When the joint venture was formed, the first task was to combine deliveries of the various brands to customers. This was a complex challenge as a network of outbases around the country was used to cross-dock product and divide it up for delivery to customers. When the two companies came together, seven different warehouses fed this network.

Once combined deliveries had been achieved, a more fundamental restructuring of the logistics network was undertaken. The most important element of this was a new national distribution centre capable of loading delivery vehicles in drop order so that the products would not have to be handled again at outbases.

Tyres are now loaded in 5m boxes, which are trunked by Salvesen and then swapped onto delivery vehicles - without the contents being touched - at multi-user depots which have replaced the outbases.

The 46,000sq m national distribution centre, known as Tyrefort, is at Fort Dunlop in Birmingham. The facility, which also includes a 4,600sq m UK head office for Goodyear Dunlop, has 47 loading doors, yard capacity for 70 vehicles, and 13m clear headroom.

The centre, operated by Goodyear Dunlop's own staff has the capacity to store over 1 million tyres and is capable of a throughput of more than 80,000 tyres a day. There are several different types of racking used to accommodate the different products which, taking into account the different types and sizes, number 1,500. There are separate areas for fast-moving and slow-moving lines.

Use of IT systems is crucial in managing the flow of tyres. Orders for next-day delivery are taken until 1730 hours on Goodyear Dunlop's SAP system and are then transferred into Salvesen's automatic routing software, supplied by Paragon.

The routing information is then fed back into Goodyear Dunlop's IT systems, which use it to form picking lists and monitor their progress - if picking of an order gets behind, the system alerts warehouse staff so that more people can be allocated to keeping the order on track. When the tyres arrive at the loading bay, they are checked against the original order by Salvesen staff before being put onto the vehicle.

The warehouse uses a system of wave picking for different areas of the country with the first vehicles going to Scotland. Once the deliveries have been made to the customers the vehicles are given a route back, so that they can pick up anything that needs to be returned to Tyrefort. All the time they are on the road their movements are tracked using satellite technology, this enables the traffic office to know exactly where they are and to warn them about serious congestion.

Goodyear Dunlop's decision to appoint Salvesen as its logistics contractor came after an extensive tendering process. Kirby says that the joint venture wanted a partner, which could help streamline the network, provide the right amount of IT infrastructure and create the right relationship with its customers.

"The way we approached it was to go out and explain to potential third parties what we were trying to achieve in terms of the business and see what people came up with. It came down to two leading contenders who gave presentations to about two dozen of our customers;' he recalls. "Once the contractors had done this we had a question and answer session with our customers so that they could have an input into the selection process. That meant we were able to find a solution that everybody could come on board with."

The contract has a reward mechanism built into it to give incentives to Salvesen to make the operation, which aims to maintain accuracy levels of 99.6%, as efficient as possible. This is calculated using a series of key performance indicators covering customer service, financial performance, people, and operational costs. In order to improve the operation and make sure it is running as it should there are weekly, monthly and quarterly meetings. Salvesen is given information about the joint venture's future needs.

Questions
1) What are the strategic aspects involved?
2) What are the operational aspects of the operation?
3) Comment on the relationship between the client and the third party operator.

(Based on: "Getting to Grips", Motor Transport 31 October 2002.)

Training Topics

It can be useful for a company considering changing the third parties used, or when reviewing existing arrangements, that they ensure that all people involved have a common understanding of what is involved.

The following is an example of the contents from one such training programme:

- What is distribution?
- What is logistics?
- What are the key drivers?
- How do we meet these?
- Why do people outsource?
- Do we fully know the current operations costs and service levels?
- What are the advantages and disadvantages of outsourcing?
- How have we communicated the decision?
- What are the agreed roles and responsibilities?
- How did we make the choice?
- What are the keys to successful third party distribution?
- How is implementation difficult?
- What responsibilities remain with us?
- Are there any TUPE issues?
- What are the agreed day to day procedures?
- What are the ingredients for a successful relationship?
- How we will develop a successful relationship?
- Will we undertake spot inspections?
- How do we manage people?
- How can we identify poor relationships?
- What are the lessons from others experiences?
- What ongoing monitoring will be needed?
- How to tackle the emotional aspects of the transition and change?

Freight Rate Structures

We have seen in a previous chapter, using the road freight transport mode as an example, what the basic and "raw" costs of transport are. We will now look at how freight rates are calculated and charged. First, some important principles can be established from the following figures:

UK Road Freight Costs per tonne carrying capacity:

Vehicle Type	7.5 T Rigid	18 T Rigid	32 T Artic	41 T Artic
Cost Index per tonne	300	160	117	100

Ship Charter Rates:

TEU/DWT	$ per day Index	Cost Index per TEU day
350/5500	100	100
550/8000	155	99
1000/14000	175	61
1700/22500	240	49

These two examples show, simply, that whilst the cost to operate smaller vehicles will be cheaper (as shown by the figures for ship charters), when the carrying capacity is considered, the cost per unit carried (per tonne or per TEU) falls dramatically. This demonstrates the economies of scale that are found in transport. For example with road transport, only one driver is needed at slightly more cost when operating a 41 tonne vehicle than the 7.5 tonne vehicle, however, the cost per tonne is three times more when using the smaller vehicle.

There are other anomalies with freight charges; distance is not always a good indicator of the rate charged, as a longer distance may have a comparatively lower rate. This can be due to many factors such as traffic imbalances on a round trip basis, the ratio of time spent moving/not moving (e.g. a ships unloading time in port, a road truck waiting to be unloaded), the competition in the market, the port charges paid by a shipping company, etc. The following comparisons show this very clearly for indexed sea freight rates for on one TEU from North Europe to destinations in the Middle East/Indian sub-continent and the Far East. The ports have been ranked from shorter to longer distance:

Dubai	100
Mumbai	125
Colombo	111
Singapore	78
Shanghai	78

It can be seen it is actually cheaper to ship a TEU to the Far East than to the Middle East/Indian sub-continent.

Variations found in Freight Charges

Freight Charges can be complex in their application: not only can the bases for charging vary between modes, but also often within the modes themselves. Additionally international freight rates are often expressed in US Dollars with variable surcharges applied, all of which can create a varied cost base which can change on a daily basis.

The following two basic rating principals are found across all freight modes with some examples indicated. We shall explain these examples shortly:

Rating by the Unit of Charging:
- Weight factor (W)   e.g. per kilo and per 1000 kilos
- Measurement factor (M)   e.g. per 1CBM and per 3 CBM
- Value factor per W/M   e.g. up to $1000 value per W/M, then $90 per W/M
- Value factor percentage   e.g. 3% of FOB Value

Rating by the Type of Goods:
- Commodity factor   e.g. Woollen rags $50 W/M
                                  e.g. Combed wool $80 W/M
- Freight All Kinds (FAK)   e.g. 50 pence per kilo
- Per Piece/unit   e.g. $2000 per 20 ft container
                                  e.g. £15 per metre on the vehicle length

Where more than one variable exists in the rate structure, then, usually, the one that produces the higher revenue is the one applied. For example, a rate of $100 W/M for cargo of 2000 kilos/4CBM is charged as 4CBM @ $100 giving a $400 charge (and not 2000 kilos @ $100).

As with many rules however, they exist to be broken. For example, air freight rates do allow for adjustments to be made to give whichever brings the lower revenue (we shall refer to this later).

As general principles, ratings are applied as follows:

Mode	W/M Rule	Value Rates	Commodity Rates	FAK Rates
Sea	1000 kilos 1CBM	some	some	mainly
Air	1000 kilos 6 or 7 CBM	some	some	mainly
Road	1000 kilos 3 CBM	no	no	yes
Rail	N/A	no	no	yes

Finally, in addition to freight rate application variations, other variables that are found are as a result of trade imbalances causing freight price variations, frequency service level variables, service supplier variables and liability. We shall now examine all these variations in freight charges by looking at each mode.

Basic Ocean Liner (Deep Sea) Rates

The majority of these are expressed as per freight tonne or per tonne W/M. For sea freight, this means the charge is per 1000 kilos or per 1 cubic metre, whichever is the greater. This W/M breakpoint is low, so the majority of freight is effectively volume measurement rated.

Some freight tariffs are published (but often not widely so) and the tariffs also include standard rules on applications. The majority of freight was traditionally rated by the Commodity and meant many hundreds of different base rates; the principle with commodity rates being one that says that a ton of gold can stand a higher rate than a ton of scrap iron. Increasingly however, basic FAK rates (Freight of All Kinds) are found, with around fifteen different base rates. For example:

For packages each under 500 kilos/1CBM:

a) Value not exceeding $1000 W/M
Consignments up to 5 tons $100 W/M
Consignments 5 - 10 tons $90 W/M

b) Value exceeding $1000 W/M
Consignments up to 5 tons $130 W/M
Consignments 5 - 10 tons $120 W/M

Container Rates
Whilst the basic ocean leg may be rated as above, the tariffs are usually structured to reflect the through movement. For example on UK Imports:
- Foreign collection haulage on a box basis or weight basis.
- Foreign terminal charge on a box or weight basis.
- Basic freight charge on the basis as above.
- UK terminal charge on a box or weight basis.
- UK delivery haulage on a box or weight basis.
- For a full container load (FCL) the freight tariff incorporates safeguards for shipping lines against the under utilisation of the container capacity.

Basic Short Sea Routes
For Europe, another variable situation is found. Whilst FAK rates are more common for the few remaining conventional services; for LO/LO or RO/RO services the FCL or FTL movements are charged for the sea leg of the movement per box or per metre respectively. For example, £1500 per 20-ft container, £35 per metre for a 13 metre trailer. For part loads, LCL or LTL movements, then an FAK rating dominates with the weight or measurement factor applied based on 1000 kilos/3CBM (and this usually expressed per 100 kilos/0.3 CBM).

Surcharges
These are a feature especially of ocean (deep sea) services. Typically, they involve upward and downward adjustments for currency and bunkers.

The currency adjustment factor (CAF) is justified on the basis that revenue is needed in one currency, typically US Dollars, but that expenses are paid in a local currency. As exchange rates vary, the CAF accounts for these.

The Bunker adjustment factor (BAF) is related to the cost of purchasing fuel oil. This is a critical cost for all transport modes and as the price of oil changes, the BAF make an appropriate adjustment.

Other surcharges can also be found:
- Congestion Tariffs are built up by calculating a normal turnaround time at port terminals. The standing cost of a ship is high (like for all transport vehicles), so if congestion is occurring regularly at specific ports then the tariffs will include a surcharge to cover for the extra costs involved in serving the port.
- War risk. This reflects the increase in insurance premiums when vessels are operating in dangerous parts of the world.

The existence of surcharges complicates the freight rate calculations. For example, 40-ft container rate is $5000.00, with surcharges of BAF 10%, CAF Minus 5%, Congestion $100 per 40 ft container.

The calculation is:

Base Rate	=$5000
BAF 10% of $5000	= $500+
CAF -5% of $5000	= $250-
Congestion	= $100+
Surcharge subtotal	=$350
Total payable	=$5350

The end of European Shipping Conferences

Most ocean trade routes serving Europe used to have a "conference", indeed some trades that do not serve Europe, still do. A conference is effectively a cartel of major shipping lines who have established a common freight rate tariff in return for established regular and scheduled services, irrespective of the shipping line operating. To maintain shipper loyalty to the conference, shippers signed an agreement to restrict their shipments to conference operators. For this loyalty, the conference gave a discount to the published tariff; for example, a 9.5% immediate rebate. If shippers decided not to sign, then a deferred rebate was payable 6 or 12 months after the shipment. Some conferences, however, choose (more simply perhaps) to give a lower basic rate to signatories. This was up to a 30% discount available for regular large volume movements.

Those shipping lines not in a conference were known as "non-conference lines" or "independents". Whilst they did not always offer such regular and frequent services as conference lines, they offered cheaper freight rates.

However, such conference cartel practices were ruled by the EU as anti-trust competitive practices, and were abandoned formally from the 17th October 2008. This means that it is unlawful for shipping companies to jointly fix freight rates or any additional charges such as BAF, CAF on a collective basis. The impact of this radical change is uncertain, and will remain so for some years. The ban also applies to sharing information, and will therefore take a degree of management culture and mind set changes that take some time.

Meanwhile, the EU expectation is for rates to fall and service levels to be maintained. It remains to be seen if this EU pro-customer-friendly practice will spread to other non-European trades.

Air Freight Rates

Airline rates also have a weight/measurement ratio, called "chargeable kilos" or "volumetric units". Generally the ratio is 1000 kilos/6CBM - usually expressed per kilo/6000 cubic centimetres; although for some areas the ratio still remains at the former ratio of 1000/7CBM (or per kilo/7000 cubic centimetres). The airlines have attempted in recent years to lower the ratio to 1000 kils/5CBM, but this was resisted by trade and lobby groups.

Within this W/M structure, airline rates are categorised as follows:
- general cargo rates (GC).
- specific commodity rates (SC).
- classification rates.

- FAK rates.
- Containerised rates (ULD).

General Cargo Rates apply for most freight. Typical weight breakpoints are:
- minimum flat charge (M).
- normal rates (N) up to 45 kilos or up to 100 kilos.
- quantity rates (Q) over 45 kilos or 100/199 kilos etc.

It is allowed to over-declare the weight to achieve the cheaper higher weight band rate, for example where the GC Tariff is:
- M   £70.00 in full.
- N   £6.00 per kilo.
- Q100   £2.50 per kilo.
- Q200   £1.60 per kilo.

160 kilos @ £2.50 = £400. But this can be rated as 200 kilos @ £1.60 = £320.00 payable.

Specific Commodity Rates offer substantial discounts to the general cargo rates. SC rates apply for large quantities of specific and named commodities moving between specific airports. For example, Kiwi fruit - Auckland/London.

Classification Rates apply to only a few cargoes. These are discounted or surcharged SC rates. For example, gold is surcharged, newspapers are discounted.

FAK Rates have been introduced onto major trade routes, like the transatlantic, where they replace the GC/SC rates. Effectively then, the SC rates are abolished and a lower GC rate structure applies.

Containerised Rates apply for ULDs. The rate is a flat FAK charge per unit regardless of weight, providing the maximum weight allowed per ULD is not exceeded. The ULD rate is usually a flat minimum rate above which a rate per kilo then applies. These rates are therefore charged per container/ULD without reference to the commodity loaded therein.

European Road Freight Rates
Full trailer loads (FTL) are charged on a job rate basis. For example, point A to point B, £1500 per trailer.

Less than trailer loads (LTL) incur a higher rate. For example, the part load shipper with 10 tonnes would pay around £1100 from point A to B against the £1500 for a FTL. The groupage shipper with 1 tonne would pay around £250. The important principle here is that the smaller the consignment, the higher the freight charges.

The basis for charging is:
- By Job/FAK for Full trailer loads (FTL)
- By FAK/W/M for Less than trailer load (LTL)
  (where W = 1000 Kilos, M = 3 cubic Metres, whichever is the greater).

Rail Freight Rates

Full trainload movements are charged on a negotiated trainload basis.

Trainload movements are provided by the privatised rail companies in the UK, principally DB Schenker, the former England, Welsh and Scottish Railways (EWS), and a few other trainload operating companies. Various freight train service providers, who act as a wholesaler by buying in bulk a trainload and then selling on part train load/wagon services, provide all other movements.

Either type of trainload service involves a terminal-to movement and will often have road providing the collection/delivery. European shipments increasingly use the Channel Tunnel, which provides the cross channel movement.

A single rail wagon or swap body or a standard ISO container incurs freight of all kind (FAK) ratings on a job rate basis. For example, point A to point B @ £1,700.00 per wagon, body or container.

Integrators rates

Integrators use rail, road, air or sea modes offering a door-to-door service.

Rates are FAK and are commercially decided between customers and the integrator. The usual way is a flat rate plus a rate per kilo.

The services are fast, often marketed under words like "express." Service levels of 24-48 hours are available to major worldwide destinations for up to 30 kilo consignments.

Determining Rates with Forwarders/Agents services

Knowledge of both the operational costs and knowledge of how an operation is performing are critical aspects to be understood in the management of freight transport. Before improvements can be made it is necessary to know what the current levels are for efficient and effective operations. Then commercial decisions/negotiation applies.

Assuming a forwarder is operating a groupage consolidation service of their own, the following examples will give some indications of how they calculate the freight charges.

Example one: Deep Sea LCL
- FAK charge terminal/terminal = $2500 per TEU of 20 tonnes/20 cbm.
- At 60 % utilisation = 12 tons w/m payload.
- Base Rate therefore is $208.33 w/m.
- Charge rate plus 10% profit = $229 w/m FAK.

Example two: European LTL
- Terminal/terminal road charge = £1500 for 20 tons/60 CBM.
- At 70% utilisation = 14 tonnes w/m payload.
- Base rate therefore £107.14 w/m.
- Charge rate plus 15 per cent profit = £123.20 per 1000 kilos/3 cbm.

Example three: European LTL
* Base charge rate as option two = £123.20 per 1000 kilos/3 cbm and it is decided that the charge out rates should be scaled, for example:
* Minimum = £55.00.
* Rates per 100 kilos or 0.3 cbm:
* 1-500 kilos   = £37.00.
* 501 to 1000 kilos = £25.00.
* 1001 to 3000 kilos = £19.00.
* 3001 to 5000 kilos = £15.00.
* Over 5000 kilos   = £12.30.

For Forwarding Agents, if they are contractually acting as an agent to principals, and charge @ cost/as paid, plus an agency fee (usually negotiable up to 5 % of the outlay on the freight cost only), then it is fair to ask for evidence of the costs paid on behalf of the principals; for example, by providing a copy the shipping lines, airlines or the forwarders freight invoice(s). Clearly here, the principal is exactly that and is using the services of an agent who is legally obliged to evidence the charges incurred in carrying out their duty as an agent.

Determining Rates with UK Road Transport Third Party providers

We looked, in Chapter Three, at how operators can determine pricing. The following article provides a most useful overview of the possibilities and the options that are available to the users.

Case Study: Third Party Charging Structures

Once a company has determined that outsourcing its non-core competency areas to a third-party logistics provider (3PL) will positively impact both quantitative and qualitative areas and a 3PL provider has been chosen the parties must agree to a mutually acceptable compensation package.

Few people are telepathic. Fewer work effectively under someone else's pre-conceived, unspoken notions. Companies must, as a rule, spell out all expectations for other parties with whom they develop relationships. Compensation is a sensitive issue, and it must be approached with the understanding that by the very nature of capitalism, people want to be paid for their effort and want to know the when, the how, and the why.

Fee scheduling should be done according to the company's current operational policies. Determining compensation schedules should be part of the detailed scope-of-work prepared by the company (and its hired consultants, if applicable), so proposals from 3PL candidates may be evaluated with those terms clearly defined.

Three methods of structuring fees are commonly practised but variations and combinations of these structures are also widely utilised. The three core methods are unit rate, cost-plus and management fee. Companies must take special care in choosing the fee structure for their 3PL arrangement, weighing the advantages and disadvantages of each alternative and carefully assessing the specific criteria, which impact the project. No black and white or absolute areas follow. Advice from consultants with experience in logistics management could be helpful in making the correct judgement call on this important issue.

1.) Unit rate compensation

In mathematical terms, unit rate compensation (URC) can be defined as cost per unit handled. In other words, the sum total of operating costs, facility costs, overheads, fixed costs and profit, divided by the number of units.

URC is a reasonably simple structure to utilise. For example, Company A and its 3PL provider, calculate the following variables:
- Operating costs = £10,000/month.
- Facility costs = £1,500/month.
- Overhead = £2,500/month.
- Fixed costs = £1,500/month.
- Profit = £250/month.
- Volume =150000 units per month (based on forecasting methods)

The unit fee therefore would be set at £0.105 Per Unit per Customer Handled. During the first month of their arrangement, the 3 PL provider handles 155000 units and therefore receives £17,050 as compensation.

Advantages of the Unit Rate Fee Structure include:
- User friendly.
- Cost change with volume..
- Volume guarantees can be added.
- Incentives may be provided to 3PL provider. For example, company A states clearly that if 250,000 or more, units are handled with less than two percent mishandling, a 10 percent bonus will be added.
- Motivation of 3PL provider to produce is enhanced.

Disadvantages of the Unit Rate Fee Structure include:
- Possible ambiguity unless the definition of unit is clear and unmistakable For instance, does customer handled mean a customer buying product, or customer buying a product and returning it, or customer calling just to seek information?
- Inflated cost due to addition of contingencies.
- Lack of incentive on part of 3PL provider to share in productivity gains.

2.) Cost plus structure

This is the method most open to modification. The compensation format may look like the following:
- Fee equals all direct costs (operating, material, and labour) plus flat fee (overheads plus profit). Incentives may be added to the fee for increased productivity and reduction in operational costs.

Company B and its 3PL provider agree that the cost plus structure best suits their circumstances. The flat fee agreed upon is £5,000/month to cover any overhead and £250/month is agreed upon for profit. Since Company B has had access to the financial records of its 3PL provider, information regarding operational, and facility costs is clear. There are no surprises when the invoice arrives. After 12 months of a satisfying relationship, Company B builds into its cost plus structures an incentive for its 3PL provider: reduce costs by 10 percent and receive 2.5 percent on top of the total invoice.

Advantages of the Cost plus Structure include:
- Profit is fixed, so sacrifice of service for increased profit is not possible.
- Motivation on the part of 3PL provider to enhance productivity and reduce costs (if incentives are built in).
- No padding for contingencies.

Disadvantages of the Cost plus Structure include:
- Company doing the outsourcing must monitor costs regularly and set reasonable benchmarks.

Without additional, pre-determined incentives, the 3PL provider has no reason to lower costs and increase productivity.

3.) Management fee

Though the simplest to define, the fixed management fee compensation structure has the most barriers to acceptance. It is rigid and often based on inaccurate or unreliable information. The fee is equal to everything associated with the 3PL outsourcing activity, or to direct costs plus a management fee wherein the management fee equals overheads plus profit.

It is interesting to note that aggregate management fees are rarely chosen, as they do not reflect cost volatility, or do they invite enhanced.

Company C chooses the management fee compensation structure because of the nature of its business. As provider of a number-crunching software package called Elsten, Company C realises that volume and shipping trends are difficult to forecast.

For example, after a trade-show, Elsten might be shipped to 100 customers for next day delivery. Three months after the trade-show, two people may lackadaisically telephone the customer service department requesting that Elsten be sent to them 'whenever you get round to it'. Then two weeks later, ten friends of those two people 'absolutely needed this software yesterday'. With this situation and with the fact that Company C owns the distribution facility but is outsourcing its staff, Company C and its 3PL provider decide on the following management fee schedule:

Fee per year equals £250,000 to cover all overhead and profit with direct costs billed monthly to Company C.

Advantages of the Management fee include:
- Reductions in debate over expenses and costs.
- Helpful when volume and shipping are speculative.
- Fixed overhead and profit levels.

Disadvantages of the Management Fee include:
- Barriers to acceptance often difficult.
- Setting the initial fee may be based on inaccurate, inappropriate, or unreliable data.
- No incentives on part of the 3PL provider to improve on present operations.

4.) Combinations of fee structures
Often, companies choose to combine and make variations on these three traditional fee structures. Company D, for example, may have a 3PL provider (No.1) operate a large distribution facility owned by No.1 in its own city. Company D chooses to pay No.1 a unit rate to ship its product. Company D has employed the services of another 3PL provider (No.2) in another city to operate Company D's warehouse. Since No2's employees staff Company D's facility, Company D pays a management fee to No.2 for operation of its own facility.

Finding a suitable fee structure may prove just as involved and frustrating as choosing a 3PL provider. Unbiased, external resources such as consultants, recognising trends and understanding the ramifications, may prove valuable assistance in determining the when, the how, and the why of 3PL compensation.

(Source: Logistics Manager May/June 1997)

Costing/recovery of freight charges by suppliers/shippers/senders

Suppliers and shippers often (and strangely) handle the method by which freight costs are incorporated into the overall cost/charges that are made to customers. Whilst we referred earlier in this chapter to the concept of Total Acquisition Cost (TAC), which emphasised that freight and transport costs are only part of the equation, the examining and impact of freight cost must be correctly assessed. We looked earlier at the variations that are found in transport rate charge structures; meanwhile some points to be considered when costing/recovering the freight charges are as follows:

- **Average freight costing:** A highly dangerous method, and the range that is involved in calculating the average is always useful to look at. Too often however when average costing is used, the range is large and the average costing is less than helpful. Average forms of costing can mean that, say, smaller delivered quantities are being subsidised by full load movements. If the larger full load movements volume decrease, then the smaller movements are exposed to higher costs. Such forms of cross-subsidising need to be a conscious and closely monitored decision.

- **Percentage of product value:** Here for example, a year's total freight costs are divided into the year's total ex works sales price, to give an average freight cost figure. A dangerous practice, unless perhaps we are dealing with high valued products like diamonds, where the percentage cost is miniscule. Whilst this method is commonly used to assist in establishing, for example, delivered prices from a known ex works prices, the reality of this figure needs to be monitored against the actual costs incurred. It is very rarely found that the product value will equate directly to freight costs incurred, as, simply, freight costs are based more on the weight and the volume and there is rarely a correlation between these factors and a product value.

Exercise - Global Tobacco

Global Tobacco (GT) has a global presence in buying tobacco, manufacturing and selling the finished products. A major aspect of the business is to balance supply and production with the demand.

The UK operation has a freight transport and warehousing spends in excess of £100 million per annum. The operation briefly comprises of supply of raw tobacco from seven countries (Brazil, USA, Kenya, Zimbabwe, India, China, and Turkey) and is received in 40-foot containers at the GT Oxford store.

Here it is made up into blend sets and sent on as required to the GT production sites that are located in Peterlee, Co.Durham and in Crewe, Cheshire. Here the blend sets are processed and packed in an automated operation.

All the finished products are then exported to:
- 10 % to Europe
- 15% to Africa
- 10 % to the Middle East
- 65% to the Far East

Tasks
1) How would you propose the purchase of import and export freight is conducted?
2) What are your recommendations for custom controls?
3) What more information would you require to assist you to give a more complete answer?

Trade imbalances can affect freight charges

Movement of goods are driven and determined by market forces. Transport is the economists classic derived demand. So with no economic activity there is no transport service. From the viewpoint of the provider of the transport service (the shipping line, the airline, the road hauler, the rail operator) - they wish to maximise the utilisation of the equipment - (the vessel, the aeroplane, the tractors/trailers etc). If they are successful at this - on a round trip basis there and back - then they can offer competitive rates and make more profit.

This balance between economic activity and freight tonnages moved can be a delicate one. More freight moves into Scotland from England, therefore outbound rates from Scotland are very low in comparison to the inbound rates. More freight is imported from the EC into the UK than is exported, and, for example, the trade with Spain can show a split of 80% import into the UK against 20% exports during the main seasonal Spanish fruit import season. On a European basis, the share of trade between UK registered vehicles and other countries registered vehicles shows an imbalance. The major trades for road freight movements to and from the UK are, in order, to France (number one), Germany, Benelux, Italy and the Netherlands. The traffic carried by UK registered vehicles has shown the following patterns in recent years:

Country	Out	Back
France	45%	40%
Germany	75%	60%
Benelux	80%	70%
Italy	85%	75%
Netherlands	45%	35%

The share of other than non-UK registered vehicles in some trades is significant, for example in France and the Netherlands.

On an international basis, more freight moves from the Far East into Europe, and for every TEU sent full from Europe to Far East, around 2.5TEUs come back full. For example, on Transatlantic trades, however, the pattern is reversed as more TEUs are sent from Europe, and around 30% more are sent to the USA full than come back full. Clearly this has implications for the shipping lines and means empty containers have to be positioned; accordingly "swapping" an empty TEU for a full TEU freight rate means a marginal rate is available. As examples, rates from Europe to the Far East have been around 50% cheaper than the rate from the Far East; and those from the US to Europe have been around 40% cheaper than the rate to the US from Europe.

Meanwhile, to illustrate the dramatic changes that can occur on freight rates; the Far East European trade is one of the most competitive and busiest in the world and in 2008, due to reducing traffic levels, this meant that operators became engaged in a price fight for a larger piece of a smaller cake. The rates therefore fell between May 2008 to September 2008, from USD900 to USD350 per TEU; truly unbelievable figures. (**Source: International Freighting Weekly, 6th October 2008**).

All these trade imbalances in a market economy will affect freight rates; and for example with airfreight, the specific commodity rates for a specific route give an indication of how this industry has adjusted freight rates to encourage freight traffic.

Packing & Security
The prime function of packing is to ensure product protection. The two basic types of packaging are as follows:

Outers
•   fibreboard boxes/cartons.

- nailed/screwed wood boxes/crates.
- steel or fibre drums/kegs.
- wooden barrels/casks/kegs.
- fibre/fabric bales/trusses.

Unit Loads
- wood or plastic pallets/skids.
- plastic slips.

The packaging outer should be clearly marked to enable identification, taking care however not to advertise the contents to potential thieves. Effective marking ensures safe arrival at the correct destination, a speedy identification, compliance with regulations (for example, hazardous cargo), damage prevention and compliance with any customer requirements, for example:

Standard Shipping Package Outer Markings

Line 1	Initials or abbreviated name	
Line 2.	Reference number	
Line 3	Destination	
Line 4	Package Numbers	
Example:	SAE	ABCD
	12147	0161
	LAGOS	MANCHESTER
	1/25-25/25	1/16-16/16

It is useful to follow a procedure for packing using the following stages, and consider especially packing for the toughest leg. The author has many unfortunate experiences of viewing LCL cargo in Nigeria that was already received badly damaged in the container, simply because it had been packed for a short domestic journey in the country of shipment - too often it seemed packed for a journey only in the back of someone's car!

The following flow chart will help to ensure correct packing is undertaken.

Packing Flow Chart

1.	Study the product, the journey, the transport mode. Pack for the "toughest" leg
2.	Select the most suitable external packing outer
3.	Stow goods well inside the packing outer
4.	Small packages should be consolidated into one load
5.	Consider any effects of co-loading or stacking with other products during the transit
6.	Secure, strap, band all packages
7.	Select an effective marking/labelling scheme

Once goods are packed and are ready to be loaded, the following procedures can be followed during loading:

Guidelines: Loading Container Units/Trailers
- Inspect interior for damage, water-tightness, cleanliness and adequate fittings, fastenings/lashing points.
- Inspect exterior for dents/tears and the doors/openings for secure locking and sealing.
- Observe safe working loads (SWL) of all equipment, including any weight limitations of the unit/trailer.
- Observe any special cargo regulations for example, hazardous cargo, temperature controlled freight.
- Have all cargo and stowage materials ready before loading.
- Put heavy times at the bottom and lighter ones on the top.
- Distribute the weight evenly.
- Arrange a compact stow.
- Stow tightly to prevent movements whilst ensuring ease of unloading at the destination (such as forklift openings facing doors, stowing in the reverse order for the desired discharge, etc.)
- Avoid mixing incompatible cargo.
- Keep the stow with the unit/trailer dimensions.
- Secure and tighten any load restraining equipment.
- Close and lock/seal.

Security and minimising loss
Particular modes of transport have specific security requirements. Airfreight requires regular (or so called "known") customers to give written certificates confirming they have packed and prepared air cargo to an acceptable specification. For some shippers, this known customer will be their freight forwarder, who in turn will have arranged appropriate cover from their shipper client. "Unknown" cargo will be subject to security process, before it can be loaded by a listed agent and again, this could be the freight forwarder, a freight handling agent or by the airline themselves. The inspection process will involve a hand search or x-ray. Listed agents can also inspect and examine "known" premises to enable verification and the training of individual personnel.

For transits through the Channel Tunnel, there is a legal requirement for freight to be checked for terrorist explosives. On the port to port shuttle, random screening occurs. For through intermodal movements, then the checking takes place at the point of loading. Companies undertaking this loading have to register with SACTFF (Security Approved Channel Tunnel Freight Forwarders). Inspections and training similar to those for Air are involved.

On the physical loss of product on international trades, insurance experts advise that loss is due to the following factors:
- Fortuitous loss 20%, for example Acts of God, crashing, fires, collisions
- Preventable loss 80% for example:
  - Theft is 40%
  - Handling damage is 30%
  - Water damage is 10%

With almost one-half of preventable losses attributable to theft and pilferage, and therefore non-delivery to clients and customers, the wise shipper will take the following simple precautions:

- Use only new, well-constructed packing for products. Early deterioration or collapse of flimsy or previously used cartons, boxes or bags invites pilferage through exposure of the contents.
- Use of uniquely patterned gummed tapes will make possible the quick detection of tampering.
- Corrugated fasteners will add to the security of wooden boxes.
- Shrink wrapping, strapping and banding will further contribute to package security.
- Don't advertise product to thieves and pilferers.
- Descriptive labelling, illustrations or prominent display of trademarks and well-known company names on any type of cargo simplifies the pilferer's task, so the use of coded markings and changing the codes frequently is advisable.
- The ultimate retail customer/consumer will very rarely see the shipping package and therefore any 'en route' advertising certainly does not impress him.
- Use cautionary markings both in English and the language of the country of destination.
- Use of international handling symbols provides added effectiveness because handlers who lack the ability to read can readily understand graphic illustrations.
- Clear, concise and complete delivery and handling instructions should appear on at least three surfaces of the exterior package.
- Limiting marks to only one or two surfaces invites rolling, tumbling, and flipping of the packages in the search for marks and delivery information.
- Bright colour coding of sides or corners of items in the same shipment facilitates identification and minimises the parcels "straying".
- Utilise various-sized boxes, crates and pallets to consolidate small multiple or non-uniform parcels into single load units.
- Unitising and palletising as well as use of ISO containers will help keep cargo together and also make it inconvenient to thieves and pilferers.
- Process documents and customs papers expeditiously to avoid unnecessary delay in pick-up or delivery.
- Insist on prompt pick-up and delivery. The longer cargo rests on piers/dock areas, in terminals or in truck bodies, the more it is exposed to loss by theft and pilferage.
- Make immediate reports of losses or non-delivery to law enforcement agencies, carriers and the insurer.
- The quicker you act, the greater the probability of recovery.

Cargo handling in the various air and seaports of the world ranges from highly professional to totally unskilled. Rough seas, turbulent air, heavy traffic and substandard roads subject cargo to every imaginable kind of motion and impact. Remember to pack for the toughest leg of the journey! The following are points to be remembered:

- Wise selection of packing depends on the nature of the cargo.
- Items which completely fill the box or carton and contribute to the strength of the package are normally the easiest and most economical to package.
- Articles which do not completely fill the selected container must be cushioned,

braced, fastened or blocked to prevent damage to the article itself or destruction of the container.

- The capacity of the box, bag or carton should not be exceeded.
- Any inner bracing or blocking must distribute the contents' weight over interior surfaces, rather than concentrate it on one or two critical points.

Unitised, palletised or assembling cargo into the largest practical unit consistent with handling, weight, and dimension requirements, will assist greatly the handling. A unitised load of 50 cartons adequately wrapped, strapped and provided with a pallet or skid base will have a much greater survival factor than 50 cartons which must be handled individually. Unitised cargo invites the use of mechanical handling equipment, which substantially reduces exposure to the inherently rougher, man-handling techniques.

Water Damage, rain, high humidity, condensation and seawater (separately or in combination) can reduce otherwise stable cargo into a ruin of soggy, stained, mildewed, and rusty merchandise. A rain-swept Customs compound, an open truck on an airport apron in a torrential downpour, the insidious dripping of condensation from the chilled interior of a ship's hold, or sweat forming on the cargo itself, are all common hazards. Each different commodity has its own unique characteristics which react differently when exposed to water. It should be noted that containerisation does not guarantee protection against wetting. As containers age, "leakers" become more commonplace. Containerised or trailer cargo must be packed to the same degree-of water protection as with most general cargo.

The following are some guidelines to follow:
- Cargo should be protected from water damage from external sources such as rain, seawater, high humidity and ship's sweat by adequate preparation and packing.
- Apply preservatives, corrosion inhibitors or waterproof wrapping directly to the item.
- Provide waterproof or vapour-proof barrier liners in individual packages.
- Use of desiccants (moisture absorbent materials) in conjunction with vapour-proof barrier liners and wraps is particularly effective in protecting moisture sensitive items.
- Shield cargo on the top and the sides by use of waterproof shrouds.
- Crates and other large containers should have drain holes in the bottom to preclude collection of water within the packing. This is of particular importance where the cargo itself is subject to formation of condensation (cargo sweat).
- Indelible inks, paint, and water repellent labels should be used to preclude obliteration of marks, shipping instructions and handling symbols.

Transport Excellence

Transport is the one area of company that will touch all the links of the supply chain. It is important therefore for transport to operate effectively and the following areas of best practice can be used to determine if this is so:

Basic aspects
- Lowest cost for optimum service levels.
- Reliable service levels.

- Professional management ensuring equipment is productive in terms of both utilisation and performance, for example: management fully monitors fuel efficiency and vehicle turnaround times.
- Friendly approachable drivers and staff.
- Client/customer "aware" driven.
- Clean appearance of vehicles and staff.
- Tracking and pod trace availability.
- Responsive to special requests.
- Conducts legal, safe and secure operations.
- Takes a total supply chain view and has as the appropriate knowledge of supply chain management involving, buying, production, warehousing and marketing considerations.

Investigation areas
- Alternatives modes/carriers are continually being investigated.
- Key performance indicators are monitored and used to improve operations.
- All the supply chain supplier and customer deliveries are examined for synergies.
- Other companies and organisations are monitored for best practice applications.
- Pooling of resources and "partnering" with other companies.

The following case study illustrates an award winning example of "working together":

Case study: DHL and Morrison's: Forecourt Challenge

DHL and Morrison's won the coveted Motor Transport Partnership Award in 2007 for their innovative melding of teams to revolutionise Morrison's' petrol retail business.

The Morrison's-DHL relationship started in 2000 when DHL began an operational trial with two vehicles carrying fuel for the supermarket's forecourts from Immingham. The relationship blossomed and in 2004, DHL won the national contract for distributing Morrison's' forecourt fuel, collecting at the terminals and delivering to filling stations.

Coming together
However, the concept of partnership between the companies was developed when they viewed the huge integration project that faced them following Morrison's purchase of Safeway. Bringing together the two petrol retail businesses was highly complex, with three different fleets and workforces needing to be integrated into one under DHL.

The integration of the forecourt delivery system across the newly-expanded Morrison's was another important factor, and the companies decided that a successful and efficient system could only arise from their working together more closely than ever before.

DHL and Morrison's jointly developed a definition charter, which dearly specified the key objectives and outputs required by both companies, but went a stage further and identified key areas where a joint approach would pay dividends on producing a good result when it was needed.

The key joint objectives were defined as:
- Improved operating efficiency and cost reduction.
- Improved delivery service operating 24/7.
- Timely/accurate inventory reconciliation. To achieve these, the cornerstones of the partnership were created:
- A single integrated logistics team based in Morrison's' headquarters in Bradford.
- A collective procurement team.
- A single management team for health, safety, environment and quality (HSEQ), HR and communications.
- A jointly created IT platform.

Technology

Morrison's now needed an IT system that could efficiently schedule and monitor fuel deliveries and give real-time stock reconciliation. Both companies reviewed the IT systems they were using, kept the elements from each that may be useful, and then brought in external specialists to complete the package.

A six-way alliance developed between the retailer, the freight supplier and technology companies Lomosoft, HTec, Isotrak and Touchstar Technologies.

How it works

Information from the individual fuel storage tanks is collected and sent to the mainframe by telemetry where the Lomosoft product WinDMS then creates the orders, prioritising deliveries store by store. The logistics team reviews this data, amending and checking afternoon deliveries in the morning for greater accuracy.

WinDMS then notifies DHL's Exel Supply Chain Petroleum inventory Control System, which allocates orders to the appropriate section of multi-compartment tankers, so that each compartment has exactly the right amount of fuel for the forecourt tank it is intended for.

The fleet is managed using Isotrak's Interactive Resource Management, which interfaces with the other systems and makes sure the tankers are fully utilised, with real-time capacity tracking as the deliveries progress. HTec's role is to monitor the fuel levels in the tanks. Upon request, HTec takes readings that are delivered to the driver's Touchstar handheld unit; the HTec software then works out a delivery order, tank by tank, for the driver to follow and can verify full tanks when the job is Complete.

HTec sends a daily report to the logistics team at Bradford and WinDMS puts all the necessary orders through the Morrison's accounts system, cutting two days off the cash to cycle. This means Morrison's can process payments to fuel suppliers quicker and receive early payment benefits.

The benefits

Apart from the vehicle travel distances saved by the JIT system, and the resulting reduction in carbon footprint, the DHL-Morrison's integrated logistics team saw other benefits to their close collaboration.

The team works as a single company when it comes to health and safety, recruitment, processes, management and communications. As well as saving money, says DHL, there have been a number of soft benefits including reduced incident rates.

High quality training programmes have been jointly developed and rolled out across the staff, leading to improved staff and driver retention, better morale and greater commitment.

Key savings

The ability to read store stocks and balance the loads accordingly has improved in the following areas:

- Average loads size improved by 2.74%
- Kilometres rim reduced by 8-16%
- Product returns reduced by 74%
- MPG improved by 1.96%
- Productivity improved 15.18%

Efficiency

The companies both list significant benefits from the integration of their teams, but none so large as the waste reduction and fleet efficiency brought about by the IT system. "It saved vehicle kilometres and reduced carbon emissions because the fleet was no longer running product to forecourts that didn't need it, nor were they returning product that hadn't been needed. It was a truly just-in-time (JIT) system, industry-leading in that we know exactly what product was in the ground and when to deliver," says DHL's Les Bargh.

The system managed and tracked every aspect of DHL's 50 tankers on the Morrison's' account, servicing the 285 petrol forecourts. "Everything we had was visible to Morrison's and everything Morrison's had was visible to us," says Bargh, "It was a very open relationship." He believes that without this transparency between them, and the intermingling of other teams, the project would never have been so successful. "It enabled us to understand the vision that Morrison's had for their forecourt business, and they understood our strategy in turn," he says, "it was definitely the partnership aspect that enabled us to be so effective, delivering more savings and efficiencies than we could have done otherwise."

Transparency

For Bargh, the DHL-Morrison's experience was unique, "I have never experienced a relationship so founded in partnership and transparency with any client company before," he says.

That openness and collaboration, continues today. The companies jointly talk to staff, with drivers' meetings attended by representatives of DHL and Morrison's. "It isn't down to individuals in the management teams to foster this special relationship" says Bargh. "It's just part of the shared culture."

Phil Maud, director, petrol filling stations at Morrison's, says: "This truly demonstrates what can be achieved in creating a totally integrated supply chain by two companies working as one. Our combined vision and innovation has driven efficiency and shared benefit throughout all areas, while creating a 21st Century IT system."

Source: Motor transport 12 June 2008

6: People

Transport can use all the best and most efficient equipment, but without effective management, the operations will fail. Management is ultimately all about people, and getting the best from them is a major and critical task. This is not always going to be an easy or automatic process, as people operate firstly as individuals "in their own right," also in "collective" groups and teams who will then "combine" into a company/culture.

Additionally in supply chains, the following trends and resultant changes can be noted in recent times:

From Old Ways	Towards New Ways
Technology/product / supply	Customer/Market/Demand
"Push" product flows	"Pull " product flows
Product Sells	Customer Buys
Manage People	Manage Messages
Specialist Skills	Broad Skills
Bureaucratic control	Empowerment
Instruction/telling	Consulting/Selling
Job for life	Portfolio jobs
Earning a living	Learning a living
Adversarial	Partnership
Fire-fighting	Fire-lighting

All of the above can mean that existing skillsets need updating, and "the way we do things round here" may need to be changed. This essentially involves looking at management and the total management process.

Management

Management has various definitions, some of which are as follows:
*   "Getting people to do things".
*   "To Achieve a Task, Build a Team and Develop Individuals".

Managing involves dealing with the four fundamental management activities: planning, organising, directing, and controlling. These activities involve the following:

Planning
*   Identifies the current situation.
*   Determines the outcome required/desired.
*   Sets aims and objectives.

- Prepares budgets and develops standards.
- Determines what has to be done.
- Sets deadlines and timescales.
- Establishes policies.
- Develops programmes and procedures.
- Sets plans of action.

Organising plans into action involves:
- Determining what resources to use (money, machinery, and materials, methods, time).
- Determining how to make the best use of resources.
- Defining and designing jobs responsibilities and authority levels.
- Structuring work relationships.
- Designing systems of work.
- Allocating work.

Directing actions to achieve results by:
- Developing communication channels.
- Co-coordinating actions with teams/groups.
- Assessing leadership styles of individuals.
- Training and developing individuals.
- Identifying opportunities for learning.
- Recognising what needs to be learnt.
- Determining the effectiveness of operation and people.
- Knowing what's going on.

Controlling the outcomes/results of actions by:
- Using standards to monitor performance.
- Creating controls and measures.
- Evaluating results.
- Recognising problems.
- Continually monitoring.
- Conducting appraisals of performance.
- Taking corrective action.
- Making improvements.

These four functions cover all supervisory and management tasks. It may be that some activities are carried out more than others, for example, a specific job function, such as a work planner/scheduler, may determine that some activities are undertaken more than some of the others.

However, over time, all the four activities will usually be undertaken, often many times per day, and the way that individuals undertake these management activities will vary as each person has their own style.

Management styles

The way people actually undertake the four management activities can differ, as individual people have a "style". Styles include being aggressive, being passive and being assertive, and will be looked at shortly.

Management styles themselves are subject to change and for example, the "old" and the "new" ways of management can be seen in the following view:

Managing, or Command and Control Style
- keeps control.
- people are "held onto".
- judgmental.
- "tells".
- see though a "pinhole".
- directive.
- "push" approach.

Coaching, or Empowering Style
- lets people try.
- people are given a "self release".
- non-judgmental.
- "sells".
- sees the wider view.
- supportive.
- "pull" approach.

People differ

People will differ, for example some people are more orientated to planning, or organising, or directing or controlling, some are more autocratic and directive, some are more democratic and want a consensus view, some are more charismatic and supportive and some are "utility players" and flexible. As people are different, a key principle to be recognised by all managers is to build and develop on individual strengths, whilst recognising the need to manage their weaknesses. Unfortunately some managers continually concentrate on their peoples' weaknesses and leave them wondering what their strengths are; such managers getting the praise/criticise balance wrong.

Therefore, understanding how people behave is fundamental to understanding people and being able to manage them more effectively.

Behaviour
First a few definitions on behaviour and on related matters:
- Behaviour is "what we say or do".
- Attitudes are the "way we see and think about things".
- Beliefs/Values are "what we believe to be true".

- Habits represent repeated and learned behaviour.

Identifying the incentives that motivate and create action/behaviour, towards that which satisfies needs, will often change a person's behaviour. However, people will view in different ways the incentives and their needs. People will see these differently as "perception is 90% behind the eyes", "whether you see it wrong or see it right, you are right", and "as a person thinks so they are."

People can individually behave differently, when they face common circumstances. Three general types of behaviour patterns have been identified: passive, aggressive and assertive as follows:

Aggressive and autocratic behaviour: these people are hard positional negotiators who:
- drive and push people but are not a leader.
- has a "single", "my" viewpoint.
- one-way communicator.
- demanding "do it my way, now".
- takes "fixed my way positions" and engages in a contest of will.
- makes threats and applies pressure.

Passive and procrastinator behaviour: they are soft positional negotiators who:
- abdicate from taking decisions.
- use group viewpoints.
- indecisive and believes is always being democratic.
- "what do you all want to do, whenever".
- changes positions easily and avoids any contest.
- makes offers and yields to pressure.

Assertive and charismatic behaviour: they are partnership negotiators who:
- pull more than push.
- two-way communicator.
- people follow naturally, is a leader.
- makes concessions, "I think this, what do we think".
- problem solves and explores interests.
- partnership views and reasons.
- looks for objective criteria and yields to principles not pressure.

Key points here are that individuals differ in their own style, and also that individuals will also respond differently to other styles. Therefore, a manager who "does things one way with everyone, is like the clock that has stopped; it is correct only twice a day." Selective adapting and responding is needed, as well as recognition to change the way "things currently are."

Managing change

Change is the one constant of modern life. As the world changes, so does work. The only certain aspect of the future is that it will be different; a future of stable turbulence. It is in the dealing with the uncertain future that managing change becomes a key management function. In today's intensively changing world, a central management challenge is involved in managing change; and at the same time, ensuring people continue to contribute to company goals by being willing participants with trust and commitment.

Sources, reactions and dynamics to change

There can be many sources of change. Some of these general categories are as follows:

- Political, e.g. trade agreements.
- Economic, e.g. currency fluctuations, inflation levels.
- Social, e.g. lifestyles, increased leisure time.
- Technological, e.g. IT.
- Legal, e.g. legislation.
- Organisational, e.g. take-overs, closures, new start ups.

Change can be dramatic and can, if handled wrongly, be traumatic and cause a company to become extinct. A choice often has to be made whether the response needed is to be either revolutionary or evolutionary.

Change will always impact on people at some time. The impact will vary, but all those people involved will experience the same stages – usually at different times. The following table shows the stages involved and some typical responses; stage one commences when a person first hears about the change.

Stage	Comments	"Here" to "there"
1. Shock, immobilised	"They can not do it"	Past orientation
2. Denial	"We will never do it"	Past
3. Frustration and defensive	"It is just too difficult"	Past
4. Acceptance and discarding	"I might try"	Past/ Future
5. Testing	"Lets try"	Future
6. Search for meaning	"It seems to work"	Future
7. Integration	"I can do it"	Future

People's attitudes to change will therefore vary in any group of individual people. These attitudes can be very emotional and wide ranging; for example:

- Stimulating to Resisting.
- Exciting to Denying.
- Dynamic to Fear.
- Anticipation to Anger.
- Enthusiastic to Stress.
- Exciting to Concern.
- Challenging to Worry.
- Opportunity to Certainty.
- Visionary looking forward to Staying with the current situation.

It is critical appreciate that all people will go through such emotional responses to change, but they do it differently and at different times, as people have to change one at a time. The dynamics of change are found in any change situation. There are two forces involved, the driving and the restraining forces:

Examples of Driving forces are:
- Job enrichment.
- Upgrading.
- Broadening.
- More Responsibility.
- More Reward.
- More Status.
- Better Conditions.
- Easier work.

Examples of Restraining forces are:
- De-skilling.
- No discretion.
- Changed jobs.
- More difficult work.
- Degrading.
- No promotions.
- Redundancy.

One force represents the "foot on the gas"; whilst the other one represents the "foot on the brake". A key action therefore is to identify the driving and restraining forces in a change situation/context and, then to recognise that if we move forward by increasing the driving forces, resistance may well increase to maintain the balance. Consequently, the best way to move forward is by analysing the restraining forces and trying to minimise their impact.

Resistance to change can also be minimised when the change:
- Is agreed by all.
- Is owned by individuals.
- Is supported by management.
- Follows culture and values.
- Decreases current problems.
- Increases new experiences and interests.
- Emotions are understood by management.
- Reactions are allowed to be discussed with Management.
- Does not cause personal security to be threatened.

Managing change will be a routine activity in a changing future, which involves learning to learn and being continuous learners with active continuous personal development plans. Managing change also involves the full and complete management repertoire; unfortunately it is estimated that the majority of change fails. Such a statement is also about the poor quality of management.

Some case study examples on change follow to show it is not impossible for some companies to get change "right":

Change Case Study - Manufacturer (1)

The "Problem"
- Long established stable company in an industry that was changing.
- Had traditional structure with top down communication.

The "Future" was identified as needing:
- Team work across the functions.
- New plant and machinery.
- New annualised hours, therefore abolishing overtime wage structure.
- New graduate managers to be the core management.

The "Approach"
- Coaching one to ones.
- Business application workshops.
- Group meetings of coaches to build common purpose/plans/projects.

The "Results"
- All changes made on time.
- Moved from "problem performer" to a "star performer".

Change Case Study - Manufacturer (2)

Important points identified:
- Tailored approach was needed
- Top management commitment was vital
- Long term view needed
- Communicating was very important
- Involvement
- Listening (more than anticipated)
- Partnership with true union
- Third party facilitation and assistance
- Visit/learn from others
- Training needed

Change Case Study - Retailer

The "Problem"
- Not customer focused.
- Low quality product.
- Family focus ownership of a PLC.

189

The Plan used was:
- Establish a mission statement, E.g. on value for money, customer service, friendly environment in stores.
- Establish a set of values, E.g. trust, respect, communication.
- Planned the change programme, E.g., current and future cultures identified.
- Worked on the top managers behavioural style, E.g. less "tell".
- Work on the mid managers behavioural style, E.g. teams, interactions.
- Worked on branch managers/department managers behaviour style, E.g. customer service.

Other initiatives were:
- Focus groups, internal cross-functional, external on customer service.
- Annual conference.
- Monthly area meetings.
- Weekly trading meetings.

Managing change is a skilful process; and a key skill in dealing with change is communication.

Communication

Communicating involves sharing information between people, "up/down and side/side", with the objective being to prevent misunderstanding. Unfortunately much of what passes for communication is actually one way, and makes no attempt to check on whether it has been understood, for example as demonstrated in a FTSE 100 company who renamed all their notice boards to communication boards (= wrong thinking to this writer).

The following questions therefore focus on how communication should actually work in a company:
- Is there evidence of an interchange of ideas?
- Do employees know the reasons for the job they are being asked to do?
- Can changes be introduced without major upsets?
- Are ideas used that are put forward and if not, is it explained why?
- Are those nearest to the job consulted on matters affecting them?
- Are new employees carefully inducted?
- Do all people know what their jobs are?
- Do people show a sustained interest in their jobs?
- Is there a smooth flow of work?
- Are people seldom bypassed in the flow of information?
- Is the "grapevine" a very small one?

The objective of communication is to therefore to prevent misunderstanding and to do this effectively, involves the following:
- Not "telling" propaganda, but "selling" proper communication.
- Informing at all stages.
- Asking questions to uncover feelings.
- Listening carefully to answers.

190

- Using written communications only where appropriate. Concentrate on face to face methods.
- Consulting wherever possible.
- Admitting any mistakes and learn from them.
- Celebrating individuals and group success.
- Being as open as you can.

Communication at work involves giving and receiving feedback on work related issues. Managers will get more out of people if they are sensitive to their situation and treat them like adults by concentrating on their behaviour and not on personal traits/characteristics. It is necessary to balance both positive and negative messages and not just to concentrate on weaknesses but always balance these by emphasising strengths and directing towards the behaviour that the person can do something about.

It will be necessary to choose the appropriate tone and language and to check, at the end, for understanding, for example, by asking them to repeat the feedback given. Always end on a positive note. **The Communication Toolkit**, by Stuart Emmett (2008) has more detail.

Consistency in management

Finally some steps of consistency for managers; it can be seen that communication is only one part:

- Develop an awareness of your impact on others.
- Try always to involve people in decision making.
- Believe that teamwork is the best approach.
- Have a consistent management style.
- Spend time coaching and developing.
- Build a positive climate in the team.
- Empower and support team members rather than control them.
- Develop appropriate performance reviews systems and methods.
- Set challenging but achievable and measurable objectives.
- Communicate one on one.
- Reward success.
- Agree improvements and personal development plans.
- Give regular feedback.
- Tackle poor performance.

It is critical therefore to involve people, communicate, listen, give people chance to air objections, and to give people time to adapt.

Teams and Transport

Teams are a small number of people, who have a common shared and accepted goal. The goal is the "performance purpose" and the team players, the people, have a complimentary contribution with mutual accountability. Teams are a place where the team is put before individuals. The following sayings are true of teams:

- "Individual success is dependent on others".
- "Work out problems together, individual blame is banished".
- "Where the whole is more than the sum of the parts".
- "Teams require individuals to connect to something bigger than them".
- "Where you need to be awake, aware and in tune with others".
- "United we stand but divided we fall".
- "There is none of us as strong as all of us".

Teams are not a universal cure all for everything. For example, they are not suitable when creativity is needed with individual specialised talent, and where there is committee/group working with no unified common goal.

It can be difficult to get team working in transport in the same way that it can be in warehouse operational activity. In transport, the core personnel involved (transport drivers) are, by job requirements, not together at the same place of work all the time, and therefore not a "collective" workforce. In warehouse operations, this collectiveness is more readily available, and therefore having the work coordinated to give effective teamworking is much easier to manage. It is also interesting to note that many management styles and approaches rely on face-to-face management contact at any time during working hours. With transport drivers, again this is not always possible and effectively means that face-to-face contact with drivers will need handling much more effectively during the limited time that is available. Managing warehouse operatives and managing transport drivers can therefore be very different.

Teams and Sports

Sports teams offer good analogies for work teams, and the following aspects from the British Lions Rugby team of 1997 can be checked and compared with teams in business and in companies:
- Inspired leadership.
- Clear goal.
- Meticulous planning.
- Picking the right players.
- Clear communication.
- Excellent team spirit.
- Committed team member.
- A learning culture.
- Desire and passion.
- Focus on results.
- Shared values.
- Self and team belief.
- Confidence in ability.
- Pride.
- Celebrate success.

A key principle that is also demonstrated here is that teams require the right blending of unique individual strengths. When managing people, it is important to be able to build and develop on strengths, and to recognise and manage weaknesses. Diversity is, therefore, a strength, and means that people differ, with some being better at planning, some in organising process and methods, some being able to meet deadlines, some to be directive, or be creative and thoughtful, or be supportive or to be more "utility players" and flexible. After all, if all people were exactly the same, then we would all go fast in one-direction and cause casualties en route! Meanwhile **The Team Management Toolkit**, by Stuart Emmett (2008) has more details.

Company Culture

Individual people's behaviour and the collective of individuals working in teams both come together to make a company. Here people working for specific company will find that it has its own way of doing things. Those people, for example, who leave one company to join another company to do a similar job, very soon have to appreciate the urgent need to "fit in". A company has its own culture, which can be defined as the "way we do things around here."

Formal culture
The formal expression of company culture maybe seen in statements of Vision, Mission, Goals/ Objectives and Rules/Procedures, for example:
- Vision incorporates the timeless values and beliefs.
- Mission incorporates the purpose, policies, and power structures to achieve the task.
- Goals are the strategic, tactical and operational objectives, right down to people's individual roles and responsibilities.
- Rules and procedures set the standards of conduct and show the way people should behave by clarifying what is expected.
- Procedures are also needed to help people keep to the rules and establish the methods used to deal with the rules. Procedures maintain/apply the standards, demonstrate a fair/consistent approach and also bring clarity.

Informal culture - unnamed values and beliefs
However, culture is also often covert and informal, with values and beliefs that can remain unnamed. For example, contrast the difference between a charity and a private sector company, between the army and a football team, between the civil service and a retailer, between the Royal Mail and TNT. As well as things like dress, office styles, types of buildings, differences will be found in the human "software" represented by the attitudes, values, and beliefs that operate behind the scenes and run and determine how decisions are made.

In all forms of management, there are involved both hard and objective and clearly defined ways of managing and there are also more subjective beliefs and values and soft skills involved. Is the "culture" climate, friendly or unfriendly?

Friendly	Unfriendly
People take the initiative	People feel boxed in
Team work flourishes	Friction and a lack of appreciation between team members
People understand their contribution	People have little understanding of there role
Clear direction is found	Conflicting goals are found
Good communication exists	Mixed messages and little understanding
An even workload allowing for individual skills/abilities	Work is spread unevenly
Teams knows other team members skills/abilities	Little understanding exists on what makes the team tick
Work environment is conductive to good performance	Physical environment prevents good performance

This quick test will show the management tasks that may be needed to improve work, for example:

- Communicating regularly, for example: what do people think about their work and what do they want to do?
- Creating a shared vision, for example: so that everyone knows where they are going.
- Improving the physical environment, for example: lighting.
- Using ideas from the team to make improvements to the work.
- Using people playing to their strengths, for example: consider people's skills and aspirations and allocating work accordingly.

These examples will also serve to illustrate getting the best from people, a topic at the heart of motivation:

Motivating people

Motivation is a topic seen by many managers as central to them being able to get the best from people. Motivation is indeed essential to improving performance, but it is commonly misunderstood. It requires the following:

- Competence, which is having the knowledge and skills, for example from training.
- Commitment, which is having the confidence and motivation to do the job in the workplace.

Competence may, therefore, be provided, but without commitment, the performance may well suffer. Simply, "telling" and "showing" will not always work, as commitment is always "an inside job".

Motivation is therefore all about the following:

- "Getting People to do things, willingly and well".
- "The Motives to Act".
- "Positive Valued Rewards".
- "Goal Directed Behaviour".
- "Getting people to do what they want to do" (Using the Carrot approach), which is the opposite to manipulation, which is "getting people to do what we want" (The Stick approach).

The results of poor motivation, at work, can be a depressing reality for many companies, as shown below:

Reduced	Increased
Quality of work	Absenteeism
Work performance	Wasted time on breaks and private tasks
Willingness of people	Gossip and grievances
Attention and interest	Disciplining
Positive company culture	"Playing the system"
Creativity	Negative compliance
Job satisfaction	Bureaucratic controls
Direction	Rule breaking
Team spirit	"Them and us"
Feedback	Unacceptable behaviour

Providing motivation at work
To provide motivation at work, according to some of the theories, on motivation, the following is needed:

Incentives "to be promoted" and to increase the sources for motivation are:
- Achievements. For example, targets, SMART objectives, interesting work.
- Recognition. For example, create heroes, appreciation.
- Participation/responsibility. For example, involvement, consensus management.
- Growth/prospects. For example, personal development, life long learning.
- Feedback/communication. For example, praise and criticise fairly.

Key aspects with incentives to be recognised are that, once provided, motivators do not last as once we get our needs satisfied, the incentive reduces its impact. So for example, money, by itself, is not a motivator. It is important, therefore, to always have the "motivation encore ready" to go beyond the temporary effect of a single motivator.

Disincentives are "to be cleaned up" so that the sources of discontent are removed are for example:
- Policy/administration. For example, paperwork, rules and procedures.
- Supervision. For example, management styles, communication.
- Working conditions. For example, heat, light, tidiness, safety equipment.
- Personal Relationships. For example, harassment, social facilities, shift patterns.
- Salary/pay/ benefits. For example, compare with others, times of reviewing.
- Job security. For example, communication, job descriptions.

Key points with disincentives are that removing discontent does not bring motivation; it just removes the discontent and stops that particular source of "groans and moans." If the discontent is not removed, it can create resentment = grows into a problem = grievance = dissatisfaction = depression = frustration = poor work = discipline procedures.

Implementing Motivation
As mentioned above, motivation does not last as there is the need to look for the "encore" and, you could run of "encores". For example, where motivation is by fear ("do or else"), or

motivation is by reward ("do this and you get a prize"); once the fear has gone, so has the motivation. Similarly, with rewards, once it has gone, then so has the motivation.

The only motivation that will ever last is one that satisfies an individual's core value/belief; for example, a belief that they will "live life to the full". This gives an internal drive, which has an irresistible momentum. This links to the way that people believe and is also shown by the following statements:

- "You are what you think".
- "You get what you expect".
- "The impossible is what no one can do, until someone does".
- "Seeing self as a 'winner'".
- "Dreaming big dreams".
- "Choosing to be what you love".

It is helpful when dealing with other people to really know them and what needs are important to them. One should appreciate that the differences in people can be interesting, and that some people need more direction and guidance than others. Seeing things from other person's perspective will also help. All of this involves a manager or supervisor being able to:

- Link motivation to specific staff.
- Plan and organise what to do.
- Develop positive habits themselves.
- Plan motivating action points, by calendar events (e.g. Christmas), by company events (e.g. new recruits), by communication events (e.g. newsletters), by personal events (e.g. five year service awards).
- Keep a record on motivation actions for specific staff.
- Review and check what happens. Modify as appropriate.

Effective motivation does really make a difference, and it has been said, "There are more chrysalises than butterflies - a manager's job is to encourage the chrysalis to hatch and to encourage the butterfly to fly. It is like getting a plant to bloom."

Motivation is not therefore what you do to someone; it is what you allow them to do to themselves. This is also what empowerment is about, as we shall see shortly. However, there is always much that can be encouraged and supported by managers in the workplace and the following Motivation Model will help to ensure this is done.

The Motivation Model: Steps One to Three

Step One: Expect the best from your people
- Believe people want to do a good job.
- Tell people what is expected.
- Have clear rules and procedures (but do not be bureaucratic).
- Set SMART objectives/targets.
- Involve people in determining these.
- Communicate.
- Be flexible, recognising that people are different.

Step Two: Eliminate barriers to "being the best"
- Check out all the disincentives, remove/improve as appropriate.
- Check out all the incentives, apply as appropriate.
- Make work interesting, meaningful, valuable.
- Ensure people have the appropriate resources to do the job as required.

Step Three: Encourage people to "be the best"
- Recognise good work.
- Give feedback.
- Be accessible, ask and listen for feedback.
- Reward with good pay, promotions, personal loyalty.

The Motivation Toolkit, Stuart Emmett (2008) has more detail.

Drivers of transport vehicles

This key people resource for road freight transport needs some special mention and attention, due to the growing reluctance of people to undertake freight transport driving. This is symbolic perhaps of many changes that have occurred but are being poorly managed by…if there is such a thing…the road freight industry.

At best such problems are dealt with incrementally and in isolation from one another by the large companies and at worst, are not dealt with at all apart from by poaching of staff with inevitable consequences for rising costs. Drivers were generally unanimous in what they used to like and dislike about their work, for example:

Like:
- Being not office or site based.
- Seeing other parts of the country.
- Independence and being their own boss; although this "like" has now been depleted by the use of telemetry, in-cab phones, GPS and all other such technology that effectively means managers "can sit on the shoulder" and know exactly what is happening in real time.

Dislike:
- Not having career prospects.
- Low status of the job.
- Remuneration.
- Pressure of meeting deadlines with road congestion delays.

Until transport management is able to tackle such aspects effectively (and some individual companies are trying), it would seem that any needed growth in freight transport will be limited and constrained by the availability of a key resource, the vehicle driver. In Warehousing, labour requirements can be reduced through automation where, for example, picking labour is the largest operational controllable cost in warehouses. As the costs of technology falls, the take-up of automated picking increases. In freight road transport, however, no such automated option is available and "the nut that holds onto the steering wheel" will still be needed: no unkind pun is intended here and, indeed it has been commented, that indeed yes, you are "nutty" to do the job these days.

In Transport, the core personnel involved, transport drivers, are by job requirements, not at the same place of work all the time and therefore are not really a "collective" working together work-force. It is also interesting to note that many management styles and approaches rely on face-to-face management contact at any time during working hours. With transport drivers, again this is not always possible and effectively means that face-to-face contact with drivers will need handling much more efficiently during the limited time that is available.

Referring to the above section on motivation, and applying this to drivers shows the following: incentives are "to be promoted", which to increase the sources for motivation. Incentives are:

- Achievements. For example, stressing the importance of the work done, and how this fits into customer/consumer requirements; increase the job status/importance; after all, it is an important and vital job.
- Recognition. For example, appreciation of overcoming daily difficulties with roads congestion ; tackling known delivery point delays and not just giving instant dismissive remarks like, "it's your job to sit there, there is nothing I can do".
- Participation/responsibility. For example, involvement in decisions that affect the job; involving drivers in what has been done over delivery point delays.
- Growth/prospects. For example, personal development plans; moves into management; opportunities for advancement.
- Feedback/communication. For example, praise and criticise fairly; what do the customers say; how the business promotes and markets itself and what the drivers can do to help on this; creating a supportive culture.

Disincentives are "to be cleaned up" so that the sources of discontent are removed, for example:

- Policy/administration. For example, removing unnecessary paperwork, rules and procedures; clarity in rules and procedures.
- Supervision. For example, improving management styles and communication.
- Working conditions. For example, user friendly vehicles, fair overnight allowances, shared workloads.
- Personal Relationships. For example, tackling un-social hour shift patterns, recognising personal needs and making adjustments; tackling negative "grapevines" by creating opposite positive cultures.
- Salary/pay/ benefits. For example, salaried pay with holiday and sickness benefits; demonstrated fair pay, terms and conditions.
- Job security. For example, communication on developments.

These examples are not meant to be exhaustive, but are meant to illustrate what can be done by effective people management. As stated in the earlier section on motivation; there is always something that can be done.

None of these examples is "rocket science", but managers do not always know what they do not know, therefore they do not do it. Ignorance, though, is really not a valid excuse these days, and ignoring such aspects is not a good management option and will ultimately lead to a poorly motivated workforce and effectively damage the company.

People management matters and effective polices can make real differences: "On one site we have cut £400 000 worth of agency costs just by retaining good people for longer through better human resource policies." **(Bibby Distribution in International Freighting Weekly 28 April 2003)**.

Why can't all companies take such a proactive approach to people management?

Training Topics

It can be useful for a company involved in managing people that they ensure that all people involved have a common understanding of what is involved.
The following is an example of the contents from one such training programme:

Understanding Management and leadership
- Definitions.
- The linking and connected activities.
- Appreciating different styles and approaches.
- Getting the balance right.

Supervising People
- Differences with people in groups and as individuals.
- Building on strengths and managing weaknesses.
- Team development, forming and building.
- Team working, roles, responsibility and relationships.
- Characteristics of performing teams.

Managing Change
- Why change?
- Attitudes to change.
- Types and levels of change.
- Moving from "here" to "there".
- Steps of change.
- Model for handling change.

The role of planning in a company
- Corporate planning.
- Operational planning.
- Control mechanisms.

Defining performance management
- What it is and what it is not.
- Why it is needed.
- Being consistent.

Understanding productivity
- Setting standards.
- Utilisation and performance.
- Financial and non-financial measures.
- Benefits of taking a "systems" view.

Objectives and goals
- Work performance.
- Objectives/goals and standards/targets.
- Authority and responsibility.

Appraisals
- Conducting appraisals (and not pay reviews).
- Benefits of appraisals.
- What managers want from appraisals.
- What individuals want from appraisals.
- Handling and conducting appraisal interviews.

Motivating
- Behaviour styles of people.
- The links between attitudes and behaviour.
- Assertive and aggressive behaviour.
- Exploring what motivates people.
- Understanding why people come to work.
- Theories of motivation.
- Practical applications of motivation.

Communicating
- Communication methods.
- Problems with communication.
- Best practice.
- Verbal and non-verbal communication.
- Body language, words, voice tone impacts.
- The difference between understanding and agreeing.
- Handling diverse viewpoints.

Employing and dismissing people
- Recruiting and hiring.
- Job analysis.
- Job descriptions.
- Job advertising.
- Interview preparations.
- Selection.
- Defining unacceptable performance, competence or commitment.
- Defining unacceptable attendance and relationships/behaviour.
- Deciding whether to counsel, coach or discipline.

- The model approach to handle typical problems.
- Interview preparations.
- Spending time on prevention.
- Recognising the improvement/punishment balance.
- Following the appropriate legislation throughout.

Financial control
- Accounting.
- Profit and loss accounts.
- Balance sheets.
- Capital.

Commercial activities
- Credit control.
- Payments.
- Financial advice.
- Funding.

Budget control
- Budgeting.
- Cash flow.

Company Law
- Statues
- Liabilities
- Contracts
- Agency
- Sole traders
- Partnerships
- Limited companies
- Starting and ceasing a business

Exercise: People improvements in transport operations

A transport company had falling productivity and rising costs. This forced an examination of work methods and the following methods were introduced:
- "Work with People" was used as a theme to break down adversary relationships
- "Everyone has two jobs - their own and improvement of their work" was another theme introduced
- The transport operation was viewed as a series of supplier/customer relationships
- 2 hours a week was allocated to discussion groups - either internal or with external suppliers/customers
- Clocking in was abandoned and uniforms introduced

Tangible results were reported as:

- Transport costs fell by 15 per cent in two years
- Productivity rose by 22 per cent in two years

Question:
What are the people strategy aspects used here?

7: Developments & Trends

Transport can often be a barometer of an economy; accordingly, any changes in industrial structures and any changes in consumer tastes and demand will all affect transport operations. As transport is involved in providing the links of supply chain management, transport is not separated from any of the developments and trends that occur in supply chain management and in business generally.

The supply chain

Clearly, transport exists to serve the various multiple supply chains of a business. In evaluating transport networks therefore, it is necessary to examine the supply chain(s) and to ensure that they are effective and adaptive and profitable. The main areas to be examined for company profitability from the supply chain are as follows:

Product and service portfolio management
- Detect product life cycles shifts and modify underlying models.
- Customer segmentation can allow for targeted service offerings that will increase margins.
- New products can capture the market potential more directly.

Working capital efficiency
- Reduction of inventory and payment cycles.
- Ensuring rapid flows of goods and information.

Cost to serve
- Cost management is reported by both product and by channel to market.
- Checking of the "planned to actual" profitability of each customer order.
- Using of total acquisition cost models by the buyers.

Asset efficiency
- Recognising that the utilisation of assets goes straight to the bottom line.
- Outsourcing can reduce the working capital.

The impacts of these profitability aspects on transport can be seen in the following examples:

Profitability Aspects	Transport Effects examples
Product life cycle shifts	Returns of unsold items
Targeted customer offerings	Smaller deliveries to "unusual" places
New products	Smaller deliveries to new customers
Reduced inventory	More frequent deliveries of smaller quantity
Rapid goods flows	Speed and reliability of delivery
Cost management	More control on costs/productivity
TAC models by buyers	Emphasis on the previous "hidden" transport costs
Asset utilisation	More productivity analysis
Outsourcing	More third party usage and more leasing/sub contracting by existing 3PL companies

Clearly these examples will vary in specific contexts. Suffice to say, however, that many impacts will be found; and whilst some will merely reinforce current known trends and developments, some also serve to confirm once again the importance of effectively managing cost, productivity and change (as explained more fully in earlier chapters).

Designing Supply Chains

In designing the supply chain and the associated transport network, the following can be noted:

Customer Demand
- Design the supply chain on market needs - it is demand that "kick starts" the whole process.
- Understand the supply chain requirement for customer segments (and tailor as appropriate).

Product
- Will vary, for example: standard, segmented standard, customised standard, tailored customised, pure customised.
- Design products for interchange ability, ease of assembly, and standardised parts.
- Assemble to order, customised products.
- Postpone final product differentiation until the product is required.

Strategic
- Need a top recognition and commitment to the supply chain purpose/vision that recognises, it is fundamental to integrate independent processes for interdependency.
- Concentrate on areas that have maximum business impact.
- Leverage e-business to link assets and process, across partners.
- Minimise fixed costs, keeping assets and resources flexible.
- As supply chains are collections of business that add value, focus on the core value drivers. Then perform more added value work.
- Outsource non-strategic and non-competitive activity (DIY or Buy In).
- Adopt and enforce common performance and quality standards throughout the supply chain.
- Use flow logistics by designing all processes for the continuous flow of goods and information, therefore minimising lead times and stockholding.
- Design and manage adaptable supply chain networks.
- Manage through a cross functional organisation and structure.
- Appreciate flexible relationships across the supply chain.
- Continually develop the people, so that they will continuously improve.

The future supply chains will be dynamic, hopefully more collaborative, and with end to end visibility being fully recognised in both the supply side (capacity, availability, compliance, fulfilment, and settlement); and in the demand side (orders, inquiries, promotions, inventory).

The following case study illustrates the trends:

204

Case Study: Global Supply Chain Trends

Executive Summary

While the survey reveals numerous strategies used by companies to manage their supply chains on a global basis, we have identified ten major trends that are driving innovative supply chain design and configuration across all industries:

1) Globalization is accelerating, leading to large structural shifts for global supply chain organizations and new challenges to successfully manage supply chain performance. While past globalization initiatives focused on manufacturing and assembly, future globalization will also target product and technology development.

2) Pressures to reduce cost and penetrate local markets are the two key drivers of accelerated globalization.

3) Despite average cost reductions of 17% per globalization initiative, many companies have difficulty realizing savings in management costs. The gap between planned and actual benefits is caused by internal barriers that prevent full support of globalization efforts, and external network partners that fail to achieve expected performance.

4) China and India continue to emerge as major targets for globalization, while Eastern Europe is catching up as a top off-shoring destination. Investments in North America and Western Europe also remain strong as companies look to secure access to local markets and key resources.

5) Product quality and safety, as well as supply chain delivery and security, are the most critical concerns when expanding the supply chain globally. Four major risk mitigation strategies – including the deployment of company resources at supplier locations – are employed.

6) Major barriers to globalization include limited supply chain flexibility and the lack of internal competency to manage partners. Better visibility and management across the supply chain are important keys to overcome these barriers.

7) Environmental sustainability is a key consideration in the development of future globalization strategies. Today, sustainability is mainly driven by the need for regulatory compliance and satisfaction of customer demand. It is not yet considered a strategic differentiator.

8) Acceleration of supply chain maturity, enabled by advanced supply chain practices, appears to have reached a plateau. Among those surveyed, supply chain maturity differs significantly across geographic regions and industries.

9) By 2010, the need for greater supply chain flexibility will overtake product quality and customer service as the major driver for improving supply chain strategy. Many supply chain leaders have developed effective strategies to improve global flexibility.

10) The COO agenda across industries and geographic regions is converging on improving supply chain flexibility and performance. Companies around the globe face similar challenges in building effective international operations and supply chain networks.

Source: PTRM 2007; Global Supply Chain Trends 2008-2010.

In operating environments of greater customer expectations on speed, flexibility and quality of products, combined with cost, speed, and reliability of delivery, then, transport and supply chain excellence will need to involve:

- Accessible, accurate, and timely customer, product, and supply information throughout the supply chain.
- Enhanced customer relationships leading to repeat business through fast, accurate product delivery, and professional customer response services.
- Integration of internal and external information and material flows.
- Flexible infrastructures and partnering.
- Analytical assessment, on demand, of freight movement, price and placement actions.
- Co-ordinated, rapid decision-making environment that synchronises any global supply chain events.

This can be summarised in the following table where it can be specifically noticed the connections and links to transport activities:

Aspect	Traditional Supply Chain	New Supply Chain
Orders	Predictable	Variable/small lots
Order cycle time	Weekly	Short/daily-hourly
Customer	Strategic customers only	Broader based
Customer service	Reactive and rigid	Responsive and flexible
Replenishment	Scheduled	Real time
Distribution model	Supply driven/push	Demand driven/pull
Demand	Stable and consistent	Cyclical
Shipment size	Bulk	Smaller lots
Destinations	Concentrated	Dispersed
Warehouse Re-configuration	Weekly/monthly	Continual
International trade Compliance	Manual	Automated

A recent example of change to supply chains is with the promotion/change to consumer buying of grocery products for home delivery. The following case study is just one illustration of the changes this can bring:

Case Study: Sainsbury's E-Fulfilment for Food and Drink

Leading supermarket group Sainsbury's has, through recent investments, become a major authority in e-tailing distribution. With e-tailing well established yet (in business terms) still in its infancy, industry standards and best practices have yet to be fully established. It is still early days for benchmarking of the market leaders. Sainsbury's has invested in a supply chain strategy that gives the company both wide local coverage and the flexibility to process orders in the most economical way. Sainsbury's employs some in-store picking by its retail store staff. This method is used where stores have the capacity to pick orders without impacting adversely on store customers; where this is not possible, the strategy is to use dedicated fulfilment centres such as the Park Royal picking facility in west London.

These centres follow the in-store-picking pattern but – as they are dedicated to on-line shopping orders – there are no walk-in customers. The dedicated fulfilment centre in Park Royal employs state-of-the-art automated and semi-automated order picking techniques.

Dedicated centre lowers fulfilment costs
The new 170,000 sq. ft distribution centre (DC) has been designed around the key objective of minimising the costs of fulfilling e-commerce orders. The DC serves an area within the M25 and is ideally positioned to serve customers in central and west London. A substantial fleet of vans is deployed at the site for making deliveries directly to customers' homes. The London, Park Royal DC, which is operational 24 hours a day, can also fulfil orders for other parts of the UK, if required, by utilising trunker delivery services to regional points, from where local deliveries are completed in smaller vans. Thus, Sainsbury's has developed an integrated supply chain solution that provides the company with the flexibility to use both DC fulfilment and in-store fulfilment to balance customer demand and logistics capacity on a day-to-day basis.

Improved picking accuracy
The handling system at the Park Royal facility features computer-controlled order picking techniques which give the DC an edge in terms of picking accuracy, thereby improving customer satisfaction. The centre acts much like any other Sainsbury's retail store, in that it orders its stock from one of the group's conventional distribution warehouses, with certain fresh items being delivered daily directly from suppliers. Items arrive, in the main, as picked cases in roll containers – again, just like any of the other retail stores. The goods are then stored in carton live storage, pallet live storage and longitudinal or lateral shelving – but never outside of the physical reach of the average human frame. The 'Sainsbury's to You' home shopping range from fulfilment centres offers up to 15,000 lines, compared to over 20,000 in a Sainsbury's superstore.

Intelligent conveyor and pick-by-light
Customer orders are electronically segregated into three distinct sections, determined by storage and transit temperatures. Ambient, chilled and frozen goods are stored, picked

and shipped separately – albeit in the same van – and only finally come together on the customer's doorstep. The three types of goods are placed into different colour plastic tote boxes, 400 x 600 x 350 mm in size. Within the tote, the goods are actually placed into standard; Sainsbury's plastic shopping bags so that, on delivery to the customer, the plastic totes can be retained. Picking for the ambient and chilled goods is essentially similar. Once the control system has scheduled a customer' s order as ready to pick, a tote box with a unique bar code is placed onto a conveyor by an automatic tote box de-stacker.

The intelligent conveyor system transports the totes only to the picking locations required for each particular order, speeding up the material flow. Once the tote reaches a required picking zone, it is discharged from the live conveyor onto a static conveyor line immediately in front of the picking faces. A pick-by-light system identifies the tote and the quantity of each item needed to fulfil its order. As each order line is picked, a completion button is pressed until no more pick signal lamps are lit. Once all the picking at that particular station is complete, an order confirmation button is pressed and the tote is pushed back onto the live conveyor to be transported to the next pick station required for that order.

Delivery at the right temperature and the right time

Stock awaiting picking is mostly stored in carton flow racking and within the goods area there are approximately 80 picking stations on two levels. The chilled area has some 50 picking stations, again on two levels. The frozen goods are picked from static shelving within a special cold chamber. After order picking, totes of frozen goods are loaded into insulated roll cages, which are individually charged with dry ice to keep them at the required temperature until the point of delivery. Roll cages of ambient and chilled goods plus thermo-tainers of frozen goods are loaded into the delivery vans, with the chilled and frozen items being placed within a refrigerated section. Computer software plans the delivery routes, taking into account the customer's specified delivery window and the need to minimize distance travelled.

Automation and flexibility: the keys to success

Automation and computer control ensures that handling costs at Sainsbury's Park Royal facility are minimised. Intelligent conveying systems combined with pick-by-light technology have resulted in high rates of productivity and picking accuracy. Sainsbury's strategy of utilising a combination of fulfilment methods has resulted in an enviable degree of flexibility. Computer control of order processing allows this flexibility to be exploited by directing customer orders to whichever fulfilment centre in the network will complete the order within the given time frame at the lowest cost.

(It should be noted that this DC subsequently closed as Sainsbury changed to the making up/picking of home delivery orders in the retail stores; a method being used by its competitors).

Source: Warehouse News 22 July 2002

The management of the supply chain therefore affects how transport is planned and controlled and some of the developments and trends have been noted above. Meanwhile the third party sector will not be separated from such changes, and the following has been seen as the 3PL service provider market in 2015:

Provider types	Service requirements of customers	Key features required	Pricing methods	Market in 2015
Integrated/ Strategic	End-to-end scope. Shared SC strategy	Strategic relationship	Shared risk and reward	5-10%
Lead/ Wider service	As below, plus Optimisation. Single contract	As below, plus Economies of Scale	Shared risk and reward	20-25%
Core/High process conformance	KPIs. Continuous improvements	Execution focus.	Open book. Some sharing of gains.	30%
Basic/ Commodity.	Operational efficiency.	Tactical buying.	Transactional.	40%

Within the transport activity there are also developments that will in turn impact the supply chain; we shall look at some of these now.

Risk

As supply chains become more responsive and integrated with lean and agile responses, then, with any disruptions to this leanness, the supply chain could become fragile with no flow, with slow or at worst, stopped supply chains. Also, as supply chains become more lean and agile and deliver smaller quantities with lower stock holding and an increased volume product range, the demand they are satisfying is susceptible to breaks in the links. A chain is as strong as its weakest link, and transport could become the weak link.

Small changes in one part of the supply chain can cause massive changes elsewhere. Uncertainty exists and plans need to be made for this. This means identifying where the weak and choke parts are in a supply chain, and developing contingency plans, for example, alternative methods and back-up carriers. Focussing only on internal contingency planning is not enough as there are also risks from lack of supply and from other external factors, such as terrorism, for example. The key is being able to have a full knowledge of the way the supply chain works, and how it is managed internally and externally by all players and participants, and to have both the internal and external contingency plans available.

Roads

In the UK road congestion is a major growing concern, and the impacts of traffic congestion on journey times for freight traffic are expected to be dramatic, unless there is fall in economic and social activity. Journeys that take longer mean more vehicles are needed to carry the same freight volumes, a simple basic point that can be easily illustrated by any transport scheduler. Road congestion can mean late arrivals, delayed deliveries, missed book-in times, rejected deliveries, stock outs, lost sales and loss of customers; leading to higher costs, falls in productivity, unreliability and to that major supply chain major disrupter, uncertainty.

In recent times, road building has not kept up with the growth in road traffic, and in the last 50 years, the number of cars has increased by some 15 times, whereas goods vehicles have increased by 5 times (although large good vehicles became much larger in this time). The freight industry, meanwhile, notes that there are around 26 million licensed cars compared with around 450 000 freight vehicles, and believes that the way forward is determine a combined transport policy aimed at encouraging motorists onto public transport, especially at peak times.

The car issue is an important one here. Brought about by improved quality of life and the personal freedom that such transport brings, car growth has been virtually exponential since the late 20th century. As more cars are used, more road space is used; causing road congestion. Lower car parking space availability, due to the growth in car usage, in turn causes congestion in urban areas, leading to increased journey times with less reliability and predictability; a vicious circle that in turn leads to actually lowering the quality of life. Also the perceived "savoir" of public road transport is affected, and is slowed down by the increased use of personal car transport, which means fewer people use it; public transport then attracts lower investment, leading to an inferior availability; and another vicious circle is completed.

This car problem is therefore a complex one and is not a "one solution fits all" issue. In a market economy, the price mechanism is usually brought into play, for example, responses like the congestion charge in Central London. How far such market pricing level activities will continue, is beyond the scope of this book. Suffices to say, however, one wonders how soon it will be before road congestion causes freight transport cost increases, which are passed on to the consumer in price increases on, say, their packet of cornflakes. After all "if you have it, then a truck has brought it".

Road capacity is determined by the speed of vehicles and the gap between them. At slow speeds, then the flow increases. But as speeds increase, then so should the gap that is left between vehicles. When traffic is free flowing, then drivers will usually widen the gap between vehicles to allow for more breaking distance. The effect of this is to lengthen the amount of road space that is occupied by each vehicle, so as vehicle speeds increase then the road capacity will decrease as fewer vehicles can fit into the space.

To illustrate this, imagine a motorway with free flowing traffic and the maximum speed for cars of 70mph. As more vehicles join the motorway, then the speed will decrease until the road reaches its maximum designed capacity. As more vehicles continue to join, then the traffic flow becomes unstable, the speed reduces and the capacity falls until such time as it stops moving. Those who stop soon move off again, but as the following traffic is still heading into the congested area, a queue forms at the rear, whilst at the front, the traffic is accelerating away. This is why many drivers wonder what has caused them to stop; the answer is too simple. Assuming no accident or careless driving has occurred, it is simply due to the volume of traffic that is using the motorway. Traffic has to adjust to allow vehicles to enter, which then causes knock backs to following traffic…and so it continues, often many miles back from where the traffic joins. Traffic flows are, therefore, dependent upon the speed of vehicles on the road and the gap between successive vehicles. Road design for single lanes with normal breaking distances, at 20 mph allows around 2000 vehicles per hour, for speeds of 50 mph, around 1400 and at 70 mph around 1100 vehicles per hour.

When designing roads, the designer assumes safe speeds and safe gaps, but the fact is that drivers do not always follow these, and, accordingly, a higher flow is actually produced. This causes motorways to be barely working, because most of the drivers are driving unreasonably close to the vehicle in front; a dangerous situation indeed.

Rail

The UK rail network has a poor coverage and requires transhipment to road or to multimodal, often at both ends of a journey. Most of the UK track network is unable to take normal continental freight gauge wagons and the network conversion is patchy and slow. There is little sign of any major investment or extension of initiatives to encourage rail freight usage in an industry made more fragmented since rail privatisation. In the market "free" economy, rail offers no viable alternative to road freight transport in the immediate future for the majority of freight that is currently carried by road.

Whether the "free" market will remain, or whether some form of subsidy to move freight to rail will happen, or whether punitive measures will be taken against road traffic to force such movements, remains to be seen. Meanwhile, no doubt ad hoc and occasional schemes for rail freight may appear to be providing alternatives, however, history has provided a constant reminder of this "start, stop and failure" of the rail freight "saviour", accepting of course, that history is not always a correct predictor of the future.

Environment and legislation

The environmental impact of transport will continue to be noted by legislators, and changes in legislation can be expected to sponsor cleaner fuels and cleaner engines. This may also involve restrictions to operating methods as well as in the technical aspects of vehicle design. The effect of the Work Time Directive on the road transport freight industry had some impact on transport operations and forced companies to look more closely at how they can better use that increasingly scarce key resource; the driver. This for example meant some changes to operations such as 2 drivers working a vehicle separately over 7 days, the use of 3 shifts in 24 hours, and vehicle/trailer interchanges. However the anticipated greater increased use of flexible drawbar/ swap body techniques did not materialise.

Technology

The technology involved with transport in the future would seem to be one that pursues closer monitoring of vehicle performance, either in terms of satellite location technology, or in the technical aspects of the vehicle design. All such technology currently exists, even if it's not universally used. Tagging and identifying of individual packages is technically available, and if the time sensitive/reliability aspects of supply chain management continue, then increased usage of such technology will occur.

People Development

Competence is not a constant, therefore keeping up with 'what's new' is a critical function for individuals in companies and for companies to acknowledge and therefore encourage and support peoples learning. One way to advance learning is by following a process of continuing professional development (CPD).

One definition of CPD is: the systematic learning and improvement of knowledge, skills and competence throughout a professional's working life. Personal learning lies at the heart of CPD which is the method and process which uses personal power, knowledge and experience to:
- Make sense of things (by thinking).
- Make things happen (by doing).
- Bring about change (by moving from one position to another).

Learning is not a passive activity or an automatic process; it requires an active and thoughtful approach and it can be hard work.

Nobody is likely to force individuals to learn and develop. CPD is therefore all about individuals being committed to their own growth, success and survival. Many people may think that personal learning does not need to take place. In the current climate of change, continual challenge, and new developments, this view is both out-dated and dangerous. In a changing and developing world, development needs to be dynamic in order to keep up with factors such as rapid developments in technology, new and shifting markets and requirements for better standards faster and at a lower cost. Those people who abdicate responsibility for managing their own development will surely be less valuable to companies in the future.

All these changes place emphasis on the continuing need to be professionally competent. Those who remain in the past can quickly have outdated knowledge and skills. A company only develops and learns through its people. Individuals are the constant in companies' learning and development and it is individuals who do the learning in companies. It is therefore clearly the responsibility of individuals to promote their own learning. **The Learning Toolkit** and **The Developing People Toolkit**, both by Stuart Emmett, are of value here.

Political Influences

The EU has a view on transport policy, and the following represents a summary of the key issues they see. Most of these have already been commented on, but this will serve as a summary of the future possible influencing events for both operators and users.

Growing conflict is foreseen for transport, due to the increasing demand leading to worsening congestion, poor quality services, environment damages and safety.

The issues involved here are:
- Imbalance in transport modes with road being dominant.
- Rising congestion, unless something is done.
- Growth in demand.
- Integrating transport into a sustainable development.

Possible strategies to solve this are seen as:
- A reduction in mobility.
- Redistribution amongst modes.
- Road freight charging "taxes".
- Revitalisation of other modes.
- Targeted investment in networks.

These effectively look to shift the current balance of transport and will also need to considered in the context of other EU polices; such as those on economics, land use, social and education working patterns, budget and fiscal, competition and research. Some of the policy guidelines that have been made are as follows:
- Framework directive on principles of charging.
- Harmonise fuel taxes.
- Rail: to be integrated by allowing cabotage, setting high standards, creating a dedicated freight network.
- Air: to have common regulation on air space, rethinking of airport capacity, encouraging intermodality with rail.
- Water: to simply port rules and for inland waterways, to establish better links.
- Intermodal: to create favourable technical conditions and standardise swap bodies sizes. This involves considering the use of European Intermodal Loading Units (EILU) which are seen as combining the benefits of ISO shipping containers (solid and stackable) and with those of swap bodies (greater capacity) and offer stack ability and top lifting for road, rail, sea and inland waterway use. They will have the maximum internal space for goods; for example, the proposed EILU of 13.2 metres carrying 33 euro pallets or 26 UK pallets in contrast to normal 40 foot containers of 25 and 22 pallets respectively. It is proposed that essential requirements for security, interoperability, safety, handling, securing, strength, coding and identification of the EILU will be made with standardisation rules for maintenance, transhipment operations and in an increasingly "fearful" of terrorists and security minded age, the specification for anti intrusion devices. There is no intention that the use of EILUs will be made compulsory and the fit into global and world trade transport operating methods and systems seems to be not happening on any major scale.

How far the political will is able to further these proposals remains to be seen. Clearly, this is an involved and a dynamic situation, and readers who wish to keep up to date can monitor the EU website at www.ec.europa.eu/transport.

Transport Improvements

The following represents not only a continued way to ensure improvements in transport methods, but also represents potential ways forward in times of change and continued developments:

Labour related
- Work hours/shifts/annualised hours/overtime.
- Absenteeism levels.
- Managers who manage by walking around and by "leading from the front".
- Training & Development.
- Effective people policies (Critical).

Method related
- Preloading.
- Delivery frequency.
- Turnaround times (Critical).
- Journey times.
- Fixed routing.
- Unitisation of products.
- Drop sizes.
- Performance standards.
- Vehicle fill.
- Scheduling.
- Vehicle and Operational records.

Equipment related
- Specifications.
- Lease/Buy options.
- Fuel economy (Critical).
- Utilisation.
- On board computers/communications.
- Maintenance programmes.

Finally, the following represents key elements of Freight Transport Excellence, with some specific examples for road transport:

1. Reliable service levels.
2. "Value for money" costs.
3. Professional management, which at least, monitors vehicle fuel efficiency and turnaround times.
4. Friendly, approachable drivers and staff.
5. Clean, tidy appearance of vehicles, premises, drivers and staff.
6. Consignment tracking and POD information availability.
7. Customer/Client "Aware" Driven.
8. Responds to special requests.

9.   Takes a total supply chain view.
10.   Conducts safe and secure operations.

It all looks simple, but "the devil is in the details". I hope some of the detail has been shown in this book and that readers are able to better see how they can continue to improve and become excellent in freight transport methods, processes and activities.

Appendix 1: Transport Modes Summary

Summaries on transport modes follow:

Transport Modes by Cost, Speed and Capacity

Factors	Sea	Air	Road	Rail
Cost (per tonne/km)	Low	High	Low to medium (up to 400km)	Low to medium (over 800 km)
Speed (average mph)	Slow (20 mph)	Very Fast (500 mph)	Medium (30 mph)	Medium (45mph)
Capacity (per vehicle as stated)	Post Panamax container ship: 100000 tonnes/ 1500000 cubic metres	AN 225 aircraft: 254 tonnes/ 1130 cubic metres	44tonne/drawbar unit: 29 tonnes/130 cubic metres	Rail wagon UK: 70 tonnes/ 120 cubic metres

Transport Modes by flows, costs, distance, time, products

Mode	Material flows (dealt with)	Product cost (usual)	Distance	Transit time (door to door)	Products Moved (main type)
Road-parcels	Low flows	Low to high	Short	Fast to slow	Finished goods
Road-pallets	Low	Low to high	Short	Fast to slow	Finished goods
Road-full loads	Low	Low to high	Short	Fast	Finished goods
Rail in UK	High	Low to high	Short to medium	Slow to fast	Commodities and finished goods
Air-consolidation	Low	Medium to high	Long	Fast to medium	Finished goods
Air-charter	Low	Medium to high	Long	Fast	Finished Goods (FG)
Sea-conventional	Flexible	Low	Long	Medium to slow	Commodities and FG
Sea-lift on lift off	Flexible	Low	Short to long	Medium	Commodities and FG
Sea-roll on roll off	Flexible	Low to high	Short to long	Medium	Finished goods
Sea-hi speed	Flexible	High	Short to long	Fast	Finished goods
Multimodal-courier	Flexible	Medium to high	Short to long	Fast	Finished goods
Multimodal-Containers and trailers	Flexible	Low to high	Short to long	Fast to slow	Finished goods

Source: after IJTM October 2002

Transport Modes by Users Access (UK)

Mode	Public/Private ownership (Third Party/Own account)	Time (For 400 miles)	Network	Services (Available from third parties)	Users Access
Road	75%-35%	10 hours	Over 200000 miles and fixed /built with terminals at the users	Extensive	Casual and contract
Rail	99%-1%	5 hours	10000 miles and fixed/built and needs terminals	Full train loads only	Mainly contract
Air	99%-1%	1.5 hours	Extensive, natural/ "free" but limited by Terminals access	Domestic routes are limited by the short distances	Casual and contract
Sea	90%-10%	15 hours	Coastal is extensive, natural/ "free" but limited by access to terminals	Regular only to Islands/Northern Ireland	Casual and contract

Appendix 2: Example contract for third-party freight forwarding services

An example follows, covering forwarding requirements, reproduced with permission from Added Value Logistics Consulting Limited (Contact: alanslater@avlc.co.uk)

Warning:
This example contract is not intended to be used directly as a template, but as a guideline only. It will not substitute either for negotiation or for legal advice.

BUYERS OF THIRD-PARTY FREIGHT FORWARDING SERVICES SHOULD CONSULT THEIR LAWYERS BEFORE FINALISING ANY DOCUMENT OF THIS KIND IN PRACTICE.

While every effort has been made to ensure the accuracy of the statements and material in this example, it is supplied on the express condition that neither the author nor the publisher will be liable for loss or damage suffered as a result of any inaccuracy, error or omission it may contain, whether or not resulting from negligence, and that the reader or user of anything contained in it will take proper legal advice and exercise and rely exclusively on his or her own skill and judgement and that of his or her legal advisors.

Context of the example

This example contract is defined as being between an importer of clothing (the Company) and a freight forwarding operation (the Freight Forwarder).

The Company have their head office in the UK and sells their branded clothing to High Street Retailers throughout Europe either directly from their own warehouse facilities in the UK, Holland, Germany and France or via wholesalers/agents in other European countries. Their product is sourced from independent factories in China, Taiwan, Singapore, Vietnam (in Asia), Poland, East Germany and Portugal (in Europe) and India.

Typically, product is designed in the UK, samples made overseas, retail buyers show the samples, initial orders are placed on the overseas factories and top-up placed once initial sales have sold through. The lead time from design to sale may be between 3 months and 12 months plus, depending upon product and source. Preparation, collection and delivery of samples are critical and they tend to be air freighted. Other product, unless late in production, will be sea freighted with the Company providing up to 12 weeks buffer stock in the country warehouses.

All products is packed either flat pack in wrappers of 5 items which are in cartons of 100 items or separately flat packed in cartons of 10, 20 or 50 items. All cartons are packed loose into containers. Selected customers require added value work in the form of ticketing, labelling or price tagging and this work is carried out either at the factory, at the consolidation point or in the Warehouse facilities. Some customer orders may go direct from the consolidation point in Hong Kong to the customer, particularly if they have added value work included, which ensures they are for a single customer only.

The Company has no dangerous goods or hazardous product.

The freight forwarding agent has been selected by the Company following on a competitive bidding process based upon an "invitation to tender" prepared by the Company. The Company is prepared to offer a two year term to the Freight Forwarder which may be extended based upon the achievement of some agreed performance measures.

This Agreement was prepared by the company and represents their requirements and the services they expect. This Agreement with the Freight Forwarder is to provide the legal and operating framework in which the work is to be undertaken and the consideration to be paid for the services provided.

Agreement for freight forwarding services

Between

(the company)

And

(the freight forwarder)

This agreement is made on the ....day of....................200_
Between

(1)   .... a company incorporated in England and Wales

with registered number ………….. whose registered office is at …………………..

(the Company): and

(2)   .... a company incorporated in England and with

with registered number ………………. whose registered office is at ……………..

(the Freight Forwarder).

Whereas: the Parties hereto wish to enter into an Agreement under which the Contractor shall in consideration of payment by the company to the Freight Forwarder provide those freight forwarding and associated services described herein and in the Schedules hereto attached for the term specified and subject to the terms and conditions referred to therein.

It is agreed as follows:

1. Definitions and interpretation

1.1 In this Agreement the following expressions shall, unless the context otherwise requires, have the following meanings:

a) "Bonded Warehouse" shall mean point at which the Goods are held for such Logistics activities as:
De-stuffing, re-organisation, containerisation and despatch without the payment of customs or excise duties and where input quota restrictions do not apply.

b) "Commencement Date" shall mean the start of business at 06.00 hrs (GMT) on the
....

c) "Consignee" shall mean the person entitled to receive the Goods from the Freight Forwarder or their nominated Service Provider.

d) "Delivery" shall mean handing over the goods to the consignee or the placing of the Goods at the disposal of the Consignee or their nominated authority.

e) "Freight Forwarder" shall mean the person undertaking the Freight Forwarding Service.

f) "Freight Forwarding Services" shall mean the planning and control of those Logistics Activities required in the movement of Goods from the Point of Origin to the Consignee. The Freight Forwarding Services shall also include all those administrative, ancillary and advisory services in conjunction with the movement of Goods including, but not limited to, customs and fiscal matters, declarations and exchange controls, procurement of insurance and the collecting of payments for either goods or Logistics Activities.

g) "Goods" shall mean any product or property including containers, pallets or packaging materials not supplied by the Freight Forwarder.

h) "Logistics Activity" shall mean the tasks undertaken by the Service Providers involved in the movement of the Goods, including collection, unloading, acceptance, storage, stock control, order handling, de-stuffing, consolidation, palletisation, preparing for shipment, loading, assembly, labelling, invoicing, shipping documentation, exchange control information, provision of customs information, delivery and the provision of shipment tracking and tracing details.

i) "Insured Level" shall mean the sale value of the Goods to the customer or [£25,000] (twenty five thousand pounds sterling) per kilo.

j) "Logistics Centre" shall mean a location at which one or more Logistics Activities is undertaken.

k) "Mandatory Law" shall mean any statutory law the provision of which cannot be departed from by contractual stipulations.

l) "Mode of Transport" shall mean whether by sea, air, road, rail or multi modal means of carriage.

m) "Port of Origin" shall mean the country at which the Freight Forwarder is asked to arrange collection of the Goods which may, or may not, be the country of manufacture.

n) "Service Provider" shall mean the person who performs all or any part of the Logistics Activity.

o) "Shipping Reference" shall mean an order, or part order, with a specific reference number, point of origin, date for collection, destination and target date of arrival at that destination. A Shipping Reference will be issued by the Company to the Freight Forwarder.

p) "Working Days" shall mean all calendar days except public and national holidays in the territories concerned.

1.2 The responsibility for the Goods shall pass to the Freight Forwarder from the time the goods have been handed over to their nominated Service Provider and accepted until these Goods have been accepted by the Consignee.

1.3 The Freight Forwarder will also be responsible for the planning of the Logistics Activity from the time that the Company informs the Freight Forwarder that specific Logistics Activities are required for a specific Shipping Reference.

1.4 In this Agreement the following expressions shall, unless the context otherwise requires, have the following meanings:

A) a reference to a statute or statutory provision shall include a reference:
1) to that statute or provision as from time to time is consolidated, modified, re-enacted or replaced by any statute or statutory provision.
2) to any repealed statute or statutory provision which it re-enacts, with or without modification; and
3) any subordinate legislation made under the relevant statute.

B) words in the singular shall include the plural and vice-versa;

C) a reference to a person shall include a reference to a firm, a body corporate, an unincorporated association or to administrations;

D) a reference to a clause, sub-clause or Schedule (other than to a schedule to a statutory provision) shall be a reference to a clause, sub-clause or Schedule (as the case may be) of or to this Agreement;

E) if a period of time is specified and dates from a given day or the day of an act or event, it shall be calculated inclusive of that day except in the case of a defined Time window (a local time);

F) notifications, instructions and claims made by telex, facsimile or electronic mail shall be deemed to have been made both orally and in writing provided such evidence can be produced;

G) reference to any English legal term for any action, remedy, method of judicial proceedings, legal document, legal status, court official or any legal concept or thing shall in respect of any jurisdiction other than England be deemed to include what most nearly approximates in that jurisdiction to the English legal term.

1.5 The headings in this Agreement are for convenience only and shall not affect the interpretation of any provision of this Agreement.

1.6   The designations adopted in the recitals and introductory statements preceding this clause apply throughout this Agreement.

1.7   It is recognised by the Parties that variations may be needed to this agreement in the light of operational experience, and to that extent neither Party shall unreasonably withhold its consent to variations recommended by the other, provided that such variations are reasonable and commercially acceptable to both Parties. Such variations will be recorded and signed by both Parties.

1.8   This Agreement and the documents referred to in it need to be read as a whole including those Schedules attached.

2.   Scope

2.1   Subject to the terms and conditions contained herein, the company appoints the Freight Forwarder as a supplier for Freight Forwarding Services and Logistics Activities for the company's Goods world-wide.

2.2   The Company reserves the right to appoint other Freight Forwarders and specifically to do so during any period of notice to terminate, where either Party exercises its right, contained herein, to terminate the agreement.

2.3   The Parties hereby undertake to comply with all Mandatory Law.

2.4   The Parties hereby warrant and undertake that the performance by them of the Freight Forwarding Service will not result in the contravention of the provision of any other contract or agreement to which they are party. In addition, they will, throughout the term of this Agreement, comply with the provisions of all such agreements and will, in particular, obtain all licences, consents and permits as required for the performance of the Freight Forwarding Services.

3.   Term

This Agreement shall be effective from the commencement Date and shall remain in force for a minimum period of two years. Thereafter, this Agreement will continue indefinitely on a rolling basis until terminated by not less than (60 days) notice in writing by either Party to the other.

4.   Early termination

4.1   Either Party shall have the right at any time during the period of this Agreement by giving written notice to the other to terminate this Agreement forthwith in any of the following events:

A)   if the other party enters into either administration or liquidation whether compulsory or voluntary otherwise than for the purposes of amalgamation or reconstruction or entering into a composition with its creditors or has a receiver appointed over all or part of its assets;

B)   if control of the other party shall pass to any third-party (and for the purposes of this Agreement "control" shall mean the right to exercise more than 50% of the aggregate voting rights attaching to all the shares in the capital of the Freight Forwarder or the company (as the case may be); and

C)   if the other party commits a breach of any of its material obligations under this Agreement or is persistently in default of its other obligations under this Agreement and if such breach is capable of remedy fails to remedy the same within [14] days of written notice being given to it specifying the nature of the breach.

4.2   Without limitation to Clause 4.1.C material breach on the part of the Freight Forwarder shall include:

A)   loss of the Freight Forwarding Service for more than [10] working days either consecutively or cumulatively in any [2] year period.

B)   failure to maintain reasonable practices and procedures to control the Logistics Activities as agreed by the Parties;

C)   any loss or damage to Goods within the Freight Forwarding Service in excess of [£100,000] at Sales Price in any [1] year, which was caused for reasons within the reasonable control of the Freight Forwarder and their Agents.

4.3   On termination of this Agreement by the Company upon breach by the Freight Forwarder (the date of such termination being referred to as the "Termination Date"), the Company shall be liable for no other payments to the Freight Forwarder other than that for the Freight Forwarding Services provided to the Termination Date.

5.   Obligations of the freight forwarder

The Freight Forwarder will provide, or procure the provisions of the following Logistics Activities to support the Company:

5.1   To progress the completion of individual factory orders and if required, arrange shipment to a Bonded Warehouse for sortation and onward shipment to Consignees. To undertake all the Freight Forwarding Services required to achieve the supply chain process from any Point of Origin to any Consignee world-wide in a manner a agreed with the Company from time to time.

5.2   To implement a "tracking and tracing" system for all the company's Goods in transit from the Point of Origin and provide both the location and relevant data on the Goods at any time until confirmation of receipt is received from the Consignee.

5.3   To implement an "issues reporting" system by which the Freight Forwarder reports to the Company all shipping references where problems are known either to have occurred or be likely to occur. Of specific importance is where a shipment of Goods or the documentation relating to such a shipment will not reach the destination of the forecasted or due date.

5.4   In relation to each Shipping Reference to pay all costs incurred on collection, freight, terminal handling, added value and delivery charges due to Service Providers on behalf of the company. Such payments must be checked and validated, paid and a detailed invoice rendered to the Company for payment.

5.5   For each shipment to provide all Customers documentation required and to pay all Customs (and excise) duties payable on behalf of the Company and re-invoice the company for these charges.

5.6   To ensure that the following performance targets are both obtained and reported upon in terms of:

   A)   collection of Goods from Point of Origin within 3 to 5 working days of the issue of a Shipping Reference by the Company (or within 3 working days of a Shipping Reference issued with a date for collection more than 5 days ahead of the Shipping Reference date).

   B)   Advise the Company within 6 working days of receipt of the Shipping Reference upon Port of Departure and Date of Departure (including Mode of Transport and Vessel name if by Sea Freight) and the Port of entry and date of arrival in the process of delivery to the Consignee.

   C)   Reporting weekly and maintaining the "tracking and tracing" process for all Shipping References in progress from the Point of Origin to the Consignee and report any changes to the Company on a "daily basis".

   D)   Ensuring all Goods are delivered to the Consignee on the delivery date given to that consignee by the Freight Forwarding Company no less than 5 working days before such a delivery.

   E)   Ensuring that in the event of Goods requiring consolidation, sortation and re-packing in a Bonded Warehouse that these Logistics Activities and all other related Logistics Activities are completed within 3 working days of arrival of the Goods in the Bonded Warehouse.

   F)   Reporting by 15.00 hrs (GMT) to the UK Office all collection from Point of Origin and deliveries to Consignees on a daily basis. Report all known Freight Forwarding issues by a similar time.

   G)   Specifically inform the Company within 1 working day of any Goods rejected by the Consignee at delivery.

5.7   Provide in the UK Head Office of the Freight Forwarder a staff of three qualified Freight Forwarding staff who are dedicated to the provision of Freight Forwarding Services to the Company.

5.8   Provide a single suitably qualified person in each of two locations as point of contact; firstly in Hong Kong (to cover Asia) and secondly in Holland (to cover Europe and India). In addition, there should be a back-up for these persons.

5.9   Provide all the computer links (plus hardware and software) between the Freight Forwarder's premises and the Company. Maintain the computer system to provide information and data as agreed such that the communication links will be available at all times and not fail for more than 4 hours in any one working day other than for reasons beyond the control of either Party.

5.10   Provide "Proof of Delivery" or "Proof of Collection" notes within 10 working days if requested by the Company.

5.11   Raise detailed invoices to the Company for the Freight Forwarding Services provided and for any payments made to Service Providers or Customs on behalf of the Company.

6.   Obligations of the company

The Company will:

6.1   Provide the Freight Forwarder with a rolling annual forecast of Goods throughput, Product by Product and destination on a monthly and a quarterly basis to indicate potential movement requirements. Such a forecast of movement should be for guidance purposes only.

6.2   Provide computer data as a download of individual Shipping References for action.

6.3   Provide, by means of the purchase order or instruction to a re-packer the Goods in sound packaging, properly labelled at the place designated for collection and the Shipping Reference.

6.4   Provide the Freight Forwarder with all relevant documentation and data to enable them or their Service Providers to undertake the Logistics Activities required.

6.5   Provide the Freight Forwarder with product data for each of the Goods, including their physical characteristics, pallet stacking method and any special logistics requirements.

6.6   Warrant that the Company is the beneficial owner of the Goods to be moved or has the consent of the beneficial owner or has the right to authorise the Freight Forwarder to move the Goods for the purposes of this Agreement.

6.7   Provide the Freight Forwarder with instructions within 2 working days (of being informed) of action to be taken in the event of a Consignee rejecting Goods delivered. The Freight Forwarder will be expected to return rejected Goods to the Logistics Centre awaiting instructions from the Company.

6.8   Pay the Charges in accordance with Clause 10 (Payments) of this Agreement.

6.9   If the company by reason of any major change in business which deem it necessary to reduce or discontinue any or all of the Freight Forwarding Services, the Company may do so upon giving the Freight Forwarder not less than 2 months notice of such reduction.

7. Force majeure

Either Party shall be relieved of any liability or obligation herein the fulfilment of which is prevented as a consequence of an Act of God, War, Fire Riot, Civil Commotion and/or any statute of Government rule, order or obligation or any other cause beyond the reasonable control of both Parties.

8. Insurance

8.1 The Freight Forwarder will full indemnify and keep the Company indemnified Against the following (including costs, expenses and interest);

A) third-party claims in respect of death and/or injury to persons or damage to property due to the negligence or failure to fulfil the obligations set out in the Agreement by the Freight Forwarder, the employees and its servants or agents or Service Providers or Freight Forwarder demonstrably caused by any of the equipment used for the provision of the Freight Forwarding Services.

B) claims by Employees under statute or common law provided that nothing in this sub-clause contained shall impose on the Freight Forwarder any liability in respect of claims arising out of the negligence of the Company, its employees, servants or agents; and

C) any losses of or damage to the Goods resulting from any actions or omissions of the Freight Forwarder, the employees, its servants or agents or Service Providers including loss or damage caused during the loading or unloading of aircraft, vehicles, vessels or rail wagons unless such loss or damage has arisen from:

1. an Act of God;
2. any consequence of war, invasion, act of foreign enemy, hostilities (whether war be declared or not), civil war, rebellion, insurrection, military or usurped power, confiscation, requisition, destruction of or damage to property by or under the order of government or public or local authority;
3. any act, negligence or default of the Company, its servants or agents; the Freight Forwarder is liable to exercise due diligence and take reasonable measures in the performance of the Freight Forwarding Service and any failure due to a breach of the Freight Forwarder's duty of care may lead to a claim for compensation;
4. seizure under legal process;
5. riot, civil commotion, lock-outs or strikes, other than by the Freight Forwarder or their Service Providers, servants or agents.

8.2 The Freight Forwarder will not be liable for any loss or damage where such loss or damage has arisen from poor packaging or labelling of the Goods.

8.3 Subject only to the exclusions set out in Clause 8.1.c and 8.2 of this Agreement the

Freight Forwarder hereby undertakes that it will accept all responsibility for damage to or loss of Goods supplied by the company to the Freight Forwarder.

8.4 Subject to Clause 8.1, 82 and 8.3 the Freight Forwarder shall have no further or other liability save that in the case of death or personal injury caused by the Freight Forwarder or their Service Provider's negligence.

8.5 The Freight Forwarder shall provide on behalf of the Company:
A) adequate insurance in respect of the Goods against all loss or damage caused by such risks as it shall consider prudent whilst in the care of the Freight Forwarder by their Service Providers, but only where the same is the express responsibility of the Freight Forwarder under this Agreement up to the Insured Level; and
B) provide the Company with a copy of the Freight Forwarder's Policies on request, complete with receipts for premiums. The Freight Forwarder will, in addition, provide the company on request with details of such insurance on an annual basis.

8.6 The Freight Forwarder will provide:
A) limited employers' liability insurance of not less than [£10] million sterling.
B) Public liability insurance of not less than [£2] million sterling;
C) a financial extension to their public liability insurance to include financial loss (including consequential loss) to a minimum level of [£20,000] per claim and [£10,000] sterling per annum;
D) an "indemnity for principals clause" should be included in their insurance which protects the company from claims which are the responsibility of the Freight Forwarder; and
E) Fidelity Insurance in the sum of [£3] million sterling per occurrence.

8.7 If no loss or damage is notified by the Company to the Freight Forwarder within [90] days of such loss or damage or within [30] days of the company's financial year end audit, the Freight Forwarder, its employees, servants or agents shall be deemed to have no liability in respect of such loss or damage.

8.8 The Freight Forwarder will be responsible for any acts or omissions of any Service Providers and will fully indemnify the Company in the event of an occurrence while the goods are in the care of a Service Provider.

8.9 The Freight Forwarder, its employees, servants or Service Providers shall not be responsible to the other party for any loss of profit or other pure economic loss, unless the company specifically and in writing, defines their obligations to the Freight Forwarder and the penalties that the company has agreed to in the event of failure.

8.10 The conditions in Clause 8 apply to all claims by the company on the Freight Forwarder whether the claim is founded in Contract or in tort.

9.   Pricing

9.1   The Freight Forwarder will maintain separate records relating to the expenses incurred on behalf of the Company. These records will be subject to audit by the Company, its servants or agents.

9.2   The Freight Forwarder will make the following Charges based on the costs agreed in the Schedule of Charges – Schedule 1:

A)   "Standing Charges" which will include payments made by the Freight Forwarder as specified below, particularly:
1)   Gross wages for staff permanently on the company account at UK and overseas offices of the Freight Forwarders.
2)   Rental of 2,500 sq.ft. at the Bonded Warehouse.
3)   Cost of a Customs Bond at [£250,000] sterling
4)   Insurance for Goods and public liability; and
5)   The Management Fee

B)   "Operating Charges" will cover all other costs incurred by the Freight Forwarder including:
1)   Costs incurred by Service Providers undertaking Logistics Activities
2)   Overtime by staff (9.2 (A) (1))
3)   Consumables including pallets; and
4)   Added value work required by the Company.

C)   "Specific Charges" which will cover itemised costs incurred by the Freight Forwarder:
1)   Customs Duties; and
2)   Quota costs

9.3   In the event that there are unforeseen circumstances in one or more Movements and the Freight Forwarder acting in the best interests of the Company incurs additional cost, then these costs will be paid by the Company.

9.4   This Agreement will be subject to annual price reviews (where costs may rise or Fall). The first such review will be [12] months from the end of the first full month of specification after the Commencement Date. For the purpose of such a review the costs will be divided into elements and amended with effect from each review date as follows:
A)   Standing Charges; and
B)   Operating Charges

After the first year from the end of the first full month of operation after the Commencement Date in the event that the forecast workload or requirement changes by more than 15% (plus or minus the original figures), then either Party shall have the right to re-negotiate rates as appropriate to reflect any upward or downward movement in costs from the date of such an occurrence. However, no cost increases will be accepted retrospectively by the company.

9.5   All charges referred to in the Agreement are exclusive of Value Added Tax and any fee or charges imposed from time to time by any Government or other authority and are subject to the addition of Value Added Tax at the appropriate rate.

9.6   The Company may wish to introduce a penalty and reward scheme were:
   A)   in the event that the Freight Forwarder was not regularly achieving the parameters agreed for the budget then a penalty will be offset against the management fee.
   B)   in the event that the Freight Forwarder was regularly performing better than budget against the agreed parameter then the Freight Forwarder would be paid by the company a proportion of the savings achieved.

A full penalty and reward scheme would be agreed between the Parties if appropriate no earlier than six months from Commencement Date.

10.   Payments

10.1   The Company shall pay punctually to the Freight Forwarder the charges in the manner following:
   A)   the Freight Forwarder shall submit monthly invoices to the Company in respect of the standing charges; invoices shall be paid [30] days after the invoice date.
   B)   the Freight Forwarder shall submit weekly invoices to the Company in respect of the operating charges.
   C)   the Freight Forwarder shall submit invoices to the Company on the day they raise a cheque in payment of specific charges which invoice shall be paid [4] days after the invoice date.

10.2   All sums payable hereunder shall, if applicable, be subject to the addition of VAT at the rate prevailing from time to time.

10.3   All charges due to the Freight Forwarder and unpaid for one calendar month following the due date shall be liable to an additional interest charge of 2% per annum above the base rate of the National Westminster Bank plc prevailing at that time, such interest being charged from the date of the payment fell due to the actual date of payment, except the Freight Forwarder will not impose such interest on outstanding invoices against which the Company has logged a genuine written query.

10.4   The Company shall make all payments due to the Freight Forwarder without any reduction or deferment on the account of any claim, counter claim or set off.

10.5   The Freight Forwarder shall, to the extent of any outstanding payment not paid after 90 days, have a general lien on any Goods or documents relating to the Company business and may enforce such a lien in [30] days after informing the Company in writing they would do so.

11.   Disputes

11.1   In the event of any dispute or difference between the Parties hereto arising out of this Agreement, the Parties shall meet to try to resolve the dispute without resort to proceedings. The meeting will be held within [7] working days of a written request from one party to the other, which request will set out brief details of the dispute. Such a meeting will be attended by a director from each party.

11.2   If the dispute of difference is not resolved as a result of such meeting, the Parties may agree that negotiation be entered into with the assistance of a neutral advisor (the "Neutral Advisor") and the dispute be decided by arbitration. If so,

A)   The Parties may then, within a further [7] working days, agree on the appointment of the Neutral Advisor or may apply to the Centre of Dispute Resolution at 100 Fetter Lane, London, EC4A 1DD ("CEDR") or another agreed third-party to recommend a binding procedure for the resolution of the dispute and to nominate the Neutral Advisor.

B)   The Parties shall within [7] working days of the appointment of the Neutral Advisor meet with him in order to agree a programme for the exchange of any relevant information and the structure to be adopted for the negotiating session(s). If considered appropriate, the Parties may seek assistance from CEDR to provide guidance on a suitable procedure.

C)   If the Parties reach agreement on the resolution of the dispute, such agreement shall be recorded in writing and, once it is signed by duly authorised representatives of both Parties it shall be binding on the Parties. Failing agreement on the resolution the parties may agree to invite the Neutral Advisor (acting as an expert and not as an arbitrator) to provide an opinion in writing and such opinion shall be binding on the Parties hereto. The costs of the Neutral Advisor shall be shared equally by the Parties hereto.

11.3   If the Parties do not agree to resort to arbitration, either Party may issue proceedings in the English courts.

12.   General

12.1   The Freight Forwarder shall not disclose, copy or permit to be disclosed to any person, firm or company, any trade secret, confidential information or knowledge or any financial or trading information of or relating to the Company or its group companies. Without prejudice to the generality of the foregoing, the Freight Forwarder hereby acknowledges that all information relating to the operation of the Company's business including but not limited to the volume of sales, the identity of any supplier or customer and the nature and operation of this Agreement together with its content and the information is confidential information or knowledge of the Company. The Freight Forwarder undertakes to advise all of the

Employees, servants, agents and Service Providers who are provided with this confidential information of the prohibitions against the disclosure or improper use of such information and acknowledges its responsibility for any such disclosure or improper use by any of the Employees, servants, agents and its Service Providers. Any confidential information of the Company's will be returned by the Freight Forwarder upon the termination date or at any time if requested by the Company.

12.2   Each of the Parties hereto shall pay its own costs incidental to the negotiation, preparation and completion of this Agreement.

12.3   No announcement in connection with the subject matter of this Agreement shall be made by or on behalf of any of the parties hereto without the prior approval of the other.

12.4   This Agreement is personal to the Parties hereto and no Party shall be entitled to assign or in any way dispose of its rights or obligations arising hereunder without the prior written consent of the other Party which consent shall not be unreasonably withheld.

12.5   This Agreement shall be governed by English Law and the Parties hereto hereby submit to the non-exclusive jurisdiction of the English courts.

12.6   Any notice required or authorised to be given hereunder and any process to be served in relation to or arising out of this Agreement (hereinafter called "Notice") shall be in writing and may be served personally or delivered to the address of the relevant Party as specified below or to such other address as either Party may from time to time notify to the other for this purpose. Any Notice may be sent by pre-paid recorded delivery letter or facsimile and shall be deemed to have been served 48 hours after posting or simultaneous transmission (subject to the production of confirmation of transmission if requested).

(A)   if to the Freight Forwarder:

Address:

Post Code:

Tel No:

Fax No:

Attention of:

(B)   if to the Company:

Address:

Post Code:

Tel No:

Fax No:

Attention of:

12.7   During the continuance of the Agreement the Freight Forwarder and Company will fully and in good faith co-operate with each other in order to provide with all possible expedition all information required by the other to take all reasonable action as is necessary for the efficient transmission of information and instructions and to enable each of theirs to fulfil its obligations under the Agreement and to benefit from its terms.

12.8   This Agreement does not constitute a partnership or joint venture between any of the Parties.

As witness the hands of the Parties hereto or their duly authorised

Representatives the day and year first before written.

Date: ....

Signed by: ....
(For and on behalf of the Company)

In the presence of: ....

Signed by: ....
(For and on behalf of the Freight Forwarder)

In the presence of: ....

Schedule of charges has not been included.

The above example contract is not intended to be used directly as a template, but as a guideline only to what may be involved and what should be considered. It will not substitute either for negotiation or for legal advice.

Reproduced with permission from Added Value Logistics Consulting Limited (contact: alanslater@avlc.co.uk)

Bibliography

Journals and magazines:

Emmett, S. November 2001. **How to Improve Your Freight Transport & Warehouse Operations,** in *Control.*

Getting People "Right" in the Supply-Chain, in *Focus.* April 2003.

International Journal of Transport Management (IJTM). October 2002.

International Journal of Logistics Research and Applications. Volume three, number three. November 2000.

Tracking the load down. *Logistics Europe.* July 2000.

Third Party Charging Structures. *Logistics Manager.* May/June 1997.

Partnerships or Partnershaft. *Logistics Manager.* April 2003.

Getting Personal. *Motor Transport.* 3-10 August 2000.

Getting to grips. *Motor Transport.* 31 October 2002.

New Look. *Motor Transport.* 29 August 2002.

Ikea. *Motor Transport.*10 April 2003.

McKinnon, Alan. July 1999. **The Effect of Traffic Congestion on the Efficiency of Logistical Operations**, in *International Journal of Logistics Research and Applications, Volume 2.*

Morrison's and DHL. *Motor Transport.* 12 June 2008.

Post Kogelo. *Motor Transport.* 27 March 2008.

Supply Management (CIPS). 29 June 2000.

Crime and Punishment. *SHD.* August 2004.

Wallace, Mark. **Taking the Medicine**, in *SHD.* July 2004. NYK Logistics.

Paragon Software enables Raleigh to reduce order cycle and increase fleet efficiency. *Warehouse News.* 2002.

Books, Manuals & Internet

Cudahy, Brian. 2006. **Box Boats.**

Cheltenham Tutorial College. 2002. **International Logistics** (for Chartered Institute of Purchasing & Supply qualification).

Cheltenham Tutorial College. 2002. **Stores and Distribution in the Supply Chain** (for Chartered Institute of Purchasing & Supply Professional Stage qualification).

Code of Practice: Safety of loads on Vehicles. 2002. www.dft.gov.uk

Driver Hire Nationwide. www.driver-hire.co.uk.

Driving at Work. 2003. Health & Safety Executive and Department of Transport.

Emmett, Stuart. 2008. **Communication Toolkit.** Management Books 2000 Ltd.

Emmett, Stuart. 2007. **Customer Service Toolkit.** Management Books 2000 Ltd.

Emmett, Stuart. 2008. **Developing People Toolkit.** Management Books 2000 Ltd.

Emmett, Stuart. 2005. **Excellence in Warehouse Management**. John Wiley & Sons.

Emmett, Stuart. 2003. **How to Mentor and Support Learning.** Spiro Press.

Emmett, Stuart. 2002. **Improving Learning for Individuals and Companies.** Chandos Publishing (Oxford) Ltd/Spiro Press.

Emmett, Stuart. 2008. **Learning Toolkit.** Management Books 2000 Ltd.

Emmett, Stuart. 2007. **Motivation Toolkit.** Management Books 2000 Ltd.

Emmett, Stuart. 2008. **Team Management Toolkit.** Management Books 2000 Ltd.

Emmett, Stuart. 2007. **The Discipline Pocketbook.** Management Pocketbooks.

Eye for Transport. 6th European 3PL Summit.

Guide to Maintaining Roadworthiness. 2007. VOSA.

IBM. 2006. *Building value in logistics outsourcing.*

Institute of Logistics and Transport (ILT). **Open Learning Material for the Introductory Certificate in Logistics.**

236

Will, Murray. 2003. *ILT Transport Forum* newsletter, Issue 1, 2003.

PTRM. 2007. **Global Supply Chain Trends 2008-2010.**

www.berr.gov.uk

www.ciltuk.org.uk

www.cips.org.uk

www.dft.gov.uk

www.europa.eu

www.export.org.uk

www.freighttransportbestpractice.org.uk

www.hmrc.gov.uk

www.internationaltrade.co.uk

www.roadtransport.com

www.sitpro.org.uk

www.transportgistics.com

Index